THE
WONDER
OF IT ALL

THE
WONDER
OF IT ALL

Rediscovering the Treasures
of Your Faith

BRYAN CHAPELL

CROSSWAY BOOKS • WHEATON, ILLINOIS
A DIVISION OF GOOD NEWS PUBLISHERS

Names of individuals and occasional specifics are changed in some personal accounts appearing in this book to respect the concerns and wishes of those involved. My debt is great to those who have taught me the Gospel of grace with the testimony of their lives.

The Wonder of It All

Cover design: Big Picture Design/D² DesignWorks

Cover photo: The Image Bank

First printing 1999

Printed in the United States of America

Library of Congress Cataloging-in-Publication Data
Chapell, Bryan.
    The wonder of it all : rediscovering the treasures of your faith / Bryan Chapell.
      p.   cm.
    ISBN 1-58134-061-3 (TPB : alk. paper)
    1. Christian life. II. Title.
BV4501.2.C4756 1999
248.4—dc21   98-53804
                                          CIP

15	14	13	12	11	10	09	08	07	06	05	04	03	02	01	00	99
15	14	13	12	11	10	9	8	7	6	5	4	3	2	1		

For Gordon

CONTENTS

*Discussion questions are included with the Introduction and each of the following chapters so that this book may be used for twelve- or thirteen-week Sunday school quarters, as well as for small-group Bible study or personal reading.

PREFACE

FALLING IN LOVE AGAIN

ჟ

"I fell in love with Jesus." That is the way one of the dearest Christians I know explains her conversion. She does not use traditional terms such as "being saved," "coming to faith," or "accepting Christ as Savior and Lord." When she does not feel constrained by others' expectations or fear their judgments if she uses unconventional terms, these words naturally burst from her heart.

Now mature in years, this woman had been in and around churches all her life but says that she "fell in love" when a neighbor helped her understand who Jesus is and the kind of life he offers despite her flaws. "That he would care so much for me when even I hated who I was made me fall in love with Jesus," she says. Not only does the genuine glow that envelops every aspect of her demeanor when she says these words confirm the woman's sincerity, but it also makes others long for the love she knows. Yet, for many of us, that love seems remote, inaccessible, and unreal. Too many do not know what to love. This book is designed to help.

The following chapters explore truths God provides in his Word that assure Christians that a wonderful relationship with him is possible and precious. If you have been in church all your life and yet have never fallen in love with the Savior (or the love you once had has grown cold), then these soaring truths can help relieve deep aches in your heart.

Understanding who God is, what he has done, and the ways he

works in and around us can make your heart glow with fresh love for Jesus. Before we examine these truths, however, we need to share a confession with each other: Many of us do not know what we believe anymore. It is hard genuinely to love someone whose character and ways are unfamiliar or obscure. Yet that is precisely the situation many of us confront when we honestly examine our knowledge of the truths in the Bible that are supposed to reveal God to us.

Recent studies and surveys from a variety of perspectives and camps confirm what we hate to confess. With the well-documented erosion of biblical literacy over the past two generations has come a corresponding decay in the understanding Christians have of their faith distinctives. Cultural analyst Russell Chandler writes, "As Christian believers are barraged by secular influences which in subtle and not-so-subtle ways threaten to drain the credibility of their witness, many are uncritical or even unaware of the distinction between culture-based values and values that derive from the Gospel of Jesus Christ."

Efforts to halt the deterioration of a biblical worldview among Christians have not succeeded according to any large-scale measurement available. *Doctrine* reverberates like a dirty word in our sanctuaries. Attempts to inform congregations of the historic commitments of the Church so echo the divisive denominational power struggles of previous generations that few preachers can speak of such matters without facing resentment.

The result has been to replace preaching and teaching on the great truths of the Christian faith with "practical lessons" that show what latest psychological therapies, relational cures, or management techniques echo in biblical passages. The Bible has become a source for illustrating what people want to hear rather than a standard of evaluating what they hear and determining what they do.

This "use" of Scripture not only reinforces the notion that the Bible on its own has no immediate application to everyday life, but it also robs people of the ability to think "Christianly" about their lives. When they have poorly developed biblical reference points by which to orient their lives, decisions, and views, Christians are forced to navigate the world according to secular considerations. Such believers begin to think of their churches solely as places of ritual and retreat rather than as institutions to equip them emotionally, intellectually, and spiritually to confront the issues of real life. Religion gets relegated to the realm of sanctified opinion, and tolerance of diversity rather than commitment to truth becomes the unifying ethic of Christian convictions.

Deprived of commitment to clear faith concepts, Christians think about life no differently than the rest of the world, and they inevitably question whether their faith offers anything other faiths do not. As a result the Bible's great truths either get lost in a syncretic mishmash of Christianity, cultural do-goodism and religious fads, or these truths get relegated to obscure corners of personal conscience where they cannot offend prevailing social sensibilities nor address life's daily challenges.

Some will argue that the solution to the demise of Christian convictions in our society is a resurrection of "solid" Christian teaching on the distinctives of our faith. "Solid" in this case means in-depth, systematic, and regular instruction in the Church's historic understanding of Scripture. While I sympathize with such sentiments, I must also admit that I believe they are naive. Trying to beat into people's heads more details of what they have already indicated they do not or cannot appreciate is a doomed enterprise.

People will seek a deep understanding of Christian truth only when they appreciate its significance for their lives. That conviction is the catalyst for this book. I defer to other writers for the formulation and systematization of the Bible's affirmations. While I deal with a number of the essential truths of our faith, my foremost concern has *not* been to prove, define, or defend those beliefs. I have attempted to show *why* they are important.

Throughout the writing of these chapters, I have kept one question foremost in my mind: "What difference does it make?" Whether the issue is as apparently remote as "heaven" or as seemingly abstract as "revival," I have tried to put myself into the life situations of everyday Christians and there expose why it is important for them to know what Scripture teaches. I want people to understand clearly what they will lose if they do not claim God's instruction and to appreciate how much richer their lives will be with a firm grasp on the treasures in his Word.

My goal is nothing less than to encourage Christians to fall in love with their faith again. I pray this process of rediscovery will lead people to a fresh appreciation of the preciousness of biblical truth. This book can be an important first step in a rewarding journey toward the recovery of individual commitments that grant meaning and worth to life's greatest challenges. When we learn to cherish what God says, we will ever long for more of his Word and in its depths will always find more of his embrace.

INTRODUCTION

DO YOU BELIEVE IN MAGIC?

⌁

Do you believe in magic? Most of us do not hesitate to deny serious faith in a stage show's "amazing" wizardry. We do not really think that top hats produce rabbits, that pigeons materialize under shirt sleeves, or that people will levitate at a wand's wave. Yet despite these mature denials, something childlike in each of us still longs for some magic transformations of reality in our lives. From our earliest years we may even learn to depend on a little bit of magic.

• A four-year-old falls down, bumps her knee, and screams bloody murder. Her mother asks, "Do you want me to kiss it and make it better?" As if a kiss could make the hurt disappear. Yet what happens when Mom kisses the knee? The child stops crying. Amazing!

• When my son Jordan was little, he sometimes said that he was so tired that he could not clean up his room. Yet if his mother draped an ordinary bathroom towel over this child's shoulders, suddenly he became "Super Jordan," able to clean up bedrooms in a single bound. Amazing!

Adults, too, have their magic—the expectation that someone will have just the right words, the secret formula, or the special touch that will transform their lives. The magicians of our adulthood, however, are not dressed in tuxedos and black capes but wear the garb of doctors, lawyers, psychologists, and stockbrokers. We expect these professional prestidigitators to make our problems vanish, and we are disappointed—even angered—when they cannot. Listen to our surprise when the charms of our adult magicians fail:

• "What do you mean, my mother won't get better? This *is* a hospital, isn't it?"

• "Counselor, we've been coming to you for six months, and our son is not any more cooperative. What's *your* problem?"

• "You told me this was a *good* investment!"

The words may sound naive and unreasonable, but every professional recognizes they are not rare. Amazing!

Expecting our lives to change because someone has the right magic is a hope that can typify any age or any culture. Such expectations pervade our society. They even invade our churches.

• A man says, "I'm inviting my brother over to dinner Thursday night, Pastor. Will you and your wife please come, too, so you can save him?"

• A young couple on the verge of separation after years of financial imprudence and marital difficulty drop by the church's counseling center unexpectedly. The wife says, "Dr. Bridges, I told Jerry we don't have to get a divorce because you will be able to help us."

• A three-year-old hooligan terrorizes teachers and peers in the nursery. Twenty minutes into a tantrum thrown when he is denied the entire class's box of animal crackers, the boy's mother is summoned from the worship service. Her response: "If this nursery had workers as caring as those in our home church, Billy wouldn't feel the need to get my attention this way."

• The morning after committing his son to a substance abuse facility, an angry father confronts the high school youth leader: "Why is your program so lacking in competent instruction that you can't even keep a Christian teenager from a good home away from drugs?"

What some expect of their church is amazing! These people seem to think their pastor, elder, Sunday school teacher, or Christian friend possesses magic words. Such thinking suggests that a verse invoked from memory or some holy suggestion materialized from spiritual domains will—"poof"—instantly transform everything into a world without problems.

More amazing still is the fact that mature Christians sometimes allow themselves to believe the same thing. We grow too ready to conjure instant cures and too glibly stir up quick fixes from caldrons of sanctified clichés. We find ourselves using Bible verses like magic wands to create the impression that problems will vanish into thin air because of words we can quote or advice our insight will supply.

I came face to face with my own magic view of ministry the first time I tried to minister to a couple whose child was dying. For me, part of the horror of the cancer was how slowly it seemed to creep through the child's body. Yet for the parents I know the disease advanced terribly fast.

As their child grew worse, I talked frequently with the parents about the truths of the Bible. They are believers. They accepted what I said and responded with a godly faith I still find inspiring. Not the parents' reactions but my own put my heart in anguish. My words could not "fix" anything. I was accustomed to having my speaking facility smooth over difficulties, avert problems, and control my situations. I hated facing the fact that I could not correct *this* horror.

This family's crisis was greater than my abilities to control. Even if my expressions of biblical care could make the parents feel some comfort and even smile for brief moments, I could not make their hurt or its cause go away. Their grief was too profound, deep, and prolonged for any quick fix or smooth words to cover.

Returning from the hospital one evening, I shared my distress with my wife: "Kathy, I feel so useless. I can't make this right, and I can't make it disappear." I cannot now adequately express the degree of despair I felt. I desperately wanted to help. I wanted so much for this awful disease not to hurt, not to scar, not to grieve. Yet the cancer did all of these at a depth I had not previously known.

I did not become a minister to sit by and watch people hurt. I wanted to make a difference. I needed to change things. Now this situation forced me to ask, "If my words won't avert such hurt—if I can't make this right—then why am I here? If God gives me no magic, then what am I supposed to do?"

We can easily despair if we do not understand exactly what God expects. But his instruction is simple: "Preach the Word" (2 Tim. 4:2). By urging his ministers to proclaim his truth "in season and out of season"—whether the occasion is pleasant or difficult—God signals the transforming hope that resides in his Word. This does not mean that the Bible is magic. Yet if it is rightly used and correctly understood, Scripture possesses amazing power to help us face life's greatest challenges. This book is dedicated to helping you grasp this power.

CONFIDENT PROCLAMATION

Confidence in the power of the Word grows as we recognize that our Lord has made us accountable to him for the proclamation of its truths (2 Tim. 4:1). If no one in this country could launch an atomic weapon without a charge from the president, then consider how awesome must be the power that God must authorize.

The power is evident not only in God's authorization but also in what he anticipates from the proclamation of his Word—eternal results! Truth proclaimed does not merely touch a moment. The effects of gospel proclamation stretch beyond a lifetime, beyond millennia, and beyond our ability to calibrate because God expects his Word to transform souls for his eternal kingdom (2 Tim. 4:1). This Word is amazing!

Nothing known to humankind equals this eternal force. The effects of atomic weapons, earthquakes, floods, hurricanes, and monstrous meteors all diminish with time. Yet the Word of God and its impact endure forever (cf. Ps. 119:89).

The fact that the power needed to carry such force is contained in mere words makes it even more amazing. I can never escape an "eerie" feeling when greeting those who have come to know Christ as Savior in our church. Some come from complacency and indifference. Others have been caught in a web of adultery, alcoholism, or abuse. Still others have waged philosophical war against the faith or once ridiculed its claims. Now they all come to join themselves to the body of Christ. How can this happen? How can mere words voiced with human frailty draw such people from a lifetime of wretchedness to desire eternity with God? The transitions almost seem like magic, but they are not. They are evidence of the divine power present in the Word.

God breathes his own power into the Word (2 Tim. 3:16). Its truths hold his creating, life-giving, transforming force. We cannot read Paul's words intelligently without being reminded that where God's Word is proclaimed, God's own power is engaged. The Word is surrounded by, permeated with, propelled by God himself. Thus, since God works by and with his Word, he (and we) can rightly expect the Word to influence eternity.

Hearts change, lives turn around, confidence in God's perfect plans grow, and souls destined for heaven multiply as God fulfills his intention of pouring the power of his Word through our frail expressions. If we can keep this divine expectation in view, then hardship need not intimidate us, nor should discouragement overcome us when we respond to God's charge to proclaim his Word.

CAREFUL PROCLAMATION

The apostle Paul uses the Greek word *dunamis* to describe the power the Gospel holds (Rom. 1:16). We derive the English word *dynamite* from this same original term. This word comparison reminds us that the truths of God—though they are amazingly powerful—like dynamite, must be handled with the greatest care. The Word's power to transform lives does not give Christians the right to bypass, manhandle, or abuse the dignity and thought of others. We proclaim God's Word because it is amazing, but not as if it is magic.

A sad expression of a magic view of Scripture occurred when a friend of mine was being licensed to preach by his denomination. An examiner asked what the pastoral candidate would say to a church family who had recently experienced the death of a loved one. My friend answered that he would express his sympathy, reassure family members of God's care for them, and remind them of God's resurrection promises for the one who had died. The examiner's frown and head shaking indicated he was *not* satisfied with this answer.

My friend then cited some Scriptures he might read and suggested other means that might express his sympathy. The examiner only exhibited increasing impatience with these approaches. Wracking his brain for whatever the examiner wanted to hear, the candidate began to make wild suggestions. Nothing he offered, however, was more bizarre than the final response of the examiner. When it was obvious that he was nearly exploding with exasperation, the examiner burst into my friend's continuing befuddlement with this *correction*: "What you are supposed to say is, 'The Lord giveth and the Lord taketh away, blessed be the name of the Lord!'"

This quote from Job was the one *right* answer the church official would accept. Apparently this citation of Scripture alone would make everything all right according to this examiner's instruction. The young preacher had only to intone this ritualized *Abracadabra* to make grief and pain disappear in an enchanted "poof" of spiritual magic.

You may find this examiner's understanding incredibly insensitive, but his perspective is not rare. In analyzing our own approaches to others' trials, many of us will discover how readily we, too, resort to a magic view of Scripture. We display our homage to this perspective in the sermons we heed, the advice we share, the counseling we give, and the consolation we offer. We do not use magic wands to dispense our Christian cures. Instead, our zeal for our sorcery has us take out a Romans 8:28 two-by-four (or its equivalent) to address nearly every human problem. We slam troubled people over the head with our "all-things-work-together-for-good" incantation and then stand back for the magic to work. It is almost as if we had said, "*Abracadabra*—feel better now?"

We long for quick fixes and take pride in instant solutions. Our faith in the amazing power of God's Word gets warped into a magic mind-set convincing us that if we can remember just the right verse and say it just the right way, we will conjure a solution to every ill. With deep insight into our humanity, the apostle Paul wisely reminds us that magic formulas and charmed incantations are not the business of Scripture nor its proclaimers. He will not deny that a word *wisely* spoken can accomplish amazing results because of the power of Scripture, but he requires that patience and wisdom—not magic—guide our expressions.

The apostle's instruction details two aspects of the wisdom needed to proclaim God's Word correctly. This instruction first tells us *what* to do with God's Word: "correct, rebuke, and encourage." Next we are told *how* to carry out these tasks: "with great patience and careful instruction" (see 2 Tim. 4:2). God requires us to speak with conviction, but he never allows us to abandon compassion. The Bible is rich with examples of this balanced presentation of divine truth.

• Jesus sharply rebuked Peter saying, "Get thee behind me, Satan," when the impulsive fisherman challenged the Savior. Still Jesus patiently reminded the discredited disciple to "feed my sheep" after Peter's betrayal.

• Christ often corrected indolent followers for failing to heed his instruction. Yet as the Incarnate Lord prepared to leave this earth, he showed consideration for his most avid students' weaknesses saying, "I have more to tell you, but you are not ready to hear it yet."

• Paul rebuked a legalistically inclined church writing, "Who has bewitched you, you foolish Galatians"; yet he circumcised Timothy.

• In his first letter to Corinth Paul pointed out great wrong saying, "There is sin among you such as is not even among the pagans." In his second letter to the same people, the apostle revealed great patience indicating that he decided to put off a trip to their church in order to spare it "another painful visit."

There are no *Abracadabras* in these inspired accounts. The proclamation of the Word that sparked amazing results combined courageous statements of biblical truth with compassionate expressions of human understanding.

Biblical proclamation is never one-dimensional. It requires commitment of heart as well as conviction of mind. Through Scripture we learn that we have no right to compromise truth, but we also learn that patience is not compromise—it is one of God's commands. Harried belligerence and impatient bombast betray Scripture even if they intend to support its truths.

Magic views of Scripture that offer quick solutions for the deep trials of the soul and the great battles of the heart simply do not take sin or Scripture seriously enough. Though it may sound very sanctified to suggest that a verse quoted just the right way at just the right time will instantly fix almost anything, this parade of orthodoxy will lead to heartache. The work of faithful proclaimers is never ceasing, rarely easy, and often lengthy. If we blind ourselves to Scripture's expressions of how deep, entangling, searing, and hard sin can be, then we will either grow disillusioned with the magic that is not working, rejecting of the people that resist its powers, or distrusting of our own misplaced convictions.

The Word can conquer sin in a moment, but it may require a season, or a lifetime, or generations. Our task is not to project when God's Word will work but to trust that it will perform God's purposes when faithfully proclaimed. The Lord will work through his Word in the way and time he knows is appropriate. Human assessment of the timing of God's work is not a measure of its glory. That the Word breaks hearts of stone and brings eternal life to those spiritually dead confirms its amazing power. Yet as amazing as these results are, they are not magic.

THE WONDER OF THE WORD

The amazing power of God's Word surfaced at a small church struggling for survival in the shadow of the Appalachians. A sagging local economy accompanied by a shrinking population base had crippled the little congregation but had not sapped its affection for ministry. I witnessed their commitment while preaching a week-long Bible conference they had designed to reach the discouraged people of their town.

As the conference progressed, a larger than anticipated crowd came, and the little congregation was thrilled. We prayed nightly for the different persons who visited, and we asked the Lord to open their hearts to his Word. Yet as we prayed, I noticed one attendee was never mentioned. She was hard *not* to notice. Though the punk rock movement had seen its day, this young woman came every night with spiked hair in an array of bizarre colors, and on some nights she brought a friend similarly attired. When those who gathered to pray repeatedly failed to mention this "obviously" unchurched woman, I grew concerned. Were we not praying for this young woman because the church really did not want her around? I summoned my courage and mentioned my fears to the pastor. He put my mind at rest and thrilled my heart with his explanation.

"Don't worry about her," he said with a smile. "She's not a visitor. That's our Maria."

The story unfolded. The child of disinterested parents, Maria had grown up on the streets of the small town. She had come to the church's Vacation Bible School as a child, but that was the extent of her church experience. As she grew older and her street life became more sordid, various women in the church tried to help her. Maria ridiculed and rebuffed them, but they did not stop praying for her.

In her sophomore year of high school, Maria took a field trip with her class to a state university. As she made her way through the cafeteria line there, the college student working as a cashier asked the attractive and street-matured fourteen-year-old for a date. She accepted and too soon became convinced that the charming young man was the answer to her misery. Weeks later the two were married.

Only days after the wedding Maria discovered that her young husband afforded college, a beautiful apartment, and a nice car by dealing drugs. The drugs brought to her door the street life that Maria was trying to escape. She told her husband that he had to quit dealing, or she would leave. Her street smarts had not prepared her to recognize, however, that she was dealing with a psyche more fragile than her own.

Maria's husband told her that if she left, he would kill himself. She left anyway. He did.

At age fifteen Maria found herself uneducated, unemployable, a widow, and expecting a child. In desperation she turned to the only people who had ever tried to care for her. The families of the church became the family she never had. The seeds of care they had sown in her heart over years without apparent results finally germinated. As the church instructed Maria in matters of life and the Lord, her spirit blossomed. Now she not only came to a nightly Bible conference designed to reach people in the town that had often spurned her, but she even brought a friend to hear the Gospel. There was no magic here. Maria still has much to learn, but the amazing power of the Word has done and is doing its work through great patience and careful instruction.

In our churches, neighborhoods, and families are many more Marias. They must learn with us the truths of Scripture in order to experience the fullness of life in Christ. However, we will only reach their hearts and enrich our own if we remain mindful of the Bible's instruction as we proclaim its truths.

The Word performs its designed tasks when its bearers proclaim precisely what God says and express clearly their love for those who hear. Evidence of this regard is displayed not only by the accuracy of our claims, but also by the attitudes we communicate. We must fix in our hearts the patience that is the mark of those who care for the souls God seeks as well as for the truths we teach.

In your faith history lies the record of at least one person who cared for you when you did not understand your faith, who loved you when you did not love the Lord, and was patient with you when you did not claim his truths for your life. The apostle Paul's words in this chapter not only call each of us to thank the Lord for such persons, but also charge us to reflect them in our embrace and proclamation of the truths this book unfolds.

DISCUSSION QUESTIONS

1) In what ways do people in our world seem to believe in "magic" solutions to life's problems? In what ways do Christians sometimes seem to harbor similar beliefs?

2) Why is it important to know that proclaiming God's Word is a divine charge? To whom does such a charge make us accountable?

3) What does the authorization God gives to the proclamation of his Word indicate about our right to alter or ignore any portion of it?

4) What does God's oversight of the use of his Word indicate about its power?

5) What divine expectation does God have when we proclaim his Word? How (and when) should God's expectation influence our willingness to proclaim his truth?

6) How does the power of God's Word affect the care with which we present it?

7) Proclamation includes "correcting, rebuking, and encouraging." How do these duties differ?

8) How does God caution us always to treat others with care and dignity when carrying out our proclamation duties?

9) How could you develop more patience to accompany your presentation of God's Word?

THE REVELATION
OF TRUTH

Little things can get you in a lot of hot water. I rediscovered that simple truth a few years ago when I took an Oreo from our cookie jar five minutes before dinner and unleashed a storm of controversy in our house.

Three little voices cried in unison, "Mom, why does Dad get a cookie before dinner? You said that we couldn't have a cookie." An innocent father reached for a little snack, and suddenly family justice was on trial.

Eating the cookie fast to get rid of the evidence did not help. "Mom," my accusers now complained, "Dad put the whole cookie in his mouth at once. You said we can't snarf cookies down."

My wife's raised eyebrow let me know this little drama I had created was not appreciated with dinner only moments away.

All I did was take a cookie!

My cookie-monster experience helps me sympathize with the woman at the well in the passage from the Gospel of John. All she did was go to the well for some water, and before the day was over, the whole town was in an uproar because of what happened there. Her drama began when Jesus, tired from his journey, asked her for a drink.

JOHN 4:9-26

⨳

⁹The Samaritan woman said to him, "You are a Jew and I am a Samaritan woman. How can you ask me for a drink?" (For Jews do not associate with Samaritans.)

¹⁰Jesus answered her, "If you knew the gift of God and who it is that asks you for a drink, you would have asked him and he would have given you living water."

¹¹"Sir," the woman said, "you have nothing to draw with and the well is deep. Where can you get this living water? ¹²Are you greater than our father Jacob, who gave us the well and drank from it himself, as did also his sons and his flocks and herds?"

¹³Jesus answered, "Everyone who drinks this water will be thirsty again, ¹⁴but whoever drinks the water I give him will never thirst. Indeed, the water I give him will become in him a spring of water welling up to eternal life."

¹⁵The woman said to him, "Sir, give me this water so that I won't get thirsty and have to keep coming here to draw water."

¹⁶He told her, "Go, call your husband and come back."

¹⁷"I have no husband," she replied. Jesus said to her, "You are right when you say you have no husband. ¹⁸The fact is, you have had five husbands, and the man you now have is not your husband. What you have just said is quite true."

¹⁹"Sir," the woman said, "I can see that you are a prophet. ²⁰Our fathers worshiped on this mountain, but you Jews claim that the place where we must worship is in Jerusalem."

²¹Jesus declared, "Believe me, woman, a time is coming when you will worship the Father neither on this mountain nor in Jerusalem. ²²You Samaritans worship what you do not know; we worship what we do know, for salvation is from the Jews. ²³Yet a time is coming and has now come when the true worshipers will worship the Father in spirit and truth, for they are the kind of worshipers the Father seeks. ²⁴God is spirit, and his worshipers must worship in spirit and in truth."

²⁵The woman said, "I know that Messiah" (called Christ) "is coming. When he comes, he will explain everything to us."

²⁶Then Jesus declared, "I who speak to you am he."

⨳

THE SWIRL

"I'll never go back," said the woman seated next to me on the plane. In our conversation she had learned that I was a minister, and now something in her wanted to tell me about what she was experiencing. For years she had worked for an architectural firm as a highly successful single woman. Then abruptly she had left the business and married. She wanted a different life. Her actual words were, "I wanted a *real* home and a family." Sad to say, the family she and her husband so desperately wanted never grew.

Because the couple was affluent, they sought the best that medical technology could offer to help them conceive. Their money was not enough. Despite the drugs, the treatments, and the operations, no child came. So they turned to a church that also took their money and promised them a miracle in return.

For a time it seemed their sacrifices and faith would be rewarded. The doctors said that a child was on the way. Then a miscarriage at five months dashed hopes again, and the doctors said there was little reason to expect a different outcome in the future.

All the disappointments and frustrations took their toll on the marriage. The couple stopped planning for children. She returned to work. They were considering ending the marriage.

I do not know why she told all that to me. At some level, no doubt, she still wanted counsel and comfort. So I prayed with her, tried to explain that God's eternal love was not denied by a world of pain, and pleaded with her to return to a church that would really help. That was when she said, "I will never go back." Knowing what she had experienced, I found it hard to blame her.

Another trip, an earlier time. The man on the plane next to me watched as I opened a Bible to continue frantically and belatedly preparing a message for a conference in another city.

"Are you a preacher?" he asked.

"Yes," I replied.

"So am I," he said.

He went on to explain that he was a businessman who had just been ordained by an organization in Asia. He was putting up the money for a national campaign to establish this group in the United States. When I asked what his religion taught, he said that they told people that they could be as successful as he was if they would plug into the positive powers within them that conquer life's negative influences.

One more trip. More recently I flew to the West Coast to attend an interdenominational meeting of religious educators. As I left the airport, the taxi driver asked me what I did for a living.

I said, "I'm a preacher."

"Oh, yeah?" he replied. "That's great. I think a little religion is good for you. I tell my kids, 'Religion will keep you out of trouble.'"

"What church do you and your children attend?" I asked.

"Oh, we're not particular," he said. "I was raised an Irish Catholic, but my kids got tired of that, so we tried the Adventists for a while, then the Baptists, but now we mainly watch the preachers on the TV. It's a lot more convenient, you know."

I confess I thought his approach to faith was a bit zany, but it was hard to fault him when I later observed the "worship service" of the religious educators. The program began with a hymn of praise played on a Cherokee flute and dedicated to the rising sun.

Dead churches, living cults, the new paganism—we seem to confront the same morass of differing beliefs everywhere we go. Is it any wonder that the people we know and meet do not seem to know what they believe anymore? Recently leading evangelical apologists met near Washington, DC, to try to determine how we can reach an increasingly confused culture with the true message of the Gospel. Os Guinness, the Christian writer and cultural critic, commented, "The ideas and movements of our culture are in such a swirl, Christians simply don't know what approach to take. As hard as it is to determine what others believe, it is even harder to decide what we should do to reach them with the truth."

The accuracy of Guinness's "swirl" analysis is born out in recent studies showing the increasing ineffectiveness of traditional evangelism. The old methods of preparing answers to questions people once tended to ask simply are not working. People in our culture are not asking what they did a generation ago. They are not concerned about the same issues or even reasoning the same way.

Our society possesses no consensus of values. Some people seek fulfillment in success, some in pleasure. Some are workaholics; others are recreation addicts. Some pursue meaning in personal understanding, others in a previous life. Some advocate a return to family values; others want a return to primal nature. While most of culture imbibes the old eroticism, another portion experiments with the new celibacy. Traditional religions mushroom in some corners at the same time that we experience cult explosions worldwide. Health concerns grow nearly fetish across our nation while high-risk sports fascinate millions.

Culture races not one way but a thousand. As a result our churches search for ways to share Christian truths with increasing trepidation. We cannot but feel timid about sharing the Gospel when even our experts say they are unsure what will effectively communicate.

So what are we supposed to do? We have neighbors and family members who need to know the Lord. Even if our experts are confounded, we cannot sit idle while the hearts of loved ones lie in eternal jeopardy. What are we to do? How can we penetrate the swirl that swallows souls?

The Lord answers our questions in this Scripture where he presents himself to a woman in a culture no less confused than our own. His words remind us that no matter how much confusion swirls in our culture, we can anchor the Gospel to basic truths that do not shift.

I. Truth About Persons

Jesus helps us understand how the Gospel can have meaning in a swirling culture by revealing to us the nature of a person. "Culture" boils down to persons living and acting together. For our Gospel to have power, we have to sense the brokenness of each person. Our gaze may scan masses, movements, and generations, but every culture consists of individuals whose hurt is real and who cannot be touched with the healing of the Gospel until we see the wounds each bears.

WE MUST SEE OTHERS FOR THE PERSONS THEY ARE

Because my present job takes me to many different places, I often find myself preaching to those I do not know. As a result I can easily grow more concerned for the impression I am making than for the people I am addressing. I must frequently pray, "Lord, let me see faces. If all I see is a crowd—if individual persons do not have an identity—I will not speak with the passion your Word requires." I recognize that if I stop seeing real people with real needs, the Gospel stops having real meaning even to me.

I am thankful that my challenge to see faces on my travels does not reflect a limitation my Savior shares. In Christ's earthly journeys the individual never faded from view. As he walked down the road one day, a young man clothed in finery and pride asked what he could do to inherit eternal life. Jesus could have passed by without a comment, but instead the Bible says, "Jesus looked at him and loved him" (Mark 10:21).

Once the Lord passed through a crowd, and a woman in need touched his garment. "Who touched me?" asked Jesus. His disciples scanned the pressing crowd and scoffed, "Lord, how can we determine who touched you?" But Jesus identified her (see Matt. 9:20-22; Luke 8:45-47).

Jesus went down a street so packed with onlookers that a despicable little man could not even find a curbside view. Jesus still saw him in as unlikely a place as a sycamore tree and called to him by name: "Zacchaeus, you come down for I am going to your house today" (see Luke 19:1-10).

So consistent was his compassion that when he looked over the city of Jerusalem only days before its citizens would crucify him, he cared enough for the town to lament for each sinful inhabitant as for a loved one. He cried, "O Jerusalem, Jerusalem, you who kill the prophets and stone those sent to you, how often I have longed to gather your children together, as a hen gathers her chicks under her wings, but you were not willing" (Luke 13:34). Then, as he drew nearer to death at their hands, he paused again to weep for them (Luke 19:41).

The Lord would not let faces blur into insignificance. He paid attention to individuals. This is true late in his life on earth, but it is just as true at the earliest stages of Jesus' ministry. The consistency of his personal approach tells us how important individual care remains. In this account he merely sees a woman collecting water at a well. The routine would hardly have captured the attention of anyone in that culture. Her activity is roughly our equivalent of washing dishes, picking up a newspaper, or dropping kids off at school—nothing special.

For us this woman would likely disappear as a speck of humanity on the background of her society. We would take no more notice of her than we do of a person in a neighboring checkout line at the grocery store. But she cannot escape Jesus' attention. He will not just pass her by. She possesses a face to recognize, a life to heal, and a heart to save. Jesus sees her deepest needs as clearly as we see more obvious externals of her situation. What precisely he sees in her we learn by specifics the Holy Spirit records.

Society-imposed Need. When Jesus sees this Samaritan woman, he recognizes one whose national situation automatically imposes needs upon her. Because she is a Samaritan, the prejudices of her society trap and prod her. Her nationality, faith, and situation make her a despised minority in Palestine. Her words to Jesus make it clear that she has felt the prick of Jewish animosities toward her people (John 4:9). She is hated and hates in return. She knows that if Jesus shares the attitudes typical of his people, he will not consider her to be of the right race, nor of the right region, nor of the right religion, nor even of the right gender. The culture victimizes her in more ways than she is likely even to recognize. Jesus is clearly not blind to these societal pressures, but he does not let them inhibit his interaction with her (cf. vv. 7, 22).

Self-imposed Need. Though Jesus clearly recognizes the external needs society imposes on this woman, his conversation focuses on her self-imposed needs. Jesus sees inside, too. He sees a woman who has had five husbands, and the man she lives with now is not her husband (vv. 16-19). Her personal needs have driven her to extremes the Holy Spirit clearly identifies for us. Apparently she drifts from one failed relationship to the next, not able to sustain love. Yet despite her dismal record of failed relationships, she appears driven by some obsessive passion, crazy bent, or maybe just the need to belong to someone.

She keeps trying to find fulfillment with a man. Five times she has tried to make marriage work, and now (talk about "Lookin' for love in all the wrong places") she is trying to make a life with someone not even committed enough to her to marry her. In this sixth compulsive attempt, she seeks happiness with a man who, by the very nature of his relationship with her, will subject her to the worst scorn her society can inflict upon a woman. Though she has given up on marriage, her search for some person that will offer love brands her with a growing desperation she herself may fear to face.

This picture of desperation may strike us as odd, extreme, or isolated. Yet as this woman's conversation with Jesus unfolds, her portrait grows increasingly familiar. It should. Though this woman draws water at an ancient well, her situation remains remarkably contemporary. Not only does the immorality of our day echo in her choices, but the basic nature of all persons reflects in her experience. If we will look beneath the masks of those about us, we will see many similar faces. Roving eyes betray what well-trained expressions may not disclose—a never-ending search for something or somebody that will provide relief from an ache felt at a level of being that cannot be satisfied by the pleasures and ambitions of this life.

Faces of people in need appear where we work, where we play, and where we worship. We do not have to guess whether such faces are present. Experts say that only 5 percent of the couples in our society deem their marriages as deeply rewarding, less than 25 percent of working people want to continue in their present jobs for the rest of their careers, 50 percent of those currently married will seek sexual expression outside of marriage, and a third of us will go through episodes of serious depression.

I would not want to defend the accuracy of these statistics, but what we can see every day confirms a degree of their validity. The lines at the lotteries, the gambling phenomenon sweeping the country, Publisher's Clearing House hopes, the crowds before the latest investment guru, the luxury homes on postage-stamp lots, our society's lust for passion, marriage fix-it bestsellers, body-sculpting videos, our anger over health care, our fear of economic futures, our guilt over personal pasts—each in its own way signals the deep longing we have for the things we do not have, the security we cannot claim, and the contentment we do not really know. Little evidence disputes assertions that few of us are at real peace with ourselves, our situations, or our futures. Many of us put on masks to cover up our pain and sometimes do not see our own hurting, but a deep distress remains etched in our eyes for those who will care (and dare) to see faces. Each face mirrors a deep, deep need of the Gospel.

Maybe you think you cannot see these faces. The persons behind the faces are not obvious to you. You say to yourself, "How can I know what really characterizes other persons? I do not have Jesus'

X ray eyes. I cannot just look at a person and determine, 'You've had five husbands, and the one you're living with now is not your husband.'" Such reasoning is wrong. If you are willing, you *can* see the faces behind the masks. How? Look in the mirror.

WE MUST SEE OURSELVES FOR THE PERSONS WE ARE

By his dealings with the woman at the well, we learn that Jesus came to rescue her from her sin. For whom else does the Savior come? When Jesus says, "Everyone who drinks this water will be thirsty again, but whoever drinks the water I give him will never thirst" (John 4:13-14), his words embrace more than this one woman. The "everyone" and "whoever" are broad enough to include you and me. The needs she has, we share. The thirst-quenching he offers, we need.

Though Jesus deals with this woman, he reveals much more about each of us. He first exposes her desire for physical satisfaction through her thirst (v. 15). With this desire he confronts her need for relational satisfaction—she wants a man to make her happy (vv. 16-17). She responds by exposing her own spiritual poverty—she doesn't know on what mountain to worship (vv. 19-23). She longs for water, for love, and for spiritual well-being (vv. 25-26). She thirsts, but not alone. Her needs are universal. Each of us recognizes her needs because we have experienced them.

We share something else with this woman. We share her personal inability to find ultimate satisfaction in what *she* can do about any of these needs. When Jesus says that he can provide an eternal, internal source for satisfying the needs of this life (i.e., the "spring of water welling up to eternal life" in verse 14), he highlights the limitation we all must face. Apart from what Jesus supplies, we will always be dissatisfied, needy, and longing for more. We are all in need of him. In this way we are not different from this woman. She does not appear in Scripture for our pity, our amusement, or our scorn. She is the mirror in which we should see our own faces so that we will recognize in us the needs of others. As we are like her, they are like us.

Since Jesus came to be Messiah to me as well as to her, then in a fundamental way I am like her. In the deep well of my own heart's hurt reverberates my knowledge of her. And, if in me resides the essence of what one such as her experiences, then the mirror is the place I learn to see the faces of others. They are just like me.

Only when we understand how needy we are, will we see the true nature of every person. Unless we drink from the well of eternal life, we all thirst. Our need of Jesus makes us no different than any other we may choose to serve or to judge.

I have learned a poignant way to see my true nature while partaking of the meal Christ ordained to remind us of himself. In our church we serve Communion in small individual glasses that are passed down each aisle in trays. The juice we use has to be the right dilution for this to work, but in recent years I have taken advantage of the "view" those little, clear cups provide. I have noticed that I can hold the cup of drink in one hand and use it as a lens to look at my other hand.

Through that liquid-lens whose contents symbolize Christ's blood, my own hand looks as though it is red. The image reminds me that my hands are covered with blood. I am a sinner. My sin required my Savior's sacrifice. My actions required him to die for me, and my hands are stained scarlet. Jesus died for me, not just for some others in the world who possess great need. The guilt is mine. By blood shed *for* me, rather than *by* me, I have been made a blood brother with the most vile persons I can imagine. I am like them; they are like me. I, too, would die in my guilt were it not for my Savior's death for me.

We can forget our need at times, but our God takes care to let us see how like others we are so that we will remember how gracious he is. For example, a few weeks prior to writing this, I lost my temper at work. Losing one's temper at a seminary is not exactly noble behavior. We are supposed to be perfect on such "holy ground," but

I soiled the sacred halls a bit that day with my anger. Still, because I do not usually show my anger, I may be tempted to think such things do not characterize me. My pride wants to consider this momentary failure an atypical blip on my life's character monitor.

My heart needs a better perspective of my true nature. I need to see that if events get me tired enough, if situations put me under enough pressure, if just the right circumstances or people push just the right buttons, something ugly in me comes out that is just as real as the pleasant side of my nature. Another real me lies under the surface of the polite facade I can construct. This ugly dimension of my character is just as true of me as what I want you to see and more often portray. If you scratch deep enough, you will find the monsters of my character always raging beneath the surface.

I must continually renew my vision of the internal monsters that would sap spiritual strength from me and make my soul a desert so that I will thirst for my Savior. Anger, you see, is not my only frailty. I have a wonderful marriage, but if I did not, what real me might then surface? I have a great job, but if I did not, what sins might tempt me that I now do not even consider? I have a wonderful family and faith background, but were it not for these blessings that have nothing to do with my own choices, what would I be?

Only by the grace of God does anything good characterize me. My faults are deeper than I care to imagine, but I will never see the need others really have until I dare to consider my own true nature. If I do not consider my own causes for shame, I will judge others instead of loving them. I will distance myself from them instead of recognizing how our mutual needs unite us. I will look down on them instead of embracing them. I will stand aloof, rather than eye to eye. If I stop seeing the person I really am in my mirror, I will stop seeing the faces of others; and then the care that is the vehicle of the Gospel will not flow from me.

The limitations that stem from my arrogance surfaced a few years ago when a family visited our church. Their son met our son in Sunday school, and the new boy asked to sit with us in the following worship service. I said, "Okay," and almost instantly regretted the decision. The new boy was not familiar with church, and it showed. He was dirty. He smelled. He talked incessantly. He ignored my corrections. He punched my son. He got my son in trouble for punching back. During the sermon, for reasons obvious to no one, the new boy decided to stand on the back of the pew. My anger grew and grew.

By the end of that service I wanted nothing less than the electric chair for this little demon possessing our pew. Finally, after a sermon that I am sure lasted only thirty minutes (though it seemed like thirty hours), we stood to sing the final hymn. The little monster found the page number in his hymnal, ripping pages as he turned. Finally, he stood up—late—and sang with us, "Jesus, what a friend for sinners, Jesus lover of my soul." I confess my first thought was, *Why, you little stinker, how dare you sing so sweetly and innocently.* Then I *heard* the words of the hymn I was singing and had to face my own guilt. I had been growling inside at a child who needed my Savior. Jesus died to befriend such children, and yet all this child had known throughout the service was my anger, my frown, and my scowl.

I had to question who had really been the rebellious child in this service. How sinful I had been to care so little for one who so needed the grace I was supposedly there to praise. When I saw my sin, suddenly I could see that little boy as he really was. The barrier of my arrogance between us melted, and I saw a hurting child in an awful family situation, already out of control, desperately in need of my Savior—and as such, reflective of me. Though I had glared at him through much of the service, as he sang more of the hymn, I felt as though I saw his face for the first time. Now when I looked at that rebellion smudged face so mirroring my own sin, I could see past his antics and my discomfort. I could love him because I could see he was like me. He was just like me.

This little boy reminded me of how we penetrate the swirl of cultural problems that swallows souls. We pluck souls from the swirl by loving people who may at first glance seem far different from us. We are to learn to see our neighbors, fellow workers, relatives, peers, and passersby for the persons that they really are. They are just like us—sinners in need of a Savior.

When we see that the people around us are just like us, we may for the first time shun them less, judge them less, retreat less, and love them more with the love that carries the Gospel. Let us make no mistake, whatever reasons or rationales we think ought to motivate people to embrace our faith, the door through which the vast majority will enter is not doctrinal or denominational but relational.

People will come to know the Lord through us only if they know that we really see their faces and care for them as individuals despite the awful truths of their lives. We must confess that we do not find it easy to love those that bring us discomfort, embarrassment, and pain. We must recognize that we will care for them as we ought only if we acknowledge that what is true of them is true of our own natures. We are all sinners in need of the Savior.

My mirror reflects the face of a sinner I must see so that I will recognize others who are just like me. Without this clear reflection I cannot love others as my God requires. To help you and me see the truth about ourselves, the Holy Spirit provides this troubled woman to Windex our hearts with the water from the well of her experience. She mirrors us. Look at her. When you know you are like her, then you can love her—and others like her.

II. Truth About the Word

Love is not enough, though, to rescue souls from the swirl of culture. While compassion must characterize our approach to non-Christians, we have no monopoly on demonstrations of affection. Kindness alone cannot secure souls in a world where everyone from cults to K-mart builds constituencies with promises of care. Love that lasts—love with eternal consequences—requires a foundation of truth. Jesus leaves no question about the source of that truth. He alerts us in this passage that we must not only recognize the true nature of persons, but we must understand the nature of the Word meant to reach them.

The woman at the well initially seemed most concerned about her material needs (i.e., getting enough water) and the physical dimensions of her worship (getting to the right mountain). Jesus responded, "God is spirit, and his worshipers must worship in spirit *and in truth*" (v. 24). Matters of spiritual consequence require integrity. Jesus will compromise none of the truth he needs to say to this woman. He states his facts definitely and without apology. This is surely a passage for our relativistic times when truth seems so malleable, and no one can claim to grasp it firmly without ridicule or assault. Against the swirling tide of culture that says you can only know what is personally true for you, Jesus assures us that his Word is true.

THE IMPACT OF TRUTH

Jesus underscores the importance of acting on the basis of truth by refusing to compromise God's Word even when it may offend the one he seeks to reach. When Jesus exposes the woman's unmarried living situation, there is no question that she has to be uncomfortable with what he says. In her culture this situation would stain her reputation for life. She must feel the slap implicit in his words. Yet even though Jesus reveals her sin in a miraculous way, her response is all too human. She tries to evade the impact of the truths he reveals. She acknowledges the wonder of his knowledge (calling him a "prophet" in v. 19), but then she immediately tries to discount what he says.

To dodge Jesus' identification of her need, the woman first *questions the content* of his truth. In essence she says, "What right do you have to judge me? You Jews say we should worship in Jerusalem, but our forefathers say we should worship here" (cf. v. 20). Her reasoning is transparent. She questions, "Who can say what's right? How can anyone judge when even the experts can't agree?"

We recognize her attitude because it is so typical of our times. Now every generation cries, "You can't tell me what to do." The standard retort of talk-show hosts on anything controversial is, "That's just your opinion." Coworkers say, "That's just what your church says. . . . That's just your interpretation." Politicians, professors, and Hollywood jointly declare, "You can't impose your beliefs on others."

Jesus recognizes the protests of the woman as readily as we do and cuts her short. "Woman," he says, "a time is coming and has now come when the true worshipers will worship the Father in spirit and truth" (cf. vv. 21-24). Against the cultural conclusion of her day and ours that religion and truth are separate realms of reason, Jesus claims a universal Truth (v. 22). This is not the truth of ritual and tradition or the preference of a privatized faith. Jesus speaks with divine authority about transcendent Truth that obligates all persons before God (v. 23).

The woman then takes the next obvious step for one who wants to evade the obligations of Truth. If Jesus will not accept her contention that he holds only relative truth, she will question what right he has to dispense anything more. She *questions the authority* of Christ's Word. She says, "When the Messiah comes he will tell us what's true" (v. 25).

Jesus responds, "I who speak to you am he" (v. 26).

His message is simple: His standards are authoritative because he is Lord. Right and wrong are not indistinguishable. Everyone's truth is not as good as everyone else's. God's Word obligates everyone. Truth is not relative. You recognize the earth-shattering impact of these claims only by noting how rare it is for people in contemporary culture to say they really know what is true.

THE SHOCK OF TRUTH

The woman at the well is obviously surprised by Jesus' claims. She drops everything and races to town (v. 28). Her well-studied indifference to what others think vanishes before Christ's truth claims. But her shock must be a product of more than a philosophical challenge. She must realize that if what Jesus says is true, then the King of the Universe who knows the deepest, darkest truths of her life has loved her enough to come sit by a well and tell her of his salvation (vv. 10, 29). This is the most shocking truth of all: The God who knows us truly, loves us still.

The world about us does not understand this Christian love any more than it accepts God's Truth. The world expects those who claim to hold some exclusive truth to be intolerant, bigoted, and hardhearted. Too often we fulfill their expectations. Christ exemplifies another approach. His words and actions demonstrate how we are to speak without compromising truth *or* love. We must speak plainly and unashamedly about what his Word says even if it seems those truths may offend. At the same time, we must lovingly address those who may scorn us and God's Word. No testimony is more shocking, and none is more powerful than speaking the truth in love.

I recently witnessed the effects of such a courageously balanced witness at a spiritual life conference for university students. Over 300 young people from four universities attended. Some were Christians; many others were not. When I learned the number of non-Christians present, some who drove as much as five hours to attend, I asked the organizer of the conference what made them come.

He said, "It's simple. From the time these young people are in high school, they are taught that they can trust nothing to be absolutely true. Virtually no professor on any of their campuses would dare even to suggest universal moral values or transcendent truths. University life reserves only scorn for those who say they believe in any absolutes and labels such people as intolerant bigots. So when we tell these young people unequivocally that the Gospel of Jesus Christ is true and yet we love them, it blows their socks off.

"They are a generation without ideals living for the pleasures of the moment because they have been taught all their intellectual lives that nothing is really dependable or consistent. Most of them have otopped believing anything could be ultimately true. They recognize the despair and hopelessness of what they are taught in the universities, and they know how purposeless their lives will be if their professors are right. So, though many disagree with us, nothing attracts their interest and stimulates their hope more than someone who claims something is absolutely true and still loves those who differ."

Even when they do not immediately agree with truths Christians express, these university students respond to compassionate integrity. They are not likely to be unique. In a society without truth moorings, people both want and respect caring persons who will take a stand—who believe in *something*, not *everything*. Individuals who will present God's truths with the authority he grants and the love he commands can take advantage of powerful cultural forces to compel a hearing for God's Word.

THE OBLIGATIONS OF TRUTH

The power of a Gospel that refuses to segregate truth from compassion always hangs in jeopardy. The Church remains forever poised for a fall into intolerance fueled by a commitment to purity, or for drift into compromise provoked by a desire to be winsome. We seem caught in an almost unresolvable tension today. Our churches are supposed to project friendliness and care. We view ourselves as existing in a consumer culture where we have to compete with other churches who want to project just as much friendliness. As a result we blanche if our pastors address unpopular issues, speak authoritatively, or rebuke anything.

Preaching about sin seems the sure kiss of death for a growing church. But Jesus teaches us in this passage that penetrating truth is more important than shallow friendliness in the battle for souls. Sacrificial presentation of truths that may lack popular endorsement is the ultimate gift of love, and the ultimate cruelty is to deny others the truths that will save them from hell for fear of offending them. Mere selfishness can make churches friendly because we all want the prosperity of growth and the accolades of success. Greater love speaks unflinching truth in unfailing love and then lets the power of the Gospel do its work.

Nothing offers the swirl of ideas that dominates our culture a greater challenge than the simple truths of the Gospel. At the conference in Washington, DC, when the nation's leading apologists gathered to address "the swirl," no ultimate evangelism plan surfaced. No final solution emerged that would answer every question of our culture. In the final speech the conference leader concluded, "Apparently there is nothing more effective we can do than to tell the simple story of the Gospel." Somehow I felt Jesus must have smiled at that moment.

What can you do in the face of so many confusing ideas and competing notions? Tell others that Jesus died for your sins. What if you do not know all the right words? Tell them he forgave you. What if they scorn you? Love them. Remember the words of the old spiritual,

> *If you cannot sing like angels,*
> *If you cannot preach like Paul,*
> *You can tell the love of Jesus,*
> *And say he died for you.*

You do not have to be a seminary professor to do that much, and there is nothing more powerful. Tell all those for whom Jesus died that their sins can be forgiven. This truth presented with gentleness and respect can shake the world and claim another soul (cf. 2 Tim. 2:23-26).

III. TRUTH ABOUT THE SPIRIT

Is the simplicity of the Gospel too simple? Is it not foolish to expect culturally calloused people to respond to so unsophisticated a message? No. Our expectations remain valid not because our words burn with convincing eloquence, but because of the Spirit who ignites them in the soul.

Consider how God spreads a spiritual fire in this passage. By the conclusion of this account, many townspeople believed what this woman said (v. 39). She lacked credibility, owned a terrible reputation, and had yet to acquire a Ph.D. in theology, yet when she spoke the truth about Jesus, hearts changed.

The Word of God operates miraculously, but we tend to forget the miracle. Studies show that in the first year after their conversion, Christians most often share their faith. This is not the stage at which we are most informed, but it is the time when our transition from death to life is most apparent to us. We naturally enthuse about the miraculous work God's Word has done in us. Somehow God takes these uninformed utterances and uses them to reach others.

Sad to say, as we grow more sophisticated in our faith, we often grow more dependent on our own knowledge to convince others. We can lose confidence in simplicity and may begin to believe that more studied responses cause conversions. Growing dependence on our knowledge rather than on God's power, however, will inevitably result in less effective and less frequent witness. Through this Samaritan woman God intends to reactivate our confidence in him and to renew our zeal for his message.

God does not desire an uninformed testimony. He commands us to pursue knowledge, but he requires witnesses who depend on him. The reason for this Jesus has already explained—"God is spirit" (v. 24). Salvation efforts that focus on human abilities are doomed to fail. While we must engage all the resources of heart and mind in giving a reason for the hope that we have, we must remember that we battle for souls on a spiritual plane. We cannot affect this dimension of human existence solely by our own efforts. The spiritual realm is God's. Though the temptation to do God's work in our own strength is nearly compulsive, we must always resist self-dependent service. The spiritual dynamics necessary for salvation are beyond our manipulations. Only when God unleashes forces deeper than our emotions and higher than our thoughts do our strategies for salvation really work. His Spirit makes a simple Gospel effective.

God demonstrates his spiritual power in the testimony of this Samaritan woman. To see this demonstration we must ask how a discredited, uneducated (in the things of the Gospel), prejudiced woman could have such a spiritual impact on a community that was itself hostile to Jesus because of his race. She speaks few words, and those comments do not sparkle with clarity. Yet the Spirit of God sweeps through her and blows salvation into the hearts of an entire town.

With crafted beauty the Bible reveals how someone greater than this woman opens her heart and empowers her words. Consider the passage's 9s (vv. 9, 19, 29, and 39). As the conversations in this account unfold, the characters' evaluations of Jesus constantly shift. The woman first perceives him as her enemy (v. 9). Next his revelations of her life half convince her that he is a prophet (v. 19). Then his manner and claims cause her to think that he may be the Messiah (v. 29). By the passage's close, she and the townspeople believe in Jesus (v. 39). In a few hours the perspectives on Jesus change from public enemy, to probable prophet, to possible Messiah, to the Savior of the world (v. 42).

The Spirit of God makes simple words spiritual dynamite. God reveals the power of his Spirit in this account to encourage us. We can confront the swirl of culture with the message of the Savior even if our words are simple, because the same Spirit helps us. We do not limit the Spirit by our frailties. The Spirit accomplishes what our best words could not.

Each year for new seminary students I recount a time when the reality of the Spirit's work struck me with great power. The Spirit's wonderful work overwhelmed me when I walked into a new members' class of a church I pastored some time ago. Sitting together on tho front row of the class were three young women—all cousins. Though they had promised to come, their presence still shook me.

In the previous year each of these women had approached our church for help with very serious problems. I became acquainted with the first cousin after she left her husband over frustration with his alcoholism. As an Easter-only member, he had previously expressed little use for church, but he came seeking help after she left home. He said he was willing to do anything to get her to return. They came together for counseling. He dealt with his drinking. They reunited, and now she wanted to unite with our church.

The second cousin also had fled her marriage when she came for help at the first cousin's suggestion. She was the victim of spousal abuse and had sought solace with another man. Though we reached neither man, our ministry to this woman warmed her heart toward God. Even after her husband turned to other women, she left her lover and submitted her life to God's will.

The last cousin was also married, but she worked in traveling sales and was living as though several men were her husband. An accident that injured her nephew brought our church into her life. As she witnessed the care of Christians for the child and for her (despite her initial hostility toward us), she found a love her sexual encounters had not supplied. Now she, too, came to be a part of the family of God.

The presence of all three of these cousins in our church was a miracle. How foolish it would be to think that mere words that we had said—some consonants and vowels pushed out of the mouth by a little burst of air—could account for their decisions. No amount of human convincing could have turned them from selfish, pleasure-seeking, and self-destructive lifestyles to an eternal commitment to God. Hearts hostile to his Word now wanted fellowship with him. God plucked three souls from a hellish swirl of family confusion, spousal betrayal, and personal sin. Yet as absolutely amazing and

THE REVELATION OF TRUTH 47

totally astounding as these events seem, they are easily explained. The Spirit of God made the simple Gospel work.

These truths challenge us to question whether we have seen little fruit from our outreach to others because we have pursued it without dependence on the Spirit. Have we gained knowledge that has made us less humble? Have we tried techniques that have made us trust our sophistication? Have we memorized strategies that have made us less prayerful?

The Word of God reminds us that the best evangelism is still done on our knees. We must pray. Apart from the Spirit our best efforts will accomplish nothing lasting for the kingdom of God. Understanding the necessity and the power of the Spirit, the Puritan preacher Thomas Chalmers wrote long ago, "Prayer is not preparation for a greater work of God; prayer is the greater work of God." When we pray, iron wills yield, hearts melt, minds change, the swirl gets swallowed by the Spirit.

RETREAT NO MORE

Our culture will continue to swirl, but we can reach people caught in its currents. The Bible assures us there is no mystery and no magic in how we can rescue others. We cling to the pillars of truth about all persons, God's Word, and his Holy Spirit. These pillars anchor us for works of love, testimony, and prayer that allow us to cast others the lifelines of salvation. Caring, sharing, and praying are not new techniques for spreading the message of the Gospel, but they are the only means that will keep us from retreating from the people who need our help.

When Arab extremists freed Church of England envoy Terry Waite from five years of hostage captivity in Lebanon, he spoke of the healing ministry of one who would not retreat from him. The aid came from the other hostage named Terry—Terry Anderson, the Associated Press employee held the longest of any of the hostages.

Anderson is a committed Christian who, when he was released, responded to a reporter's question about his attitude toward his abductors by replying, "I am a Christian. I am required to forgive; there is no other choice."

Waite later said that Anderson was as faithful to his convictions during his ordeal as he was before the world's press. Waite had first-hand proof of Anderson's faithfulness. The British churchman told reporters that he had a serious lung infection at one point during his captivity. Because the terrorists provided no medical care for the hostages, Waite's infection went untreated. His incessant coughing became a source of great irritation for some of the other hostages not only because it was disturbing, but because it threatened to spread the infection.

Only one hostage was not put off by the coughing—Anderson.

Waite said later, "I was near the point of death, and though he could do nothing for me medically, Terry Anderson sat by my bedside for endless hours. I learned then the amazing healing power of a caring presence. I believe he saved my life simply because he would not leave me."

The compassion Terry Anderson demonstrated, God yet calls us to express. Though we know of the spiritual infections of the people around us who have contracted the world's sin, we must not abandon them. By his patience with a sinful Samaritan woman and with us, God calls us to be a healing presence in others' lives. He did not retreat from us because we carry the taint of sin. We must not retreat from others who are just like us. We possess the Word that offers life and can seek the Spirit who saves. Though we may think there is little we can do, we must refuse to retreat from those who need the truths we have been given. Even if their actions irritate our sensibilities and threaten our spiritual sanctums, God calls us not to abandon hearts to the swirl of sinful unbelief.

Do not underestimate the power of a determined healing presence. When we know the worst about others and still resolve to "be there" for them, we become agents of eternal life. The swirl stops its

THE REVELATION OF TRUTH

stirring when we express such compassion, and God retrieves souls from its midst. As long as we can simply speak his Word and humbly petition his Spirit, our work is not done. There are souls still to be won. He will win them through us as we resolve to be an uncompromising healing presence in this world.

DISCUSSION QUESTIONS

1) In what ways do the people around you evidence being caught in a cultural swirl that threatens to swallow their souls? What are the characteristics of this "swirl"?
2) What society-imposed needs do people in your culture face? What self-imposed needs do they create?
3) How does the woman at the well reflect who you are?
4) How does recognition of our likeness to this woman prepare us to share the Gospel?
5) Why is an absolute standard of truth needed to rescue people from their cultural swirl? What must be the source of this truth? By what authority can Christians claim that what they believe is the Truth?
6) What is the attitude of most people in your culture toward claims of absolute truth? What do most people suspect are the attitudes of those who claim they know what is really true? How do Christians sometimes confirm these suspicions?
7) Does "speaking the truth in love" mean Christians need to "water down" or "fuzzy up" what the Bible says about what God requires? How can we speak honestly without speaking harshly?
8) How can something as simple as the message of the Gospel expressed with conviction and compassion really change people?

2

THE VINDICATION

OF THE FALL

Why does grass grow in my driveway and not in my lawn? Why does my drain seem to clog only when company comes? Why is it that the only time my gas gauge falls to the left of empty is when I am already late? Why is something so often so very wrong in the persons I care so very much about?

As different as these questions seem, they actually spring from a common concern. Each asks why our lives are so often filled with frustration. Why do we have to face mosquitoes and SATs, bill collectors and disease? We may want to make light of these questions, but Christians cannot ignore them if we want the world to listen to the truths we say the Bible teaches. If we will not (or cannot) explain how a supposedly good God created this world of pain and suffering, then our faith will seem futile to all but the most indoctrinated.

Apologist Jerram Barrs writes in his series on "The Christian Mind" that the problem of evil is one of the most perplexing and persistent questions non-Christians ask. He was himself consumed with the question prior to his conversion and was initially turned off to Christianity by those who told him just to believe and not to bother with such issues. Later Barrs wrote that this ostensibly well-intended instruction fundamentally lacked compassion by not offering him a reasonable basis for faith. If Christians do not have adequate answers to such basic human questions, then we should not expect others to respond positively to the truths we espouse.

We should be eternally thankful as Christians that we do not need to dread questions about the source of life's afflictions. This portion of Scripture clearly explains how evil entered our world and why it stays. Some will choose not to accept what the Bible says about the cause of evil, but the explanation God offers is the only one that will not lead to greater frustration and deep despair. In this familiar passage that follows the account of Adam and Eve succumbing to Satan's seduction, God graciously provides Christians with sufficient light to rescue our faith and our lives from the darkness of a senseless world or a savage god that are the only alternatives to this biblical Truth.

GENESIS 3:14-19

[14]So the LORD God said to the serpent, "Because you have done this, cursed are you above all the livestock and all the wild animals! You will crawl on your belly and you will eat dust all the days of your life.

[15]And I will put enmity between you and the woman, and between your offspring and hers; he will crush your head, and you will strike his heel."

[16]To the woman he said, "I will greatly increase your pains in childbearing; with pain you will give birth to children. Your desire will be for your husband, and he will rule over you."

[17]To Adam he said, "Because you listened to your wife and ate from the tree about which I commanded you, 'You must not eat of it,' cursed is the ground because of you; through painful toil you will eat of it all the days of your life. [18]It will produce thorns and thistles for you, and you will eat the plants of the field. [19]By the sweat of your brow you will eat your food until you return to the ground, since from it you were taken; for dust you are and to dust you will return."

THE SAVAGE GOD

Harvard anthropologists tell us that in our cultural heritage are people who once worshiped the moon. At each new moon the women of the Nuer tribe would look up from their cook fires with dread. From each fire's edge the women would then grab ashes, throw them at the moon, and mark their faces with ash-soiled hands. Then, as a final expression of their fear and homage, the women would chant: "Ah, Moon, we pray that you would appear with goodness. May all people honor thee. O God, let us be."

"God, let us be." The words sound so remote—so far removed from our experiences—unless you listen closely. If you listen with your heart to the primitive words, you may hear in the honor of this savage god words much closer to home. You need not go far to hear the echoes: "Leave us alone. Don't bother us. Don't hurt us. O God, please, just let us be." We know these words still. They echo the thoughts of many who suffer and do not understand the God of the Bible nor the world he has made. They may echo the cries of a heart like your own.

A forty-two-year-old father of four, including a three-day-old infant, dies of a heart attack. His three teenage children are told the news by a well-meaning grandmother who says, "God has a reason; God took him for a good purpose." The oldest daughter cries, "Why doesn't God do his good somewhere else?"

A nineteen-year-old scholar-athlete goes to college. He makes the Dean's List, the basketball team, and he makes his parents proud. But in the fall of his junior year, he contracts viral meningitis. In thirty-six hours he dies. The preacher says, "The Lord gives and the Lord takes away. Blessed be the name of the Lord." A grieving father responds, "I will not bless such a God."

When they are just out of their teens, my brother and his wife are blessed with a beautiful baby boy. But only hours after the delivery, while they are still basking in that special glow of a first child, the doctor makes an appointment to see them. "Yes," he says, "your child looks perfect on the outside, but he has severe Potter's Syndrome." The baby is missing vital organs. He dies in five days.

Eighteen months later my sister-in-law is expecting again. The doctor says the chance of a second child having the same syndrome is one in 100,000. But the unusual symptoms of the first pregnancy begin to reappear. The worry and anxiety put such stress on my brother's wife that doctors hospitalize her twice while she awaits this child. I read her eyes. I listen to my brother's well-guarded expressions of worry. He is too concerned about offending me as a preacher and big brother to say what he really feels, but I sense the questions written in the pain on his face: "Is this God's doing? What is God doing? Why?"

Then the day of delivery comes. My brother welcomes a new daughter that is perfect in every way, and the young couple voice their relief in a hardly audible sigh mixing joy and grief: "Thank God, he let us be this time."

You need not go to a primitive land or a far-off place to find a savage god in the hearts and minds of ordinary people searching for reasons for their hurt. How should we answer them or the questions we have? Does God not care about us? Can he not take care of us or his world? Is he simply as unresponsive as the moon? The Bible answers each question without equivocation. God is not silent; he is not savage; he is not still. Our God consistently acts to bring about his good in a world corrupted by sin.

I. God Is Not Silent

The Bible never tries to hide evil from us. God offers no sugar-coating on suffering—no mystical sleight-of-hand to pretend this reality is not as it seems. Cold hard facts await those who will study Scripture to understand our world. Pain, heartache, disappointment, difficulty, affliction, unfairness, and cruelty are acknowledged with unflinching candor. They are all real. God refuses to shade the hard things, so we will trust him with the hidden things. The Bible speaks plainly about the evil that is plain to see, explaining both its cause and effects.

THE CAUSE OF EVIL

Two times in this passage (in fact, twice in the same verse) God explains why evil exists in our world. Speaking to Adam, God says, "*Because* you listened to your wife and ate from the tree about which I commanded you, 'You must not eat of it,' cursed is the ground *because* of you" (v. 17). The Bible says frustration and suffering exist in our world because Adam disobeyed God. The difficulties, diseases, and disasters we face are the result of our first parents' transgression. Human sin led to earth's misery. The perfect world God created was corrupted by the evil for which Adam and Eve were responsible. As a result of this original sin, we all live in a fallen world, a world that will continue to groan with misery until the day that Christ comes to redeem creation to its original state of perfection (Rom. 8:20-22).

THE EFFECTS OF EVIL

The effects of the evil that Adam and Eve introduced into the world are just as clearly presented in this passage. The Evil One (Satan) becomes a co-resident of the earth his wiles have corrupted (v. 14). His influence will now stretch throughout this world's history, and his assaults will reach as high as the Seed of heaven (v. 15).

Our entire existence is damaged by the brokenness of our present creation. Birth is now a source of pain (v. 16). The marriage relationship and, by corollary, the intimacy of all human relationships the husband-wife bond most highly represents are forever damaged (v. 16). The world itself now experiences trauma, and our being in the world suffers as a result (vv. 17-18). We now labor against the uncertainties of life in a world resistant to our efforts to prosper (vv. 18-19). Not only must we face trial, pain, and tragedy, but we become subject to life's greatest affliction—death (v. 19).

As the ultimate statement of the ruin man has brought upon his own relationship with God, the breath God imparted from his own infinitude to give man life now becomes exhaustible. From our first moments to our final state, the corruption of creation touches and taints all we experience.

THE CHALLENGE OF EVIL

Few who are reading this book will question this scriptural explanation for the cause and effects of evil. But this ready acknowledgment does not remove the challenge that the presence of evil offers our intellects. Despite statements in the ancient creeds and confessions of Christendom that the fall of Adam brought humankind into an estate of sin and misery, the modern intellect cannot help but question if this traditional understanding is correct.

Perhaps we all should confess that at times the biblical account of the Fall seems preposterous. A modern remake of a movie like *Inherit the Wind* that supposedly chronicles the historic Scopes trial on teaching evolution in Tennessee's public schools raises doubts that are hard to dodge. Even though we know Hollywood twists facts, characters, and ideas to provide "drama" with a clear antibiblical bias, we struggle to watch such a movie without a question or two popping into our brains.

The movie's depiction of a bombastic, self-righteous William Jennings Bryan defending biblical creation accounts with foolish reasoning almost inevitably activates a small voice in some remote corner of our minds that questions whether Carl Sagan was right when he spoke so "scientifically" of a universe devoid of Eden, Adam, and Eve. Could he be right? Have we abandoned thought for dogma? Have we been blinded by fundamentalist religion? Are there no better, more sophisticated answers to a troubled world than an ancient garden tale?

The Christian's answers to these questions must be, "No!" If you abandon the scriptural explanation for any other answer, however

sophisticated it may initially seem, then ultimately instead of finding a more intellectually satisfying solution, you will create a more
savage God.

II. God Is Not Savage

We use the word *savage* to describe what is very cruel or very primitive. God must descend to one of these levels of savagery if we
ignore the Bible's explanation for the presence of evil. Either God
could have created a better world and did not, in which case he is
incredibly cruel; or God wanted to create a better world and could
not, in which case he is ashamedly limited.

So-called sophistication that questions the fall of Adam forces
God into the role of a merciless tyrant or a beneficent incompetent
whose worship is a senseless sham. I never saw this more clearly
than when I took an orientation tour of a local hospital in the small
town where I first ministered. A local pastor from another denomination who was visiting some of his ailing members saw me wan-
dering the halls and generously offered to show me the location of
the nurses' duty stations, patient roster, and counseling rooms. I
gladly accepted, and we struck up a conversation as he led the way.

My guide soon asked what church I represented. When I told him
I was Presbyterian, he made an immediate wrong assumption. "Oh,
good," he said, "I was afraid you might be one of those fundamentalist Baptists." (Maybe something about the way I dressed.) He
laughed and then caustically referred to the struggles over inerrancy
Southern Baptist brothers and sisters have faced. "Can you believe
it," he said, "some of those clowns are still arguing for the historic-
ity of Adam!" I told him I was not Baptist, but I was one of those
clowns—and we changed the subject. Still I must confess I felt a bit
deflated. I want people's respect. I want to be thought of as a person
with an intellect and a few brains. Yet for my belief in Adam, here
was a man who considered me an utter fool.

I had to think on our conversation awhile before seeing who was really acting more foolishly. If the Bible is right and there was an Adam who caused the Fall of creation, I had some basis for going to a hospital to try to comfort people with truths about God. The God I represented lovingly created a perfect world for our nurture and enjoyment. Yet even after humankind marred his wonderful creation by selfish sin that causes unfathomable heartache, my God remains loving and faithful. He continues to use all things in this broken creation to lead people to seek his forgiveness, experience his grace, and gain access to a future, more glorious world (Rom. 8:28-29). I had hope to share with people from our church—I offered a sovereign, good God to comfort them.

But what God did this other pastor share while visiting his parishioners? If Adam did not fall, why were these people in the hospital? What kind of a God would create such a world of suffering? Only a terrible God would intentionally set up such evil. Only a primitive God could not control it. For all his intellectual sophistication, this Adam*less* preacher became an advocate of the most savage of gods. By denying Adam, he degraded God. If Adam did not fall, God did. Without the Fall this world's misery stands as absolute proof of God's savagery.

THE TYRANT GOD

A teenage mother gives birth in a city hospital to a child who goes into spasms from drug addiction. He will never see nor hear. He will experience his torture in a cell of impenetrable darkness and silence. It is God's fault. Yes, if there is no Adam and this world continues unaltered from God's original design, God ultimately remains responsible.

A mother of five develops lymphatic cancer. She will die. Her youngest is eighteen months. Without the Fall, God is culpable.

A television appeal shows thousands of children starving. Flies on their eyes, stomachs distended, faces too weary for expression, limbs too weak to struggle, bodies too debilitated to save—we witness the horror with eyes calloused from the repetition of the images. But who must be even more calloused? God. If his hand did this, his heart must be hard beyond comprehension. Such beastliness does not deserve worship.

Fear, loathing, and blame are the only obeisance anyone owes tyrants. What is so sad is how many Christians willingly offer God these responses by not understanding the consequences of the Fall. If these Scriptures are not applied to our own misery, we inevitably will blame God for our hurt. If we then honor him at all, it will be by mistaking dread for worship.

For fifty years a farming couple selflessly cared for an invalid daughter crippled by cerebral palsy. As the daughter began to age, her illness became more debilitating even as her parents' advancing age made them less able to care for her. When she lost her ability to communicate effectively with them, they did not realize the daily applications of eye drops given to her to keep her eyes moist were no longer sufficient. Only when the couple took their daughter to the doctor for an annual medical exam did they discover her eyes were suffering. The doctor's announcement stunned them: "Rachel is now blind."

The couple was devastated. They grieved for her suffering. They felt guilty for their failure to perceive her needs. They feared for her future since their health was also failing. But grief, guilt, and fear were not as overwhelming as their sense of divine abandonment.

This couple had served their God faithfully for almost three-quarters of a century. That he would now treat them with so little care—that he would treat their daughter with so much cruelty—was too puzzling and too painful to dismiss with Sunday school religiosity or polite resignation. Said a father weeping in agony and anger, "I don't know what we ever did that was so wrong that God has to treat us this way. Rachel certainly never did anything to deserve this. Why does God want to hurt us so?" The question may not sound respectful, but the man had a right to ask. If the only explanation for the suffering of innocents is arbitrary divine cruelty, then God is nothing less than a tyrant.

THE GRANDMOTHER GOD

If the thought of a tyrannical God horrifies you, the intellect can provide you with an alternative explanation for evil. The remaining option is a primitive God—a God who is powerful beyond human measure, but who is still not capable of handling everything in this world. He rules over his little domain as best he can, but he can be fooled, make mistakes, and lose control. This is the god of the theologian Edgar Brightman, who a generation ago urged, "Don't get angry at God; he's only finite." This is the god also of Rabbi Harold Kushner, whose popular book *When Bad Things Happen to Good People* still attempts to comfort us with the good intentions of a god who is doing the best he can.

This finite god is no tyrant. He is better compared to an invalid grandmother who sits at her kitchen window tapping on the pane with her cane because squirrels are stealing food from her bird feeder. "Go away," she says. "Shoo!" Then sometimes the offenders go away, but other times they do not. She means well. She wants to provide for her birds, but she cannot go out into the cold every time a squirrel comes along. She will just put some more bird seed in the feeder for her loved ones another time. The birds must simply pray that she has enough seed, does not forget, and that not too many squirrels come.

Such a grandmother god may be of little comfort in a cruel world where our futures rather than outdoor fowl are at stake—but he is all the God you get if you want no tyrant and there is no Adam.

Take your choice—cruel tyrant or aging grandmother. If you disregard the Bible's account of the cause of evil, then one of these gods is the only god you have left to worship. The old couplet rings true for either savage alternative:

If God is God, he is not good,
If God is good, he is not God.

Ultimately, if there is no Adam, there is no God. God is not really God if evil characterizes or eludes him. We are hopelessly alone in a bleak existence with no real cause to expect aid from a God who either creates misery or cannot control it.

The finest minds of our culture have always perceived the despair that characterizes our world without a biblical God. Even if they do not acknowledge the God of the Bible, the most perceptive and honest intellects have consistently recognized the darkness created by his absence.

In his book *The Savage God*, A. Alvarez first chronicles the intellectual turmoil and eventual suicide of Sylvia Plath, a poet popular in the 1960s. Opening with the poignant particulars of her life, Alvarez then offers a harrowing account of his own bent toward self-destruction. The personal account preludes an amazing history of suicide among the creative geniuses of Western society. Alvarez details the intellectual spiral of self-destruction into which those with deep insight into the human condition descend when they refuse to be distracted by worldly pleasures or petty ambitions contrived to convince us our lives have some significance apart from God. Time and again those who will look into the maelstrom of human existence devoid of a sovereign God and refuse to blink see only darkness.

Author Henry James writes, "Life is . . . a battle. Evil is insolent and strong; beauty enchanting but rare; goodness very apt to be weak; folly very apt to be defiant, wickedness to carry the day; imbeciles to be in great places, people of sense in small, and mankind generally unhappy. But the world as it stands is no illusion, no phantasm, no evil dream of a night; we wake up to it again for ever and ever; we can neither forget it, nor deny it, nor dispense with it." If Adam did not fall, savage is the God who created this miserable world.

We know some will scoff at the Bible's depiction of human ori-

gins (you will rarely be considered an intellectual giant for endors-
ing this view of evil's source), but if we do not embrace Scripture,
what hope do we have? None. The dreary blackness of an uncertain
and afflicted existence becomes inescapable. We are left with the
rebel gesture of a despairing poet who can only urge,

> Do not go gentle into that good night,
> Rage, rage against the dying of the light.

When the light of Scripture winks out, only darkness remains
with this curious irony: At the apex of Western thought we end up
flailing against the blackness with the futile echoes of our most primitive roots. The poet's secular sophistication returns us full circle to
throwing ashes at the moon, raging against the night.

Sophisticates may scoff at Scripture, but we must refuse to believe
they have superior answers. The young mother with a retarded
child, the elderly spouse of an Alzheimer's patient, the businessman
destroyed by dishonesty, the teenager disillusioned with adult
hypocrisies, the pastor dismayed by personal ineffectiveness, the
parent who just received the phone call about an accident—all need
a God who is not savage. The Nuer women called the god they worshiped "Wak na-a-na." The name means, "the god who kills people."
We must proclaim another God. His name is not Wak na-a-na. The
Bible says his name is "Wonderful."

III. God Is Not Still

Our God is no impassive celestial observer—no imperious deity in
the sky unmoved by his creatures' pain. The Bible tells of a God so
unswervingly affectionate and sovereignly able that he provided
eternal life to the very ones whose sin brought all the disasters, disease, and dying upon the creation he made and the creatures he
loves. By his words and actions in this passage God reveals both his

heart and his hands. They move with a purpose that denies the possibility that God could ever be cruel or impotent.

HIS HEART MOVES

There are no more crucial words in all of Scripture than those of this text where God first enters history to promise his Son to a fallen world (v. 15). In the cryptic terms of ancient prophecy God says that through the offspring of the first woman he will provide a Savior who ultimately will crush the influence of Satan in this world. But the promise reveals more than a determined resolve; it reveals an impassioned heart. From our side of Christ's cross we know not only what the ancient prophecy intends but whom it prophesies. God will send his own Son to rescue this world from its corruption and pain. What the prophecy also indicates the Son will experience, however, is the greater revelation of how greatly God's heart moves in our behalf.

The Bible says that the serpent (Satan) will strike the heel of the promised Seed of the woman (v. 15). The poetic words thinly veil the cross on which Jesus will suffer and richly display the undying love of our God. Knowing that the actions of humankind would lead to the horrible suffering of the one he most loved, God still promises to forgive, redeem, and glorify us. This is no savage God.

Our God's love and care are beyond our capacity to quantify. Such measureless mercy must eradicate all notions of an apathetic God and erase all mental pictures of a God who sits in heaven cavalierly throwing tumor switches or dispassionately arranging automobile accidents. For our faith to remain valid (and sane), we must know at the deepest level of our being that our God sees our afflictions and is not deaf to our cries (Ps. 34:15-18).

God loved us enough to send his own Son to walk this world and endure the assaults of Satan for our sin. Such tenderness proves that our pain touches our Lord. He weeps in heaven for our tears, sympathizing with our afflictions (Heb. 4:15-16; cf. John 11:35 and Heb. 13:8). Perhaps the most memorable political cartoon ever drawn followed the assassination of John F. Kennedy. The cartoon depicts the Lincoln Memorial with the normally statuesque Civil War president bent over in his chair, head in hands, weeping. The picture appropriately reminds us of the attitude of our heavenly enthroned God when the corruption of this world strikes us. He aches for our suffering with a divine grief more profound, pure, and deep than our own (cf. Luke 11:35; Rom. 8:26; Eph. 4:30).

HIS HANDS MOVE

Still our questions are not at an end when the Scriptures affirm the care of our God. If we are honest with our intellects and our emotions, we must confess that we wonder why a God who cares so much does not do more.

Is it not a cruelty in itself for God to require the faithful to affirm his goodness while they witness evil all about them in his world? God answers in the same verse that confirms his love. Here he does not swear to remove all evil from our world, but he determines to overcome it (v. 15). In this earliest declaration of his redemptive plan, God not only promises to expose his Son's heel to the temporal strike of Satan, but the Lord also prophesies his Son will utterly crush this enemy. With this prophecy the Bible assures us that though this world's corruption will continue till the day of Christ's final victory, God presently is neither uncaring nor inactive. His hands move in our behalf. He now uses all events (even those that are the consequence of a broken world) to destroy Satan and bring about the ultimate victory of Christ Jesus.

Our minds struggle to comprehend all this. We wonder why evil survives if a good God is active. We want God to stop the pain and cannot understand why he does not eradicate all of sin's consequences *now*. Scripture supplies the answers and the solace we need in the face of these concerns.

First, we are told evil survives so that we can exist here. Were God to wipe out all evil now, then not one person's life would continue. The sin that affects our world also infects every soul, as is evidenced by the dying to which all mankind becomes vulnerable in this account (v. 19; cf. Rom. 5:12). Were God to crush all evil, he would have to conclude the existence of every descendent of Adam, including each of us.

The second reason that evil survives is so that others can exist in heaven. Were God to eliminate all evil immediately, evangelism would come to an end. Not only would every Christian disappear if God were to eliminate all evil, in addition every culture and enterprise would cease to function since, as Jesus' parable of the wheat and the tares indicates, the institutions of man would be ripped apart. So entangled is every human institution with the corruption of this world that society itself would wrench apart with the uprooting of all of sin's influences and consequences. The righteous and the unrighteous would suffer with the demise of insurance companies, police, health care providers, fire departments, lawyers, environmental watchdogs, disaster specialists, bank and security services, pesticide dispensers, psychologists, drug companies, welfare workers, and child discipline experts.

No occupation as we know it could survive in a world without sin since Scripture teaches that virtually every profession is a direct consequence of humankind's need to protect itself from sin's consequences (vv. 17-19). To pull up the weeds of the world would inevitably rip apart the soil of society in which God has planted the seeds of salvation. Without any world order the Gospel would cease to spread. One day God will come to reap his harvest, but until that day the weeds grow with the wheat awaiting the new creation required for a world extricated from sin. Sad to say, no one in the world can escape the consequences of sin until that day. The godly as well as the ungodly face disease, heartache, and brokenness (2 Cor. 11:16-12:10; Heb. 11:32-39), but from this earthly compost new spiritual life blossoms every day.

Jesus never promises to remove his people from the struggles of this life prior to our deaths or his consummation. He promises to give

us the strength, comfort, and assurance of his ultimate purposes
while we are in the world so that we may be his witnesses and face
the world's evil undaunted till he comes (John 17:14-21). God does
promise never to allow us to face trials greater than we can bear (1
Cor. 10:13), but he tells us plainly that trials will enter our lives while
we live in this fallen world (Matt. 6:34).

Were God simply to remove all consequences of evil from those
who claim to be his followers, then selfishness rather than service
would be the motive of salvation. God's servants would witness out
of arrogance and pride rather than empathy and humility if their
faith excused them from the human condition. For the present our
God graciously allows our fallen world to exist as a perpetual object
lesson of the awfulness of sin and the need for all to depend upon
him. Were the evil of this world not truly horrible, there would be no
evidence of the awfulness of sin, nor any apparent need to turn to
God for help. The evil that God allows loosens our grasp on a world
always ready to entice us with the lie that an eternal God is unreal or
unnecessary. We need not make light of this world's suffering nor
deny its true terrors to defend God. We must see evil for the horror
it is so that we will recognize the necessity of grace in our lives and
testify of it for the souls of others.

Our finite minds reel before the scriptural assertions that an all-
knowing, all-powerful God can use evil for good without himself
becoming responsible for the evil. It is not sinful to acknowledge that
our sufferings and the afflictions of loved ones often seem senseless
and without purpose. But true discipleship requires that we order
our thoughts in accord with the thoughts of God. As water runs in
the constraints of a furrow, our minds should follow the contours of
Scripture. In order for our faith to stay strong and our vision of God
to remain sane, Christians must believe that our affliction is always
an assault of Satan and never an attack by God. The Bible says God
never intends evil, never delights in suffering, never abuses his children, but "preserves and governs all his creatures and all their

actions" in such a way that he brings about their ultimate good and his redemptive glory.

The life of Joseph is a wonderful example of God's management of the evil he condemns to accomplish the glory he intends. Sold into slavery by his brothers, falsely accused, unjustly imprisoned, cruelly forgotten, and miserably alone, Joseph nevertheless becomes God's instrument of preparing an Egyptian incubator for the birth of the nation from which our Savior will come. When Joseph's brothers later quake before him in fear that their once-sold, now-Pharaohed brother will seek revenge for their betrayal, he responds with the grace his life has exemplified: "You intended to harm me, but God intended it for good to accomplish what is now being done, the saving of many lives" (Gen. 50:20).

From the earliest pages of Scripture, God assures his people that such intentions are always in effect. His hands ever move to bring about the redemption of his creation, the salvation of his people, and the ultimate crushing of the Evil One (v. 15). This does not mean we never have questions, nor that our minds will always comprehend the purposes or methods of our infinitely wise and consummately able God. But his love should itself never come into question. From the dawn of creation God has told us he intends good and not harm for us. The undeniable evidence of that love is the supreme sacrifice to which Genesis 3:15 points. The God who would send his own Son to the cross to die for the evil of which he was innocent to save those who are guilty must love the people he saves (Rom. 8:32).

IV. Sophisticate, Simpleton, or Son

The God of the Bible is neither silent, savage, nor still with regard to evil. In his Word he says a perfect world was corrupted by man. In his providence he uses the consequences of sin in this world to draw his children into his embrace. In his mercy he sent his Son to save mankind from the sinful suffering of which man himself is the cause.

SOPHISTICATE OR SIMPLETON

In this age when those who like to test traditional ideas and toy with novel notions seem to dominate our culture, it may be tempting to question if sophisticated minds need to accept the simple truths of this ancient text. You may be thought a fool by the world's philosophy and science (falsely so-called) for believing suffering is a consequence of original sin. Yet in your "foolishness" you at least share a God who is not savage. Value this privilege and do not underestimate how easily it may escape us. Without ever intending it, we can lose the concept of a compassionate God by lack of care in interpreting this account even if we believe it.

Though Christians may blame liberal theology and scientific atheism for the recreation of a primitive God necessitated by denial of Adam's fall, we may unwittingly create as savage a God. Theology depicting a God who rules by cruelty, fear, and arbitrary judgment comes from Satan. How, after all, did Satan sway Eve? To tempt her he said, in essence, "God does not have your best interests in mind. God is trying to disadvantage you by keeping you from becoming like himself. He willingly hurts you" (Gen. 3:4-5). Satan made Eve question God's disposition toward her. The Devil was not as radical as many modern theologians. He did not make Eve doubt the truth of God's Word, only its intent. We must take this distinction to heart to avoid portraying God with Satan's twist.

We may hold to the truth of God's Word and yet abandon its intent by our demeanor, emphasis, or interpretation. We commit this error whenever we say God "causes" or "desires" a tragedy, disaster, or trial that hurts his people. Such statements, even when intended to defend the sovereignty of God, confound God's people and ultimately lead them to distrust the goodness of God. Scripture carefully assigns the evil of this world to the wiles of Satan and the hand of man. While such explanations do not answer all our questions nor reconcile all the problems with which our finite minds wrestle, they do keep our faith consistent with Scripture.

FATHERS AND SONS

When I determine that only good comes from the hand of my heavenly Father, I know how to address my world. I do not have to tell the grieving parents of an only daughter killed by a drunken driver that God did this. I do not need to look in the eyes of a leukemia patient and say, "God wants this." I must never speak to a child of abuse and declare, "God desired this." Theologians properly debate how the decrees of God allow for the existence of pain, but at the most human level we must assure Christians who hurt that their God does not conjure the evil they experience.

Scripture never portrays God as the author of evil. Yet it affirms that he assigns each event its place in his eternal plan to crush Satan, renew this world, and save souls. While Satan seeks always to destroy, God works all things for good. As obvious as this instruction seems, we must clearly distinguish the roles of these two spiritual entities lest we destroy our own basis for faith.

Faith went on trial one October evening in our town when a distressed father sat at the bedside of his comatose son. The young man had been hurt playing basketball at a church picnic. Desperate to save his team's possession of the ball at a crucial point in the game, the sixteen-year-old lunged for an errant pass going out of bounds. He missed the ball but not a spectator's chair. As he toppled over the chair, one of its legs caught the young man in the stomach and damaged vital organs. Because he felt little pain, the teen continued to play the game's final minutes while he hemorrhaged internally. By the time the pain grew enough to warrant a trip to hospital, it was almost too late. The doctors worked frantically to save him. When they had done all they could, the outcome was still uncertain. The family began its bedside vigil, waiting hour upon hour for slightest signs of recovery.

Though the son would eventually recover, those awful hours of waiting forced family members to ask questions they had never before faced. The father was alone on his bedside shift one evening when the pastor visited. They talked quietly about particulars of the son's care before the conversation turned to the deeper concern on the man's heart. Trembling with emotion and a level of spiritual wrestling the pastor had never heard him express, the father asked the question that put his faith and his God on trial: "Will God kill my son to punish my sin?"

This father was a leader in his church. Neither he nor the pastor knew of any awful sin in his life that would require the life of his son for divine recompense. Still in this moment of crisis he needed an explanation for his pain. He dared to question out loud if his God would cruelly strike a child to wrest his pound of flesh from an imperfect parent. The man asked simply if his heavenly Father could act like Satan.

We should not blame the father for his question. Such wondering comes to the minds of most when we face suffering. God will surely not blame us for the question for which he so carefully prepares an answer in his Word. In a world so full of pain God knew we would have to ask.

The answer appears here at the dawn of creation and the downfall of man. God's people horribly corrupt his world. Their actions, not God's, lead to an existence in which misery and pain fall upon the unjust and the just as long as this creation exists. What is God's response? Grace—the promise of his Son to satisfy divine justice and redeem sinful man. This is not a God who would willingly hurt any of his loved ones.

The pastor now trembled to say all this in words that would comfort and grant renewed trust in the God this father now so desperately needed at his son's bedside. Somehow the Holy Spirit provided the words. "No," said the young minister, "the Lord is not punishing *your* son for your sin. He could not, because God punished *his* Son for your sin."

Yes, our minds are sometimes pressed beyond their logical limits to reconcile the workings of God's sovereignty and the consequences of man's sin. In these moments when answers seem beyond reason, we must draw our hearts to the cross to gaze on the proof of surpassing love. At Calvary are the answers to quiet our objections, calm our hearts, and confirm our faith. Pierced hands, feet, and side defy us to question our God's care or challenge his actions in our behalf.

When human minds cannot determine why God restrains some evil and gives other temporary sway, the cross reveals enough of his mind and of his heart to assure us that his choices are never arbitrary nor savage. From such a God we can take strength and sustenance. To such a God we can go for forgiveness and grace.

We need not plead with our God, "Please, let us be." His Word tells us why: "'For I know the plans I have for you,' declares the Lord, 'plans to prosper you and not to harm you, plans to give you hope and a future'" (Jer. 29:11). In a world of evil we can still turn to this God who is Wonderful.

DISCUSSION QUESTIONS

1) What are the consequences of Adam's original fall into sin? Why is this biblical explanation for the world's misery difficult to accept?
2) What modern notions challenge Scripture's explanations of evil in our world?
3) If Adam did not fall, what does evil in our world necessarily imply about God?
4) What are the consequences of believing in a tyrannical god? What are the consequences of believing in an impotent god? How does the despair in our culture confirm these consequences?

5) What evidence does the Bible provide that God is not savage? How early in time does the Bible present this evidence? What event provides the most persuasive statement of this evidence?

6) What are reasons that God does not immediately eradicate all evil?

7) Why does the Bible take such care to deny that God is the author of evil while at the same time denying that it is beyond his control? How can God manage evil without being blamable for it?

8) Why does our humanity require a God who does not delight in evil and who sympathizes when we experience it? How do we know that God can sympathize with our suffering?

3

THE PERFECTION
OF PROVIDENCE

THE WORD IN PERSPECTIVE

~

Many have push-started a car. A driver enlists a friend's muscle and push to get the car rolling and then "pops the clutch," hoping that the car's momentum will start the engine. Believe it or not, almost the same thing can be done for a helicopter. Knowing how to "push-start" a helicopter has saved the life of many a pilot. So important is it to know how to do this that if you go to an Air Force base, you can watch pilots practicing the procedure. No, they do not get their buddies in a circle and blow real hard. Air Force pilots let gravity supply the energy.

When a helicopter engine stalls in flight, the pilot lets the air rushing past the falling copter set the rotor spinning. Then when the blades are rotating fast enough, the pilot "pops the clutch." Changing the angle of the blades, the pilot uses the wind draft to reengage the engine or "flare" the rotor enough to break the aircraft's descent. The downward fall of the aircraft—as awful as it is—actually saves the pilot.

Similar dynamics may operate in our spiritual lives. We may seem to be crashing. Awful things may happen. Yet God reveals in Scripture that he can use difficulties that drop us down to the deepest depths of human experience to enable us to soar to greater heights with him. In his providence (God's infinitely wise governance of all things that affect his people), the Lord may even save souls by descents into the darkness of tragedy.

To understand how God reveals his providence, recall what hap-

pened to Job. Remember that Job suffered much (chaps. 1-2). Yet despite early personal resolve not to complain (1:20-22; 2:9-10), ultimately he lost his patience and objected to his treatment (cf. 31:35; 40:2). Because we can sympathize with his concerns when our lives are crashing, we need to see what Job learned. We pick up his lesson (and ours) in the midst of God's response to Job's complaint:

JOB 40:1-14; 42:1-6

[1]The LORD said to Job: [2]"Will the one who contends with the Almighty correct him? Let him who accuses God answer him!"

[3]Then Job answered the LORD: [4]"I am unworthy—how can I reply to you? I put my hand over my mouth. [5]I spoke once, but I have no answer—twice, but I will say no more."

[6]Then the LORD spoke to Job out of the storm: [7]"Brace yourself like a man; I will question you, and you shall answer me. [8]Would you discredit my justice? Would you condemn me to justify yourself? [9]Do you have an arm like God's, and can your voice thunder like his? [10]Then adorn yourself with glory and splendor, and clothe yourself in honor and majesty. [11]Unleash the fury of your wrath, look at every proud man and bring him low, [12]look at every proud man and humble him, crush the wicked where they stand. [13]Bury them all in the dust together; shroud their faces in the grave. [14]Then I myself will admit to you that your own right hand can save you. . . ."

[1]Then Job replied to the LORD: [2]"I know that you can do all things; no plan of yours can be thwarted. [3]You asked, 'Who is this that obscures my counsel without knowledge?' Surely I spoke of things I did not understand, things too wonderful for me to know. [4]You said, 'Listen now, and I will speak; I will question you, and you shall answer me.' [5]My ears had heard of you but now my eyes have seen you. [6]Therefore I despise myself and repent in dust and ashes."

JUST, OR JUST THERE?

God intends it for good—some good, somehow. We say the words so easily to defend the providence of God until we face the unfairness of this world. We hear reports of soldiers held in secret captivity for years, young men deprived of their youth, their families, and their careers for no apparent purposes. It is an injustice, an absurdity, an outrage of war we can hardly imagine could be true.

Our imaginations cannot, however, shut out other horrors we know are true. Tens of thousands made refugees by the avarice of their own government. Driven from their homes, living in squalor, weakened by malnutrition, they die so a political party can control an impoverished nation. It is an obscenity of governance. We watch the newsreels and ease our consciences with orthodox recitations of God's control for ultimate good.

Then the difficulties come crashing into our own world, and the words do not come so easily. A young couple cries, "We wanted this baby so much, but the doctor doesn't hear a heartbeat. We have to go to the hospital. They will take her. Thousands of people don't want their babies and abort them. We want one, and God won't let us have her. It's not fair."

A grandfather works for an engineering firm for thirty years. Two years from retirement, without a real chance of being rehired, the firm succumbs to economic pressures and closes his department. The company hands him a pink slip just when the children of a son's broken marriage are due to move into his home. Does God know what he is doing? Is this right?

A nineteen-year-old college student is thrown from a car as it plummets into a ditch. The friend who fell asleep at the wheel walks home from the hospital within days. But many days dawn before the young man propelled from the car awakes from his coma to hear a doctor say he will never walk again. Can this be just?

Multiply your own examples . . . people you know . . . the struggles you face. You know the question that is not supposed to come to mind, but it does: "Is God just, or is he just there?"

You may think that the book of Job is the wrong place to look for answers to such a question. We recognize and fear Job's trials. He loses everything—wealth, health, children, care of a spouse, respect of friends. Why? Was Job a terrible person? Were Job's afflictions just punishment for a great wrongdoing? No. Job protests throughout his trials that he might not have been perfect but he committed no great sin (cf. 29:11-17). Job's neighbors say the same (4:3-6). Even God confirms, "There is no one on earth like him; he is blameless and upright, a man who fears God and shuns evil" (1:8).

If God can demonstrate his providential care in the face of such apparent unfairness, then our basis for trusting him grows more sound. As unlikely a source as the book of Job may seem to be to establish the comforts of divine providence, we need these passages to answer our most pressing questions about God's activity in this world. No book more greatly challenges the judgment of God, and no book more certainly confirms his care. Explanations and comfort we still need lie within the principles this most ancient biblical text labors to make plain.

I. Trouble Does Not Always Mean Sin

When something horrid happens to others or to us, we tend to make an automatic assumption: Something went wrong because someone did wrong. At a minimum the book of Job impedes the swiftness with which we draw this conclusion. Here God refuses to make his blessing a direct result of human righteousness. Job suffers, but his righteousness even God will not deny (1:8). Neither Job's blessing nor his afflictions are unalterably tied to his actions in this fallen world. Any attempt to press the providence of God into a mathematical equation based on our works will fail in the book of Job. This is an important first principle we must learn if our trust in God will outlive our difficulties. Yet as early in Scripture as God establishes this principle that trouble does not necessarily indicate sin, Christians frequently forget.

Even Christ's disciples made the mistake of automatically linking personal suffering to personal sin. One day when they saw a man who had been born blind, they asked Jesus, "Rabbi, who sinned, this man or his parents?" (John 9:2). Their assumption was obvious. They thought, *If this man has a problem, then he or someone close to him must have sinned.*

The disciples believed the man's difficulty indicated that God must have been getting back at someone for something. Jesus' response undermined the disciples' presumption and laid the basis for our confidence in him. He replied, "Neither this man nor his parents sinned, but this happened so that the work of God might be displayed in his life" (John 9:3). The physical healing of this man triggered events that led to eternal healing for him (John 9:38) and others (John 10:21). Jesus used the fallen conditions of this world to bring glory to himself without blaming one who suffered because of those conditions.

We need not automatically assume guilt for the troubles we face. We live in a fallen world. While God may use its troubles to convict of wrong or even punish sin, "it ain't necessarily so." Personal trouble does not automatically imply personal guilt. Good people living in a fallen world may experience its pain through no fault of their own. We must recognize that to some degree all people face the consequences of living in this world, or else at the very moment we need assurances of our God's providence, we will presume his hatred.

While laying asphalt during my college summers, I met a man whose life and faith were shattered by his failure to recognize that trouble was not an automatic indication of God's wrath. He was a huge, hard-working truck foreman named James Hildebrand. James cultivated a tough-as-nails image with a crusty, iron-hard exterior that barely hid a very large and pudding-soft heart.

During my second summer of working for the paving company,

James's son had his seventeenth birthday. He received what every son of an asphalt trucker must want most in this world. A new dump truck—not the kind Tonka makes. The truck foreman father gave his only son a shiny new thirteen-gear, eighteen-ton mountain of motor and steel on wheels. It was the pride of the young boy's life—and his demise. One day as he hauled a heavy load, the truck developed a brake problem. The boy crawled under the truck to fix it. The load shifted unexpectedly. He was killed.

Months later James came into the scale house where I was now weighing trucks. He sat down and uncharacteristically began "wasting time" by shooting the breeze with me. I kept wondering what he wanted as we talked about meaningless things. Then I saw his eyes cloud and begin to tear. I realized that he was no longer talking to me. In my youth and in my features he was seeing his son.

A tear rolled down his cheek and unleashed the pain he could constrain no longer. "Oh, Bryan," he said, "I should never have let him do it. It's my fault." Then he explained how the Sunday before his son was killed, James had let the boy go help a friend who was in a pinch unload a truck rather than go to church.

James believed he had to pay for his sin with sorrow. It did not matter that the punishment seemed far out of proportion to the supposed wrong. In this moment it did not matter that the Bible itself grants permission for works of worship, mercy, and necessity on the Lord's day. The only thing James knew was that trouble meant sin.

What a load of guilt and pain could have been lifted if James had known that sin need not be the only explanation for affliction. I wanted to hug him and say the words that would comfort him, but I was too young and did not know how. The words I needed God now provides. He embraces us with truths needed by all tormented with the guilt they assume must be present because of the troubles they experience. The God who put the penalty of our sin on his own

THE PERFECTION OF PROVIDENCE

Son spares us from the automatic conclusion that trouble we face always represents his punishment.

We need to consider all of Scripture to understand all the dimensions of our experience. Until the Lord returns to perfect this world, we will face misery and pain. The world spares no one all its hurts. Prophets, apostles, and the Savior all experienced the horrors of this world. Their pain could not always have been punishment. Frequently their testimony in trouble was the path to others' salvation.

If trials can only be explained as God's slap, then as long as our imperfections exist, we will fear ever to face God. Instead, God invites us to turn toward him with the promise of his relief in trial. He does not offer to release us from all trouble. The God who sent his Son to die for those who rebelled against him could never be capricious or mean. This, too, we learn from Job.

II. Trouble Does Not Mean God Is Mean

James Hildebrand could not see beyond his loss. His hurt eclipsed the loving character of God and governed his perspective. Through the lens of his pain the foreman pictured God as a vindictive, hostile, and vicious being who required his pound of flesh when crossed.

We must be careful not to judge this hurting father too harshly because his attitude precisely echoes Job's. James said, "This tragedy must have happened because I did something wrong." Job said, "Oh, God, how many things have I done wrong. Please make me to know my transgression and wrong" (see Job 13:23). In essence, both plead, "God, I don't know why you are after me, but if you'll just let me know, I'll repent. Please, God, explain why are you hurting me. What did I do wrong?"

Perhaps we have all explained our difficulty by assuming God's caprice. When I played little league baseball as a child, I was what you would call an average player. You know what being an "average" little leaguer means. It means some days I literally shined on the field, and other days I was about as spectacular as the nearest clod of dirt. I remember one of the latter days. I started at third base. Then after a few less-than-spectacular plays, I was exiled to right field. There I determined to do better—to redeem myself.

Soon I got my chance. A lefty hit a lazy fly ball right to me. I took a bead on the ball arcing toward me and knew I could not miss. The ball came closer and closer. I raised my glove into position and shielded my eyes against the sun with a professional flair. Then just as the ball arrived—in a last horrible instant—I realized I had misjudged, again. I made a desperate lunge at the ball as it passed over my head. All my teammates then saw was my flashing heels as I turned to chase the ball. What they did not see as I ran deeper into the field to retrieve the ball bouncing toward a distant fence was my tears. I cried as I ran and shouted to the sky, "Oh, God, what did I do?"

I knew about God. I knew he expected me to abide by his standards. So when I faced a little-boy's nightmare, I thought that I must have offended the bogey man above. I had pictured God as he could never be—capricious, vengeful, punishing for reasons impossible to determine (cf. 42:5). Though it was a child's impression, I need to remember what I felt, because we can all mature with such a false perspective planted in our hearts, and it will blossom later in our trials. Even Job began to regard God as an arbitrary accuser who maintains his rule with capricious acts. Said Job:

> *He throws me into the mud, and I am reduced to dust and ashes. I cry out to you, O God, but you do not answer; I stand up, but you merely look at me. You turn on me ruthlessly; with the might of your hand you attack me. You snatch me up and drive me before the wind; you toss me about in the storm. . . .*
>
> *Oh, that I had someone to hear me! I sign now my defense—let the Almighty answer me; let my accuser put his indictment in writing. Surely I would wear it on my shoulder, I would put it on like a crown. I would give him an account of my every step; like a prince I would approach him. (Job 30:19-22; 31:35-37)*

God's response to these statements clearly indicates how far afield Job's perspective has wandered. God says to Job, "Brace yourself like a man; I will question you, and you shall answer me. Would you discredit my justice? Would you condemn me to justify yourself?" (Job 40:7-8).

God recognizes that Job's statements decry divine justice (27:2). The creature screams at the Creator, "I don't deserve this. Since I am righteous, my trials must indict you." The divinity Job forges at this stage degenerates into meanness in the fires of affliction. He will yet "honor" God as one obeys a tyrant, but his trouble drives the compassion of the Lord into obscurity (31:23). Job even talks to God with the combat language reserved for enemies (e.g., 29:11, 18, 19, 28; 40:2).

Because these attitudes of Job too easily breed in our own hearts when we face trial, God uses the occasion to clarify his nature to this servant and to future generations. The patience of God now unfolds with penetrating power to reveal: 1) he *never abandons* his own; 2) he *never abuses* his children; and, 3) he *always redeems* his people.

NEVER ABANDONS

Though the book of Job meticulously adopts the biblical mind-set of assigning evil to the activity of Satan (see 1:12; 2:6), Job ultimately blames God for the calamities. Were God truly the insensitive lout Job accuses him of being, then what might God do? He could just turn away. He could abandon Job to his tirade of sinful accusations. God refuses to do so.

Although his words are stern, God clearly presents himself to Job (38:1; 40:1). Simply by speaking to Job, the Lord declares his unwillingness to walk away from an angry heart. The picture of a God who refuses to turn his back on a fist shaken at heaven needs to wrap itself around our minds. When we remember that our fists have been raised, we may doubt that God would ever care for us again. Against such doubt we can thrust these abiding truths our God so carefully plants in Scripture to remind us that he refuses to abandon his own.

NEVER ABUSES

How else might God respond to Job's accusations? If God were truly the arbitrary tyrant of Job's imagination, then how might we expect God to use his power in response to Job's disrespectful accusations (chaps. 38-41)? He who can shut up the sea behind doors (38:8), shape the earth like clay (38:14), send lightning bolts on their way (38:35), command the eagle to soar (39:27), and can pull in leviathans with a fishhook (41:1) does not need to sit idle before the taunts of a man.

How would you expect an arbitrary, capricious God of such power to react before Job's accusing finger? Job's wife thought she knew what would happen if he blamed God. When Job's trouble grew nearly unbearable, she advised, "Curse God and die" (2:9). An abusive God would lash out when challenged. A vindictive God would leave only a little greasy spot in the desert where a complaining Job once stood. What did our God do instead? Though he reminded Job that he had power to punish all evil (40:9-14), God did not lay a hand on this man.

In the end Job contritely falls to his knees before God's restraint. God does not knock his challenger down. God's patience demonstrates his love for his own and his desire to bring evil to an end—even the evil that originates in our hearts. We need to remember this God when troubles assail us. He takes no delight in evil. Brutality does not reside in his being. The God of such patience and mercy cannot be cruel.

ALWAYS REDEEMS

If God neither abandons nor abuses, then what is his real nature? He is the God who carefully reveals our own inadequacies so that we will never try to depend on ourselves to escape this world's evil. God challenges Job:

> *Do you have an arm like God's, and can your voice thunder like his? Then adorn yourself with glory and splendor, and clothe yourself in honor and majesty. Unleash the fury of your wrath, look at every proud man and bring him low, look at every proud man and humble him, crush the wicked where they stand. Bury them all in the dust together; shroud their faces in the grave. Then I myself will admit to you that your own right hand can save you. Job 40:9-14*

The words sound harsh, but they have a specific purpose. They confront Job with the limitations of his fallen nature. Despite Job's protests of the sufficiency of his goodness prior to what he assumes are heaven's assaults, he must recognize that "his own right hand" cannot save him.

Job stands helpless before this world's evil. God uses the trials that Satan brings to redeem Job from false perspectives of his ability and to point the complainer toward his real hope. Consistent with his true nature, God responds redemptively to Job's accusations. In essence, God leads Job back to his own earlier confessions that he now must see with clearer vision. Once Job comforted himself with these words: "I know that my Redeemer lives, and that in the end he will stand upon the earth. And after my skin has been destroyed, yet in my flesh I will see God; I myself will see him with my own eyes—I, and not another. How my heart yearns within me!" (Job 19:25-27).

The heat and duration of his trials eventually parch this profession from Job's lips, but God allows him to reconsider his one true hope. Job's rescue from the fallenness of this world and his own nature must rely upon a Redeemer whose victory will overcome this world and transform his mortal nature. When Job again sees his need in the light of his own impotence before his trials, he turns again to the God who alone can redeem (42:1-6).

It seems as though Job's mind has been working in two separate rooms with the door between double-bolted. In one room Job counts all his hurts and blames God. In the other room Job recounts God's plan to save him from all evil and to repair this broken world. God had wonderfully revealed to Job the same Redeemer that you and I know. Why then did Job question God's kindness? For the same reason we do. In our fallenness we concentrate on the immediate.

What stings gets all our attention. We might compare our spiritual response to trial to our reactions to getting a bee sting while mowing the lawn. Though we may have been cutting in precise rows, carefully avoiding the rose bushes, checking the fuel, monitoring the clippings, and in all other ways focusing on proper concerns, when the bee stings, we think of nothing else. We forget all about the straight rows and rose bushes. In the book of Job, God reminds us that the lash that stung his Son and the nails that pierced him should hold our attention. God's redemptive purposes always remain in effect.

We should not be too hard on Job because we are too much like him. We can intellectually know of Christ's love demonstrated on the cross, and still when the trials come, we forget it all. The grace and mercy of the Lord fade into the background, and we paint him as the tyrant he could never be. As a result we run from the one we need at the hour we most need him.

The trials we face vary greatly, but the one with whom we need to face them never changes. It may seem impossible to pray to him when you feel he could have preserved you and did not. Perhaps you have been terrified of God too long for it to seem possible to call out to him as Savior and trust him as a Father. Yet his patience endures. He is the Redeemer. Even if you have fought him and turned away from him in the past, he will not abandon you. Even if you have blamed him, he will not abuse you. He received Job again. He receives all who turn to him. He is not mean.

III. Trouble Does Not Mean That God's Ways Are Meaningless

Our God is never mean, and his ways are never meaningless. From Job we learn these vital lessons of divine providence that keep our faith strong in this troubled world. Trials make hard questions unavoidable. Even if we do not believe that God causes evil, we at times wonder why he lets it touch us. Since he protects us from so much of the horror that could consume us, does his saving arm simply reach its limit when suffering comes near? No, God clearly details the infinite scope of his power in his response to Job's accusation (chaps. 38–41). Divine limitations will not explain suffering any more than divine caprice. Neither explanation harmonizes with the nature of the God that Scripture presents.

Though we will always have questions about how the Lord can use the sufferings of this world for his purposes without causing evil, a healthy faith requires us to embrace certain foundational truths. These Scriptures make it clear that God harnesses evil without ever embracing, causing, or approving it. When Satan encourages God to "strike" Job (1:11), the Scripture writer carefully indicates that the Devil's hand rather than God's struck (1:12; 2:7). God withheld his hand for a time and to a degree, but the Bible never portrays him as one who arbitrarily damages his own people.

In his providence the Lord disciplines, directs, and matures us through trial. Evil never escapes God's boundaries, never eludes his notice, never overpowers his purposes (1:10; 2:6). Missionaries David and Hazel Knowlton claimed these wonderful truths of divine providence in the deserts of Africa when they built a clinic to care for the needs of impoverished people. Initially their building plans were thwarted by the absence of gravel for a needed concrete foundation. Though sand extended for hundreds of miles, gravel was so scarce that local builders treated it like precious stone. After weeks of futile efforts to locate enough gravel for the project, David wandered into the desert one evening praying about his predicament. Shuffling his feet as he contemplated his situation, he struck his toe against a small stone in the sand. He stopped short. What was the rock doing here? He rushed back to the compound for a shovel, pushed away the surface sand, and found gravel!

The next morning David rounded up wheelbarrows and hired workers to take the "worth-their-weight-in-gold pebbles" to the building site. The laborers transported all the gravel they could find—enough for the clinic foundation as well as for the mission quarters and a storehouse.

In future weeks word of the gravel find spread to neighboring villages. Gravel "prospectors" descended on the site to stake out claims. The government even sent representatives to manage the discovery of the new resource. But no one found any more gravel. Millennia earlier when God created the world, he planted that little pocket of gravel in an ocean of sand for David Knowlton to find for this mission project. Then at just the right time, God exposed those pebbles to encourage a heart, to establish a mission, and to turn back the forces of darkness. Such is the nature of providence.

Our all-knowing, all-powerful, eternal, sovereign God uses all things as he knows best to accomplish his good purposes. Obviously Job wondered, as we do, what possible purpose his sufferings served. Yet in this man's own words and developing attitudes are the explanations of providence for which he and we yearn.

PROVIDENCE WORKS REDEMPTION OF A PERSON

As we have already seen, Job obeyed God once as one would an enemy tyrant. Scholars have long debated what this attitude indicates about Job's heart prior to the confession at the end of the book. Was he truly as blameless and without righteous peer as the opening verses of the book state (1:1, 8, 22)? Or are the opening praises intended to be seen as an ironic backdrop against Job's later declarations of his own self-righteousness (cf. 31:35; 32:2; 35:3; 38:2; 40:8)?

I do not claim to have a final resolution for this discussion. However, there is no question that Job's manner of addressing God indicates a seriously flawed faith (40:2; 42:6). Despite his exemplary outward righteousness prior to his trial, Job ultimately confesses that his understanding of God was horribly warped (42:5). By allowing Job to see his own helplessness in the face of affliction, God enabled Job to see that his salvation was not in his own hands. By refusing to respond with rage to Job's accusation, God confronted Job with the mercy that is the true source of his blessing.

The result: Job begins by contending with a god of his imagination; he ends by worshiping the God of his redemption. Through trial God providentially brings Job to spiritual health. Ultimately, Job no longer accuses in frustration nor serves in dread. He acknowledges God as the Savior that he is and then also responds with heart-felt humility and appreciation (42:2-3). God used trials to reveal himself to Job as our Lord must be seen by all who would know an eternity of blessing based on his grace alone. With the meticulous detail of definite intent, the Bible records that God restored to Job double all that he had lost *after* Job confessed that there was no goodness in himself (cf. 42:1-6, 10). Our Lord made clear to Job what all who experience his salvation must know: God's blessing is not based on our righteousness but on his mercy.

With this key of salvation now planted deeply in his heart, words that Job had mouthed earlier ring with greater heavenly implications. Job said in the midst of his trials, "He (God) knows the way that I take; when he has tested me, I will come forth as gold" (23:10). When Job said those words, he probably believed his character would produce the gold. At the end of his trials, Job more fully understood that God alone refines the gold of our redemption.

As trials worked in Job's life, so all the disciplines of God's providence must work in ours. As we recognize that our best righteousness cannot rescue us from the miseries of this world, we are forced to confess our own inadequacy. Our frailty before a fallen world thrusts us into dependence upon God's provision. Since our "right hand" (40:14) cannot rescue us from the world's hurts, we must look to his holy arm to save us ultimately from all the evil of this world—including that residing in our own hearts (Ps. 98:1; Isa. 52:10).

The fact that God sent his Son to save becomes my ultimate source of comfort and grants me ultimate confidence in his providence. Christ's sacrifice assures me of the abiding care of my sovereign God. Because he purchased my salvation at the price of his own Son's blood, I need never doubt the care or consistency of his decisions for my life. With my Savior's cross fixed in my vision, I can face the difficulties of this fallen world and still believe "that He protects me so well that without the will of my Father in heaven not a hair can fall from my head; indeed, that everything must fit his purpose for my salvation" (*Heidelberg Catechism*).

PROVIDENCE WORKS REDEMPTION OF A PEOPLE

The book of Job not only reveals how God uses all necessary means to generate an individual's spiritual health, but also helps us see how providence claims many souls. At the book's conclusion Job's siblings and friends returned to him. Their late comfort and fair-weather support were evidenced by their arrival only *after* Job's prosperity returned and by their feeble consolation: "Poor thing, what did that mean old God do to you" (42:11)? In the false comfort of these friends echoes the world's judgment of God—a judgment that would stand were it not for Job's account. Had not Job experienced God's mercy and pardon, then his trials could have been interpreted as God's cruelty. The trials of Job and all succeeding suffering would be read as an indictment against God by subsequent generations. When God blessed Job despite his lack of righteousness, the Lord not only saves one soul, but he also provides the truth to save a multitude.

Remember this is the oldest book in the Bible. Job's perspective will lay the framework of belief for all who follow. Had God allowed Job's original impressions of a vindictive divinity to persevere without the trials that would change his perspective, then not only would Job's eternity have been threatened, so would ours. We learn of a gracious God because of the knowledge Job gained in his trial. In his providence God not only allowed Job's trials, but he also blessed us with the account of them to teach us our Lord's true nature. The trials and blessings remind us that God will do what he must to claim souls.

Blessings and battles, daylight and darkness, testimony and trial are all part of the grand providence by which God reveals himself to a world in need. By troubles God keeps us from dependence upon the false comforts of this world. In the darkness he reminds us of how much we need his light. Through the testimony of the faithful he turns others to him. With the blessing he bestows despite our weaknesses, he draws our hearts to him and paints the grace that redeems a great multitude. His providence will vary with the nature of the soul he has determined to reach, but his purpose is fixed. God will redeem his people. His ways are never meaningless.

SAVING MANY

The parents of a twenty-one-year-old son injured in a car accident met me in the waiting room of the Intensive Care Unit. As we sat down, they introduced me to a friend of their son who was also visiting. Then with unrestrained gratitude the parents told of all the people who had called or sent messages saying they were praying. Christians they had not seen in years, church friends from many hours' distance, as well as local believers had called.

As the couple spoke about the many who were praying, I noticed that they kept directing their comments to their son's friend who did not herself participate in the discussion. As our conversation progressed, I realized that the parents were testifying to the young woman by what they chose to discuss. They were using their own trial to make sure this friend knew of their God.

Later when we talked, the mother also asked me if I remembered an exchange student from Germany who a couple of years earlier had stayed with their family. I remembered the polite young man who attended each church service with a slight look of bemusement on his face. She told me that when the exchange student heard of the accident, he flew to their home. He was there as the phone calls and prayer messages poured in from all over the country. The Christian response awed him. "Nothing like this would happen in my home," he said. The mother asked if he wanted to know why it was happening. He said, "Yes," and then she explained the hope of the Gospel to him again.

I marveled at the faithfulness of this couple who knew their trial was an opportunity for the providence of God to work in other hearts. Their testimony blessed me, but my greatest blessing and amazement was yet to come. As I left the ICU, a man spoke to me while we were waiting for the elevator. "Are you a neighbor of those people?" he asked, nodding his head toward the family I had just visited.

"No," I said, "I'm just a friend."

"Those are some special people," he said. "Their son's accident was only half a block from my home."

I said, "Oh, it was nice of you to come all this way to visit after just meeting the family that way."

"You don't understand," he said. "I didn't come to see them. A couple of nights after their son was in his accident, the same thing happened to my daughter. She's here, too. I don't know if I could have made it without those people praying for us. Only because I know they understand what my family is going through was I able to believe what they are saying."

What an incredible chain of events! By tragedy God put this Christian family in another man's life just days before the neighbor faced the tragedy of his own that pierced him with his need of the Lord. Because of unique circumstances, the Christians' testimony had a power the man himself could not fully explain but definitely appreciated. Others might call the situation a fluke, a coincidence, or even dumb luck, but Christians see the providence of God at work.

Eternity opens like a vast plain before us with only the momentary passing of this life available to convince others to turn from sin to salvation. The task seems so impossible with people so hardened and obsessed with the distractions of this world. Yet our God is mighty. He reigns in heaven and rules this earth with hands so caring and precise that his will cannot be thwarted. He is saving a multitude from this sinful existence. With trials so fierce that sometimes we think we cannot bear them, he sours our taste for this world and makes us thirst for the next.

I cannot explain every aspect of what God is doing, but his Word and my salvation tell me what he is. He is good and gracious. By his nature I discern his purpose even if I cannot always decipher the details of his providence. This I know: "My Redeemer lives . . . he knows the way that I take; and when he has tested me, I will come forth as gold." All my trials will be consumed with the dross of this world, and in that day when he shall stand upon the earth, I and all who claim him shall be with him shining as gold. Because he is always, even in the harshest flames, only refining his gold.

DISCUSSION QUESTIONS

1) How would you define God's providence?
2) How does affliction and calamity affect your definition of providence? How did such trials affect Job's view of God?
3) What evidence can you cite that personal trouble does not automatically imply personal sin? What would be the consequences if such biblical evidence were not available?

4) Does God ever use trial as discipline? What are the consequences of believing that all trial is discipline for sin?

5) What evidence does the book of Job offer that God's providence is still at work even when God's people fail him?

6) If God were a heavenly ogre, how should he have reacted to Job's accusations?

7) What were God's ultimate purposes in Job's trials? What are God's ultimate purposes in your trials?

8) What do God's providential actions reveal about his wisdom, power, and love?

9) How does providence serve to lead us to an appreciation of God's grace?

4

THE ELEGANCE OF
THE LAW

✄

Your high school English teacher might not have given Psalm 19 a very high grade. Its themes seem too disjointed. The psalmist begins by rejoicing that the sun and stars declare the glory of God. They pour forth speech and knowledge of their Creator in a language hidden to none. Suddenly in the midst of this topic, the psalmist radically changes the subject. Creation fades into the background, and the writer begins to describe the law of God. Did the author forget where he was going? No. He has only found another means to underline his real theme: Everything that God made glorifies him. Not only do the stars bring God praise, but so do the standards his providence provides to help us navigate through life in a fallen world. Read the latter portion of this psalm listening for the voice that expresses how God's law reveals his greatness.

PSALM 19:7-14

⁷*The law of the LORD is perfect, reviving the soul. The statutes of the LORD are trustworthy, making wise the simple.*

⁸*The precepts of the LORD are right, giving joy to the heart. The commands of the LORD are radiant, giving light to the eyes.*

⁹*The fear of the LORD is pure, enduring forever. The ordinances of the LORD are sure and altogether righteous.*

[10]*They are more precious than gold, than much pure gold; they are sweeter than honey, than honey from the comb.*

[11]*By them is your servant warned; in keeping them there is great reward.*

[12]*Who can discern his errors? Forgive my hidden faults.*

[13]*Keep your servant also from willful sins; may they not rule over me. Then will I be blameless, innocent of great transgression.*

[14]*May the words of my mouth and the meditation of my heart be pleasing in your sight, O LORD, my Rock and my Redeemer.*

๛

The psalmist uses aspects of God's law to glorify the attributes of God's nature. The actual word translated as "law" at this passage's opening is Torah, a general term for all God tells us about how we are to conduct ourselves. The Torah includes the various types of divine instruction mentioned in the later verses—statutes, commands, precepts, ordinances, and even the restraining fear (awe or respect) of the Lord he plants in our hearts. Since God created the law, it reflects his nature just as the heavens declare the glory of their Creator. The message is clear: The law does not merely reveal what God commands; it reveals who God is. By understanding these moral standards of God, we better understand God and our relationship to him. My intention in this chapter is not to enter the debate over whether certain Old Testament civil and ceremonial laws apply to believers today, but to demonstrate the continuing value of the Bible's moral instructions that God has given to guide our conduct. Without this law we have no way to understand God or ourselves.

๛

WHAT DOES IT PROVE?

Another televangelist makes the national news. What else is new? If it is not a televangelist, then some other religious leader is making headlines for some scandal, indiscretion, or impropriety. Each time the sordid accounts appear, we experience the same reactions. First, shock waves roll over us. Anger follows. Then, though we may hesitate to admit it even to ourselves, comes pleasure. As long as the scandal does not come too near home, deep down we appreciate the demise of others. It seems to prove something to us about the hollowness of their faith commitments and the solidity of our own. Though we would never confess the attitude to our neighbors, we secretly gloat: "I knew it all the time. I knew they weren't for real. Their success had to be a sham. Finally, the truth shows. How glad I am that my faith rests on a more solid foundation."

Such judgments demonstrate how little we understand ourselves. The following examples prove how susceptible we all are to serious wrongs.

Only weeks ago a pastor in my denomination stood before his congregation and announced that, though he was married, he was a practicing homosexual and had been since adolescence when his own family introduced him to this lifestyle.

In the past three months, six pastors from various denominations in our city have been dismissed from their pulpits for sexual sin.

Josh McDowell's recent national survey of the sexual habits of teens in evangelical churches indicates that almost 45 percent of *our* teens are sexually active prior to marriage.

This past year I preached a sermon in a large, well-known evangelical church on the need for reconciliation in Christian families. When I finished, the pastor asked people to come forward who wanted prayer for reconciliation. Scores came. So many wanted personal prayer that the two staff members and I had trouble speaking with them all. When we compared notes later, we discovered in *every* case where we spoke with spouses that one or both parties of the marriage had been involved in one or more extramarital affairs.

Two years ago I spent two days with the head of the largest civil litigation firm in a neighboring state. He said his fastest growing caseload involves suits against churches—specifically suits brought by parents of children who have been molested in church day care centers, parochial schools, and Sunday schools.

No group can claim that the evil typified in headlines of sexual scandal fails to touch their church, their faith, or their lives. While a local church may not have the reputation that invites journalists to publish its dirty linen, none could stand rigorous investigation unscathed. The pervasiveness of the evil in our culture and among us would seem to demand our return to honoring God's law. Yet even in our churches such an imperative often goes unheeded because we cannot agree on how the standards of God should govern our lives.

Some Christians feel they must challenge fellow church members "not to be so legalistic." If this challenge means we should not judge one another over matters of cultural preference and Christian liberty, then I say, "Amen." If the caution against legalism further means that God's people should not believe or act as though God bases our ultimate standing before him on some righteous code of conduct, then again I say, "Amen."

However, if the admonition not to be "legalistic" really means that Christians should not consistently honor, carefully study, and conscientiously obey the standards God's Word has given for all ages, then I say, "Whoa."

If the Bible gives no standards of conduct, then I neither know how to honor God nor how to choose a path for my life that does not lead to ruin. The law is God's caring hand upon my life guiding, restraining, and protecting me. I want no less of this care—but more and more. Do I want legalism? No! Do I want the law? Yes!

The psalmist was not crazy when he sang to God, "Oh, how I love your law" (Ps. 119:97). This unlikely praise results from the inspired writer's understanding that the law pictures the affection God has for each of us. By the very care with which the Lord lays out his standards in the Bible, the law reveals the degree of God's concern for our spiritual welfare. Because God wants to spare us pain and keep us from harm, he gives us careful instructions. His law keeps us *sure* about what we should do and *safe* in where we go.

So much does the Bible identify the law with the character of God that it is impossible to love God without loving his law. Any alternative would be something akin to loving brownies but not liking the taste of chocolate. The love of one necessitates a love for the other. Apart from the law, we actually have no basis to love God. Without positive regard for God's law, no one truly understands our Lord's nature, appreciates how desperately we need him, nor perceives how great is his mercy toward us. True love of God requires (and enables) every Christian to sing, "Oh, how love I your law." Here is why:

I. The Law Reveals the Glory of God.

In addition to his words, the inspired writer uses the very structure of Psalm 19 to aid our understanding. In the first three verses of this portion of the psalm, the author lists twelve characteristics of the law in a series of six couplets. The first clause of each couplet describes an aspect of the law, and then the following phrase indicates the purpose or consequence of that feature. Concentrate on these descriptive first clauses of the couplets for the moment:

> [7]*The law of the LORD is* **perfect** . . .
> *The statutes of the LORD are* **trustworthy** . . .
> [8]*The precepts of the LORD are* **right** . . .
> *The commands of the LORD are* **radiant** . . .
> [9]*The fear of the LORD is* **pure**,
> *The ordinances of the LORD are* **sure** . . .

The concluding words in this final line summarize all the preceding descriptions—we can be *sure* about the instruction of God. We do not have to wonder if God's basic standards for us are imperfect, flawed, mistaken, veiled, tainted, or subject to variation. God's standards are perfectly crafted and eternally correct (as the psalmist relates in the second clauses of these same couplets). We need harbor no questions about the faithfulness of the Lord's guidance. When we go where he directs, we walk on solid ground.

A GOD OF SURE STANDARDS

No conclusion about God's law could be more relevant to our contemporary situation and more important for ministers of the Gospel. The defiant modern heart shouts, "Since no one knows for sure, no one has the right to tell me what to do." Our response must be strong and unwavering: "Because God's Word is sure, he has the right to instruct."

Regardless of their natural abilities, preachers may speak with authority when presenting biblical standards because of God's assurance that his Word is right. This holy boldness—which comes from confidence in God rather than reliance on one's personal gifts—must well up in the hearts of all who are stewards of God's truth. Conviction of the eternal integrity of God's law grants the liberty to speak as God requires in the face of spiritual resistance. Faithful ministers of the Word do not rely on the manner of their expression or the nature of their reception to gauge the strength of their case. The law releases them from such earthly constraints. They preach with confidence, knowing their craft does not make God's instruction right. It is right.

Whether they preach artistically or plainly, gently or with vigor, as rebuke or as encouragement, pastors who speak with the assurance that their words are true minister with divine power. For while the strongest voice is not always the surest, the voice that is sure communicates a strength that variations of expression cannot conceal.

Of course, God does not provide his law simply so preachers can speak with authority. God offers sure standards so that all his people may know what he expects of them and what paths will lead to their blessing. This is no small grace in this age when the world points so reasonably and unflinchingly down other paths.

A pastor recently received a call from a good friend and former parishioner whose unmarried daughter has begun living with a man. "Would you please call her and try to make her see that this is wrong," the father requested. He acknowledged that he had run out of arguments and influence with his daughter. The father's precise words were particularly revealing of our age. "She has an answer for everything I say," he wept.

Most of us know what this grieving father was experiencing. We, too, probably have friends or loved ones who say, "Why shouldn't we live together for a while before we get married? Why not see if we can get along before making a lifetime commitment?" These arguments sound so reasonable. They *do* make a certain degree of sense.

We may try to counter such worldly logic with our own arguments: "Your lover is just using you;" "Statistics indicate that these relationships will not last;" "Intimacy prior to marriage often deprives the marriage itself of deeper intimacy, stability, and trust;" etc. Unfortunately, no matter how accurate such observations are, others can almost always counter with reasoning from their own perspective.

Similar "reasonable" arguments will accompany every sin a society has grown to accept. Ultimately the defense of our actions must lie beyond human debate. Sin is wrong because God says so. His standards are perfect, trustworthy, right, good, and pure *because he is all these*. Variance from his instruction is always ill-considered because his law is *sure*.

Perhaps the psalmist echoes the sureness of God's law so repetitively because he knows no one is exempt from questioning the necessity of obedience. The hearts of those most familiar with Scripture are often the most skilled at reasoning around its standards. The moral failure of famous preachers is no new phenomena. Three centuries ago the Puritan pastor Richard Baxter cautioned pastors, "Take heed to yourselves because you have greater temptations and more exposure to them than other men." I am frequently amused by people who talk about pastors being insulated from evil. Every caring pastor's office floods with people taken in sin. Great spiritual danger lies in this constant exposure to evil because it dulls the sensibilities to the repugnance of sin.

Counseling settings where pastors deal with the worst of sins on a routine basis can magnify the spiritual danger. In times of pastoral stress or temptation, behavior that once possessed a horror that made it unthinkable may begin to seem ordinary. This unintentional callousness combined with the minister's professional facility with Scripture can lead to a tendency to use the Bible to circumvent the law rather than to apply it. The most godly leaders who are constantly barraged with sin can begin to doubt their own need to say no to ungodliness. The psalmist helps to rescue us from this danger by reminding us that our own lives suffer when we make God's law less sure. The Lord did not give us his law so that we could search for its exceptions but so that we could discern the path of blessing by its light.

A GOD OF SAFE STANDARDS

As the psalmist further considers the nature of the law's leading, his praise expands. Reflection on the care evident in the life path God's instruction prepares leads the writer to extol the goodness of the divine ordinances. They are "more precious than gold" and "sweeter than honey" (v. 10).

But what happens if one wanders from this precious path? The psalmist's thoughts naturally turn to consider the consequences. Great danger lies off the path God provides. With this caution in mind, the psalmist launches a new theme. Not only are the ordinances of the Lord sure, but they are also *safe*: "By them is your servant warned; in keeping them there is great reward" (v. 11).

We rarely stress this theme enough. Too often Christians try to spur others (including other Christians) to obey God with the simple reasoning that good people are supposed to be good. Our moral imperatives and holy exhortations get couched in terms designed to shame others into shape. We seem to believe that by encouraging people to protect their personal reputations, they will please God. In doing so, we imply that God loves us more because we are respectable. Such teaching makes maximizing the honor of one's self the measure of holiness. The law of God then degenerates into arbitrary rules of religious etiquette that corral the spiritually elite into self-serving paths. As a result it is no wonder that so many consider obedience a bitter pill.

God would seem far less capricious and holiness far less prideful if Christians more conscientiously offered the biblical perspective— God intends for his law to protect us from harm. A life ordered by his standards knows the most blessed existence divine love can design.

A late-night shopping venture recently gave me an opportunity to reconsider the care evident in God's law. My family learned late one Friday that out-of-town guests were coming to visit early the next day. My wife quickly sent me out to the twenty-four-hour grocery store while she began a midnight whirlwind of house cleaning. I was unprepared for the crowd at the store. Warm weather and the end of a school term had kept many young people up late in a party mood. I could hardly push my cart through the crush of teenagers at the service counter. Like bees around honey, the kids had swarmed around the videotape aisle looking for ways to keep the evening alive.

When I saw the types of videos that drew them and heard the raunchy discussion of what enticed them, I grieved for these young people. I have watched too many of their peers get a first taste of sexual expression through such entertainments. Then, as immature sexual appetites are whetted and cultivated by what is aberrant and self-indulgent, young lives drift out of control with amazing speed and horribly lasting results.

"Get away from this filth that will hurt you," my heart cried out to these young people. I did not blame them for their desires, but I ached for the hurt sure to come into young lives through the uncaring compulsions of celluloid sex. No one should claim inability to identify with the powerful craving such videos can stimulate. Neither should we assume that shame will dissuade when so much of society seems to unwilling to disapprove such indulgences.

In moments of opportunity and temptation, no one's pride offers protection from the allure of such intensely self-satisfying sins. A shield of self-serving self-respect offers little defense against the compulsions to promote one's peer standing, to preserve romantic relationships, to experience sensual pleasure, and to answer questions of sexual orientation or adequacy. When concerns for self offer no clear guidance away from sin, the Bible offers no more powerful dissuasion than this assurance: "God has designed a sweeter course for you than this."

Spiritual effectiveness resides in expressions of compassion as well as in authority. We should not expect our words to affect others appropriately if we do not address them as God has spoken to us. God presents his law in the context of his love. The motive of his instruction is his care. Our words about him are credible only when people understand that we advocate God's standards not merely so that we will have a platform, position, or power, but because we love them enough to warn of their peril. We can present amazingly challenging and unpopular truths and still win a hearing when others perceive selfless care in us. Conversely, it is possible to say much less objectionable things and be perceived as only a small-town bully because it appears we are more concerned for our status than anyone else's safety.

Christians fail God when they issue warnings devoid of the love that inspired his law. When we give God's instruction without his affection, we inadequately represent the nature of the law and of the one who gave it. Consider the biblical standard that Christians should only marry those who belong to the Lord (see 1 Cor. 7:39). Young and old may chafe under this instruction when they love another outside the faith. Our society as a whole currently finds this ordinance outdated and bigoted. Still love lies behind the precept. The deep commitment God requires of all who marry creates spiritually compromising situations too numerous to count for a believing spouse (and children) when marriage to an unbeliever occurs.

The union of two whose eternal destinies are so divergent usually holds great temporal pain despite the genuine affection of the relationship's early stages. After more than forty years of ministry in which he had observed the progress of hundreds of marriages, the Rev. Wesley P. Walters reported that he had only once known the marriage of a believer and a nonbeliever to last more than five years. That one exception lasted thirteen years and then also ended. Of course, there are other exceptions. The point is that these are *exceptions*. The ordinary course of a marriage between one who loves the Lord and one who does not is pain, distance, and division. What else should we expect when the two people who are closest in life cannot share what is dearest in life?

Prejudice does not motivate God's prohibitions against spiritually mixed marriages. Compassion does. When you consider the pain and heartache for spouses and children, you, too, can perceive the care behind God's command. By his loving law, God deters us from pain and preserves the greatest treasure of human existence beyond salvation—oneness with a spouse in home, heart, body, *and* spirit. True to his nature, the standards of God's law provide safekeeping for our lives' greatest blessings.

A GOD OF GREAT HEART

A path laid to keep others *sure* and *safe* automatically grants its pilgrims insight into the one who planned each step. We can borrow the words of the psalmist to understand what these standards tell us of God's nature and concerns. He is perfect, trustworthy, right, radiant, pure, dependable. He delights to revive the soul, to make wise the simple, to give joy to our hearts, and to let us see the path laid for our blessing. The law reveals a God of great heart.

Just as the creation fashioned by God's hands extols the Creator, so also the spiritual order ordained by the law glorifies its Designer. The higher our appreciation of this spiritual design, the greater glows his glory. This process leads to an unexpected turn of expression in the psalm. As the writer's thought progresses, he speaks with increasing awe and holy reverence for the Lawgiver (cf. v. 9). The psalmist reaches higher and higher to express his praise and then arrives at a surprising apex. Though he has used the law as a window to see God, his praise now lifts the glory of God to a zenith so high that the angle of light changes. The glass now begins to reflect as much as reveal. What the psalmist sees in the law's reflection dramatically changes his tone.

II. The Law Reflects Our Condition

In the mirror of the law the psalmist sees himself, and for just a moment he despairs. His awareness of what the law says about his own spiritual inadequacy overwhelms. The psalmist must deal with the truth about himself before he can renew his praise. By leading him to understand his own condition, the divine standards ultimately guide him into an even greater awareness of his Lord's provision. His praise will reach new heights after the psalmist recognizes that the law not only reveals the inimitable glory of God, but it also exposes the inestimable grace of God.

REFLECTION OF SIN

The law is sure. The law is safe. It is a glorious reflection of its Creator's concern for his people. As a result of these considerations the psalmist muses that in keeping God's ordinances "there is great reward" (v. 11). Then the magnitude of what he has just said about the standards collapses on him: " . . . in the keeping of them is great

But who can keep all the standards

of God's nature and so past human

n fully to discern that the psalmist

confession asking, "Who can dis-

he writer uses the technical term

his next statement makes it clear

s inability to *do* all God requires.

e his "hidden faults." The words

imself does not recognize. Not

human ability to perform, but

rom us. Though the law is sure

s from our own limitations.

nsecurity grows greater in the

en sins are not all that can come

he psalm must also appeal for

sin that threatens to rule over

ible indicates that, even when

d it without God's help.

agger us. Because as sinners

ces cannot guarantee right-

parent to us, the capacity we

ellion a constant threat. By

makes us conscious of our

e of the human heart places

REFLECTION OF INSUFFICIENCY

The dimensions of our spiritual helplessness should remind us that any instruction that merely admonishes Christians to obey God opens a deep wound. Since no one—not even an inspired writer of Scripture—can do all heaven requires, earth binds us to persistent failing. This perspective should remind us that a focus on the law without an emphasis on God's provision of grace only leads to despair. Those who stress the requirements of the law as their primary means of promoting holiness will instead discourage and weaken. No one profits from a perpetual gaze in a mirror that reflects fault without hope.

When I worked as a novice newspaper reporter during my college years, I had the mixed blessing of working under an incredibly demanding editor. Though his vocal criticism made me conscious of a number of writing techniques I could correct and improve, I began to doubt I could ever write a story that would satisfy him.

One day my editor stood at my elbow while I tried to type a report of a city council meeting. I could not get through one sentence without a barrage of "suggestions," corrections, and scowls. After the first paragraph my attempts had slowed to a crawl (causing more criticism), and before I was halfway through the account, I was paralyzed. So much did I now doubt that I could write anything well that I lost the ability to write at all. Instead of improving my work, my editor's constant reflection on its inadequacies destroyed the small ability I had.

As constant criticism only increases our propensity for error, overemphasis on the requirements of the law that highlight our failures will plunge us into greater spiritual destitution. A right understanding (and use) of God's standards must take into account the traits that the Bible itself reveals are characteristic of the law. Not only do God's ordinances glorify the Creator, but they also hold the potential to devastate the creature. At the same moment that the law affirms the greatness of God who provides such perfect paths, it testifies to the helpless condition of any person who attempts to walk them.

There is great benefit in the realization of one's own spiritual insufficiency. The confession of personal inadequacy is the first real step to spiritual health. Still the joint attestation of the law and of our hearts that we are incapable of perfectly walking God's paths cannot be the only message that the law communicates. Those who listen to that testimony without any counter harmony will despair despite the words of security and safety in the song the psalmist lisps. What good comes from singing of the goodness of one who created a safe path that no one can reach? Why praise the hand no one can satisfy?

III. The Law Rescues from Despair

Recognition of the hopelessness of his condition in the face of the law's challenges forces the psalmist to look beyond himself to satisfy his God. Since he can depend on no human effort for spiritual security, he cries out to God. It only makes sense to seek the support of one whose standards evidence such goodness. Thus the inspired author appeals to the Lord's kindness, asking that the Lawgiver would accept the words of psalmist's mouth and the meditations of his heart (v. 14). In this petition for a communion of conversation and thought with his Creator, the writer in essence—pleads for a relationship. He longs for the spiritual union with divine love that the law offers but that no human hand can grasp.

THE DILEMMA

The writer's longing for a relationship with his God presents the ultimate dilemma of the psalm. The very law that exposes enough of its Creator's nature to make the psalmist want to approach his God, also reveals the creature's inability to draw near. On the one hand, the law draws the writer toward God. On the other hand, it holds the author at a distance. On the basis of the law the psalmist must question whether he or anyone can have a sure or safe standing before his God. In the light of these questions what assurance does anyone have of God's acceptance? The psalmist does not appeal to his own adherence to the law as the basis for confidence in his relationship with the Lord. He turns to the Lord himself as a Rock and Redeemer to secure the relationship (v. 14). The *support* God provides as a divine Rock makes the psalmist sure. The *supply* God offers as a spiritual Redeemer keeps the writer safe. What God brings to this relationship saves the psalmist from despair. The law has revealed enough of

God's goodness to allow the psalmist to love the Lord and place faith in him. Thus this scriptural poem that extols the law makes the relationship God establishes the focus of our praise. In the relationship God secures we find refuge. Only in the divine initiative is there hope.

Does that mean the law holds no value? No. The psalmist lists as the first of the law's perfections its potential for *reviving* (the word means to convert or restore) the soul (v. 7). The last words of the psalm reveal how the law performs this created task. The standards signal our helplessness to lead us away from ourselves to the true hope of restoration—our Lord. He is the sure and safe refuge to which the law points. It exposes him as the Rock and Redeemer our hearts desire and our inadequacies require. As God intended from the beginning, the law leads to grace by teaching us of our dependence on him. The glory of the law is that it reveals the character of one who delights to lay this path for our spiritual safekeeping.

Because the path does not lead back on itself, does that mean we should abandon it? Should we walk away from the law simply because it leads away from self-sufficiency? No. If we were to abandon the Lord's guidance, we would annul all the psalmist has used to understand his God. The psalmist shows no inclination to wander from the path that evidences and honors the love of his Lord. Why should he leave the course so faithfully laid to protect him? The grace he perceives in his God makes the psalmist all the more desirous of staying on the path his Lord designed.

THE FOCUS

The fact that human efforts do not determine divine salvation does not remove the obligation or wisdom of honoring God's law. On the contrary, right apprehension of the love behind the law should make us delight to obey divine standards. "In keeping them there is great reward" (v. 11). Apart from God's guidance, we are left to the designs of our own hearts, which candor must confess cannot even discern their own faults. In addition, while our actions do not establish our relationship with God, when our lives do not honor him, our relationship with him (and with those about us) suffers. Attempts either to form a love relationship through rules or to live in one without the rules are equally ill-conceived.

A new father once confided that he hoped to avoid his own parents' errant attempts to force love into their family. His parents had decided in his early teen years that he was not paying enough attention to them. To correct this problem they designated times during the day when the son was to greet them and engage them in conversation. For months at the appointed hour he dutifully sought out the appropriate parent and said, "Hello." Unfortunately, the discipline only further damaged the relationship. The enforced expressions of love soon degenerated into artificial gestures, minimal efforts, and resentful obedience. The relationship itself faltered by trying to forge a bond through a set of compulsory behaviors rather than through actions genuine love engendered.

After months of increasing difficulty, the family again discussed the importance of expressing care for one another, but they dropped the scheduled conversations. The relationship eventually prospered again as the parents emphasized the importance of natural expressions of affection without making them the basis of the relationship. Today the young man again delights to speak with his parents. Though he lives some distance from them, he phones at regular intervals to keep their lives knit together. No one forces him to call. His own appreciation for their relationship spurs him to maintain the contact. He recognizes that although the rules of the past could not form a good relationship with his parents, the relationship could not exist now without meeting expectations that keep them close.

Using rules to build relationships eventually divides hearts. Only relationships built on unconditional affection will elicit the desire to keep standards that express and deepen that love. The psalmist teaches us similar lessons about our relationship with God. As an expression of our love for God (and his love for us), the law is "more precious than gold" (v. 10). However, if we teach, imply, or believe that the law establishes our relationship with God, then we promote pain and division. Spiritual duress is among the poorest excuses for obedience and will produce sadly damaged fruit.

We are often tempted to cultivate such fruit. When we witness the evil in our society, nation, and churches, we want to cry, "Stop it!" Such admonitions are not wrong in themselves. Scripture demands that faithful people stand against the world's corruption. However, simple prohibitions—no matter how well intended their expression—may yield results far removed from the Gospel. The reasons people turn from evil determine whether their obedience offers spiritual health or hurt. If our words communicate that others must honor God's law so that he will love them, then we damage God's truth and possibly others' souls. Our Lord does not love us on the basis of our actions but on the basis of his own. He is the Rock and Redeemer. In him alone resides our hope.

We must derive the motive of obedience from God's love, or we will drive others from a healthy relationship with him—even if a sense of self-preservation makes them do as he instructs. Faithfulness to the scope of Scripture requires us to teach others that they must honor God's law because his love constructed this path around the dangers of ungodliness. His provision rather than our performance must remain the focus of our faith. We must always guard against the tendency in practice (if not in theology) to let the pressures of evil invert the psalmist's emphasis and consequently raise the ministry of the law to a supreme position in our faith concerns. As the law led the inspired writer to see the Redeemer's work as the ultimate focus of his praise, so we must make our Rock the primary locus of our faith (cf. 1 Cor. 10:4).

THE LOCUS

As a searching teen, I got involved in a group that was almost cultish in its concern for the work of the Holy Spirit. When I sought some outside help in sorting out my thoughts, a very wise pastor spoke gently to me. He did not try to tell me the Holy Spirit was bad or unimportant. Rather he invited me to read the words of John 15:26 to remind me of the Spirit's ministry. "The Holy Spirit should testify of Jesus," the pastor said. "If any group's message begins to emphasize the Spirit more than Jesus, then those people may be saying all the right things and still not be all God intends."

That pastor's words have helped me many times as my own faith journeys have required me to consider the validity of a number of ministries that assert their need for primacy in the Church. I have consistently discovered that what a group makes the locus (central concern or chief refuge) of their faith is often very revealing of their gospel health. Some groups, such as the one I explored as a teen, tend to make Pentecost their locus. Other groups with a social/political agenda tend to make their locus the public ministry of Christ. Strong movements in the evangelical world that are reacting to the lawlessness within and without the Church have recently made Sinai their locus, asserting the need to reinstitute the theocratic laws of ancient Israel. Periodically groups totally frustrated with the world's turmoil push their central concern to Christ's return. While each of these movements can claim much scriptural support, their emphases, more than any particular argument, expose causes for concern. The need to discern these emphases may seem nit-picky, but the tendency distinctions are crucial.

Calvary remains the only proper locus of the Gospel (cf. 1 Cor. 2:2). In the work accomplished at the cross and made evident in the Resurrection, our God rescued us from sin and death by his grace alone. This is the focus of all of Scripture. God even intended for the law to direct our vision to the provision of our Rock and Redeemer (v. 14). The progressive thought of the psalmist harmonizes with the conclusion of the apostle Paul who said that the law was to act as a "schoolmaster" to lead us to Christ (see Gal. 3:24). As our hearts consider the moral precepts that Scripture never abrogates, we recognize just how this process works. The commandments show us how we fail our God and those about us. Thus the law forces us to acknowledge the limits of our righteousness before a holy God. The Holy Spirit, then, uses this recognition of our sinful condition to lead us to the provision of the Savior as the only hope for peace with God.

The mental and spiritual processes the law triggers to turn us toward God's mercy should also alert us to the two great errors in various churches' use of the law. The first error is simply to discredit the law, so isolating the believer's focus on grace that the standards of God mean nothing. Not only does such an emphasis deny what Scripture says about the eternal goodness of the law (v. 9), but this approach also denies the believer a path to grace. If the law holds no righteous standard that can convict our consciences, then we have no awareness of sin, and God's mercy really saves us from nothing. Without regard for God's moral precepts, every person becomes a law unto himself or herself.

Christians caught in faith communities that adopt this mind-set typically speak a great deal about love that does not "judge" others, but they end up promoting a moral relativism as damaging (and even as approving) as the worst immorality in our society. Christians that ignore the law of God ultimately cannot reflect his love, because the Lord designed the divine ordinances to represent the love of heaven in an earthly context.

The second major misuse of the law occurs not when churches de-emphasize the law, but when they overemphasize the divine ordinances. The Old and New Testament writers unite their voices to declare that the law has a directive intent. It should lead us to concentrate on the atoning ministry of Christ. Yet despite this clear indication of the sweep of Scripture, certain men, ministries, and movements can become so preoccupied with certain aspects, emphases, or interpretations of the law that their primary distinction—what they see as their central purpose—is the promotion of a particular perspective on the law. In such cases, the central thrust of the Bible should alert us that these movements are out of kilter even if many of their particulars sound correct.

God did not design the law to lead to itself, nor did he create the Church to march back to Sinai. The culminative intent of all scriptural statutes and institutions is the proclamation of the Savior. We honor our Lord by living as he directs, but we dishonor Jesus when we concentrate the energies and efforts of his bride (the Church) on the task of his messenger (the law). Jesus is the purpose of the Church. Despite their usually well-intended efforts, groups whose locus is law rob Christ of the glory due him.

When does a de-emphasis on the law become sinful disregard for it, and at what point does zealous concern for God's standards translate into legalism? Obvious extremes may not inform us as much as we might wish. We readily recognize as sub Christian those groups that have no biblical compass and communities that devise a code of conduct guaranteed to win God's acceptance. More typical of the challenges we face are those ministries whose emphases cannot be determined in a single service, document, or sermon. We grow to know their locus by the themes, echoes, tone, and fruit of their ministries (Matt. 7:15-20).

Time alone may enable us to discern whether Christ is a ministry's central concern—not only by what its leaders affirm, but also by the actions and attitudes of members. Pursuit of God's holiness with humility characterizes those who love Jesus and know their righteousness before him is not a product of their efforts. Frustration and judgmentalism identify those who have been denied the sweetness of the path marked by God's ordinances, or who are subtly (or even unintentionally) instructed to revel in the righteous standing their observances of the law can gain. Their frustration is a result either of pursuing paths less fulfilling than God designs or of failing to achieve what one feels is necessary to gain God's approval. Legalism also necessitates judgmentalism, for only in comparing oneself favorably to others can one measure the attainment of personal piety. Of course, such an estimation ultimately leads to self-delusion or despair, since no human righteousness can stand divine comparison.

These human processes indicate why spiritual pride and personal despair (often coexisting) among an organization's members are the tracer elements typically marking consistent misapplication of God's standards. While it is beyond the scope of this chapter to try to define all the considerations churches must weigh to offer a balanced perspective on biblical law, these echoes of the heart—listened for over time—rarely deceive. Hope of spiritual health resides only in those who reflect the attitude of this psalmist who extols the beauty of God's standards while using their instruction to make God's grace the preeminent message.

When the pastor in my denomination mentioned at the outset of this chapter confessed his sexual sin to his church, the leaders there lovingly disciplined him as the Bible instructs. When he felt the genuine care in their chastening, the minister's trust of his brothers in the Lord grew enough to tell them that there had not been a single day within the past several years that he had not contemplated suicide. His failure before God's law, and the judgment it contained, bore down upon him with such weight that he nearly lost all regard for the life he could not control. In the light of these years of despair while his sin was secret, he related how strange it now felt for his heart to break free with the confession he had felt sure would destroy his last reason to hold to life.

Though he did not request nor receive the continuation of his ministerial status, the now-former pastor has begun to share with others the tremendous release he is experiencing. He says, "For the first time in years I am not thinking of suicide, because I know I have the forgiveness of my Lord. And, for the first time in my adult life, I believe I have power over my sin because I have come to see how much my God wants to help me." With these words my friend has expressed in the most personal terms what the psalmist told us many centuries earlier about the goal of our Lord's statutes. Those who do not turn from God's way but follow it to the heart that gave the law find grace.

When the law of God leads to its right conclusion, the beauty of the Lord breaks upon the human soul. The psalmist has described the process. The biblical statutes first obligate us to behaviors that glorify God. The loveliness and safety of life ordered by these precepts then reveal the nature of the one who designed them. God is love. He never intends for his ordinances to serve as capricious boundaries on human behavior that can exile us in regions beyond divine care. The paths that guide to holy goodness challenge our abilities and make us aware of our own faulty footing. Our best efforts cannot keep us from falling from heaven's ways. As a result the law that leads to blessing performs the added function of convicting us of our need for aid beyond our own strength.

Were the paths that convince us of such personal failing characterized by vicious challenges and cruel hurdles, then despair would await all who traveled them. Yet because what truly identifies these paths is infinite wisdom and undying care, the paths naturally lead us to seek the aid of the very hand that designed them. So the law instructs us. It not only reveals the sure Rock on which we can stand, but also the Redeemer whose safekeeping we need when we slip.

Assured of the surety and safety of their Savior's intent, even those who have fallen will find the strength to rise again. The burden of a law that leads only to dread and depression will melt in the realms where the full light of God's Son reaches. At that altitude the clouds of the world's distortions dissipate, and we share the clarity of the psalmist's vision. The law no longer appears as a thundercloud darkening the human landscape with capricious threat and arbitrary rule. Instead, above the world's mists it reveals itself to be a stream of mercy flowing from the heights of God's love to nurture and guide all who follow its flow. Those who will trail this stream back to its source may

116 THE WONDER OF IT ALL

be amazed not only to discover that its pools offer refreshment for their journey, but that they reach their destination deep in the heart of God.

In this heavenly vision that the psalmist provides is the grace that allows us to love God's law. Through biblically enlightened eyes, we discover that this law is neither the club the world portrays nor pretense anyone can ignore. God's standards ultimately lead us to the safety Christ offers. From the security his arms provide we find we can embrace the law as he desires. That which witnesses to the glory of God and testifies to the grace of our Savior will still elicit the ancient song from our lips: "O How Love I Thy Law."

DISCUSSION QUESTIONS

1) Why are Christians sometimes pleased with the moral failures of others? What does this pleasure indicate about the faith of these believers?
2) What are some of the attitudes Christians have toward the law of God?
3) How do God's standards glorify him? What do they reveal about his character?
4) Why is it important to know that God's law is sure? In what ways is it sure?
5) Why is it important to know that God's law keeps us safe? How does the law keep us safe, and how important is it for us to communicate this?
6) What does the law reveal about the condition of our hearts? Why should this revelation not lead us to despair?
7) What does the law ultimately force us to consider as the basis for our salvation? To what (or whom) does the law lead? How?
8) What errors can churches make in their emphases regarding God's law? How can these errors be discerned?
9) What is a biblically balanced perspective for Christians to hold today regarding God's law?

5

THE EXTRAVAGANCE
OF THE ATONEMENT

Strings of Christmas tree lights now sell with built-in computer chips that play a tune as the lights blink. We do so much to make the message of Christ's coming into the world cheering that it can be difficult to remember the sacrificial purpose of God's intent to send his Son. Perhaps this difficulty helps explain why, when God spoke to the people of old to cheer them with the message of Christ's coming, it was not of a tree he spoke nor its lights. Rather, God spoke of a branch and its lineage. These words offer a peculiar image of cheer because God presented his message through the prophet Jeremiah, who was sent to the rebellious people of God in Judah to let them know that they would be cut down by their Babylonian enemies. He is often called the weeping prophet as a result. Yet through Jeremiah's tears a hope still glistened in the image of this branch. The branch represents a continuing grace for all whose sin and failures still make them weep.

Such weeping comes upon all who dare to answer a question put to God's people in all ages: "[W]hat does the Lord require of you?" The answer given in Scripture and memorialized even now in children's songs is, "To act justly and to love mercy and to walk humbly with your God" (Micah 6: 8). These words that summarize the requirements of God's law come quickly to mind and roll readily off the tongue. In fact, the words are so easy to state that we may not sense how difficult they are to fulfill. Initially we may even be tempted to think that the ability to meet these obligations lies within us. When we begin to meditate deeply upon the full implications of these standards, however, we will be as tempted to despair. We will soon recognize that full obedience to God's standards is beyond us and that we are as undeserving of divine love as were the people of Judah. Jeremiah's mission is to convince us that while we are no more deserving of God's love, we need not despair.

As the psalmist in the preceding chapter would not describe God's law without a reference to our Redeemer, Jeremiah will not tell God's people of the coming discipline for their failures without reminding them that God must provide the righteousness they lack. Jeremiah furthers the psalmist's theme by planting a reference to a sprouting branch that will take the place of the covenant nation being hewn down in punishment. This prophetic reference to Christ's taking the place of a failed people in order to provide a righteousness they lack is the germ of the message of the Atonement. When God atones for our sins, he makes a provision to cover the guilt that is rightly ours with his own goodness. Jeremiah's message, and the heart of the Christian Gospel, is that God not only requires our righteousness, but he also provides it. When the inability of God's people to meet his holy standards would deny us any right to his love, he atones for our weakness and rebellion so that his promised love may grow in the unlikeliest places.

JEREMIAH 33:14-16

[14]"The days are coming," declares the LORD, "when I will fulfill the gracious promise I made to the house of Israel and to the house of Judah. [15]In those days and at that time I will make a righteous Branch sprout from David's line; he will do what is just and right in the land. [16]In those days Judah will be saved and Jerusalem will live in safety. This is the name by which it will be called: The Lord Our Righteousness."

Tinsel for Twigs

In our town at the intersection of streets named Clayton and Ballas, a tree is growing. It is not a very grand tree. It really is just a sprout growing out of the concrete. On the little triangular island of raised curb where they mounted the yield sign for traffic turning right, this twig has somehow taken root in a crack in the concrete. In the winter this little tree is so forlorn looking that you cannot help but doubt that it will survive till spring. Surrounded by yards and yards of barren concrete and dwarfed by the traffic signs that tower above it, the twig gets de-leafed by the winter cold and whipped mercilessly by the winds of passing cars. It is the most ignorable little stick you could imagine. And yet I noticed it.

We were driving home from Christmas shopping at the mall where the lights glittered and the music blared when the twig caught my eye. A piece of tinsel had been blown from some neighboring trash can or outdoor display and had entwined in the tiny branches of the twig. As a result the wind from passing cars repeatedly lashed the sprout into a frenzied flutter. No one else in the world seemed to notice, but as that little tree waved its tinsel banner, it spoke to me more clearly of the real import of Christ's coming than any of the glitz we had spent the day enjoying.

Though the tinsel was just a castoff of the season, its presence on the little tree signaled what Christ's coming was all about. Sure it was just tinsel, but its presence meant that God had not gotten so busy in his workings of the universe that he could not pay attention to this insignificant, ugly little sprout. God had picked up that discarded sliver of silver and woven it in the hair of an ugly twig to make it beautiful to himself. That act is so typical of our God—to make the forlorn glorious. As the tinsel on the twig signaled the nature of God's care, it also served as a wonderful beacon of hope for any who would notice. The intention of this passage and of the prophet Jeremiah is to make us notice that God provides tinsel for twigs of all types—the ignored, the ugly, the despised of this world. When our actions or the estimations of others cause us to think that there is no beauty left in us, God reminds us of the hope that is in his own nature. He loves to decorate. Through the atoning work of Jesus Christ, our Lord drapes us with his purposes, covers us with his love, and makes us shine with his glory. Faith in these designs can again make the forlorn glorious.

I. Draping the Despicable

How does God drape us with his purpose? By using us. Jeremiah promises that God can drape even the despicable with divine purpose. The prophet presents God's own word that he will bring forth one who will do what is just and right in the land (v. 15). This is the promised Messiah. But from where will the Messiah come? God says that he will make this Messiah, the one he calls "a righteous Branch," sprout forth "from David's line." The wording is important because it illustrates how God can use the insignificant and failed things of this world to accomplish his ends.

USING THE INSIGNIFICANT

The image Jeremiah calls to mind indicates that God is willing to use the insignificant things of this world for wonderful purposes. The "righteous Branch" Jeremiah pictures had already been mentioned in an earlier prophecy of Isaiah. The previous prophet said: "A shoot (or twig) will come up from the stump of Jesse; from his roots a Branch will bear fruit" (Isaiah 11:1). Anyone who has cut down a tree in his yard and then sees twigs start shooting up from the stump can understand Isaiah's image. Though in some contexts the image might be a symbol of new life and hope, for the Hebrews the image only symbolized shame.

Jesse in Isaiah's prophecy was the father of David, the king of Israel in its first great days of glory. In that time of the nation's initial significance, God promised David a royal kingdom and lineage that would be eternal (2 Sam. 7:13-16). Israel—thinking only in earthly terms—expected material and military greatness to follow. And it did, at first. Under David and his son Solomon the kingdom grew and flourished. Then the people forgot who had blessed them and turned away from God. There was an ensuing division of the nation, followed by an Assyrian attack that wiped out the northern kingdom of Israel. Now Jeremiah comes borrowing the words of Isaiah to prophesy that Babylon will also demolish Judah, the southern kingdom. The once-grand kingdom of Israel has been whittled down and will be cut down. In his prophecy Jeremiah looks forward to what the nation will be, and, for all its present pride, all he sees is a stump. In Jeremiah's vision the nation will be an insignificant nothing—a joke and a source of derision for the enemies of God's people.

Yet in his vision, from this stump of shame where the tree of Israel's national pride had been, Jeremiah sees something else arising. A twig, or branch, will shoot up to restore Israel. Jeremiah then personifies this branch saying "he" will do what is just and right in the land (v. 15). We recognize the promise of the coming Messiah in these words, of course, but it is important to see what the words can also signify for us.

Jeremiah says that the Savior of the world is going to come from this stump of a nation. There could hardly be stronger evidence that God can use the despised things of this world for his purposes. Even Jeremiah himself, scorned by his own people for his message of judgment, is an example of one despised but used for a noble purpose by God. Our Lord is always doing this sort of thing. The apostle Paul says that God uses the lowly things of this world—and the things that are not (significant) to nullify the things that are" (1 Cor. 1:28). To display his care for the world's despised, God uses the insignificant things of this world to do amazing things for heaven's purposes.

Jesus, the King of the universe, was born as a spitting baby in a dirty stable in an obscure village called Bethlehem. Regardless of what we may know now, this was not an auspicious beginning. In his bestseller, *All I Need to Know I Learned in Kindergarten*, Robert Fulghum ends a section on his seasonal cynicism about Christmas by questioning the big deal we make of an infant in a manger: "Babies and stables both stink. I've been around both and I know. Bethlehem is a pit according to those who have been there [sic]." We may not like the words, but they are true. God did not pick great things to glorify his Son. He used his Son to glorify the insignificant things.

By his birth Jesus brought glory to an impoverished town and heaven to a stable. He made what was insignificant and smelly so beautiful that we sing songs about it. In a later time he would even make a branch of thorns—so despicable—a crown of glory and save souls by it. God drapes the sparkling tinsel of holy purpose on the most insignificant things. The words Jeremiah used to prophesy the Savior's coming and the images that surround his birth should remind us of how beautiful God's designs can be for what the world rejects.

USING THE FAILURES

God also uses the failed things of this world for wonderful purposes. God's design shines more brightly in the realization of the nature of Israel's insignificance. The nation's coming ruin is a sign of failure. She had a past of greatness and the potential to be great again. That she would be reduced to a sprouting stump from so great a tree is a mark of terrible failure. Jeremiah's "branch" image became synonymous with failure in the Hebrew mind and vocabulary.

The word *branch* is actually the root word behind the name of Nazareth, the town where Jesus grew up. How clever of God to see to it that the prophesied Righteous Branch grew up in "branch town." Still the derision Jesus received for being from Nazareth indicates the disdain the Jews had for the reminder of their former greatness. That is why, when Jesus said he was from Nazareth (twig city), the people snickered and said, "Can anything good come out of Nazareth?" (John 1:45-46). Yet by weaving his life into Nazareth, our

Lord again indicated that he was willing to dignify with his presence the most disdained.

Knowing that God can use insignificant failures to accomplish his glorious purposes can grant us hope in the face of our own worst indignities and failings. Some time ago I traveled to speak at a conference for a well-known church in the evangelical world. I stayed in the home of the pastor—by all accounts a very devoted man. During one afternoon as I was preparing my message for that evening's meeting, I could not help hearing the sounds of the pastor's children playing outside. I guess you could call it playing. One child, the nine-year-old son, dominated the rest of the children with cruelty, profanity, and intimidation. It was hard to listen to and even harder to study through, so after a while I walked out of the study to take a break.

My room opened at the bottom of a stairway. As I stood at the door, a movement caught my eye. I looked up and saw the mother of the boy watching him out the window at the top of the stairs. She was almost a silhouette against the window, which made her obvious pain a more poignant picture. With her shoulders drooped and head down, she flinched at the latest profanity shouted by her son. Then she turned toward me, and I realized she was crying. She knew that I must have heard her son, and through her tears she said, "I don't know what to do with him. My husband doesn't know either; all we know is that we have failed. He's only nine years old, and we have already failed."

Many of us know the pain of failure—with children, with a marriage, with a career, or with our walk of faith. More than once in my life I have been haunted by the lyrics of a sixties pop song: "I've had beautiful beginnings, but beautiful beginnings are all I've had." Most of us know what it means to have had beautiful beginnings and painful endings. We understand what it means to be like Israel—to begin with promise and joyful expectation and then to face desolating failure.

I have a friend who manages a retail franchise at a local shopping mall. A year ago the shopping center had extensive renovation, and the crowds flocked to his store. Though he was new in the business, my friend's store was a huge success, and he set company sales records. But after the Christmas crowds diminished, local gangs moved in. Six months ago a murder at the mall received extensive news coverage. Area shoppers, fearful of more gang violence, came in increasingly fewer numbers. Store operators at the mall speculated that another murder would ruin all their businesses. Recently there was another murder. The shoppers have not returned. Thus in one year my friend has gone from having phenomenal success to being a business failure.

Knowing that God does not abandon us in failure does not necessarily make the problems melt away, but it does keep us from measuring our potential by our pasts. God can use insignificant failures for his purposes. Nothing is more true of him. We may be tempted to give up on ourselves, but as long as the God of Israel lives, so do his purposes. He does not give up on his people. If he had no purpose for us, then he would have no reason to continue our lives, to make us aware of his Word, and to give us relationships with others so that we can help make them aware of him and his blessings.

Simply having life today assures us that God is preparing us for his purposes tomorrow. We cannot predict what these purposes are, but in a new day is new hope. In new days there will be new responsibilities, new opportunities to serve him, and possibly new avenues to address past failures. Even if past failures cannot be addressed, however, knowing that God has not limited our futures by our pasts enables us to move on from negative experiences with greater wisdom for positive contributions to the people and purposes God will yet put in our lives. Our God uses earth's failures for heaven's purposes.

II. Loving the Unfaithful

God underscores his willingness to use those who may even be despicable to themselves by showing that he can use those whose shame is their own fault. The promised care for the people of Israel is all the more remarkable when you realize that their plight is a result of their own sin.

THE FAITHLESS

Why is the nation being cut down? Because of the people's own rebellion. Their failure to live up to past glory and to future potential is not somebody else's fault. Unlike my store manager friend at the shopping mall, no one else is to blame for the Hebrews' crisis. They are. Yet God promises to develop the lineage of his own Son from this unfaithful people. From the decadent nation will come the Savior who will cover their sin. *God promises to cover faithless people with unfailing love,* and in doing so he gives us hope for the future even when we have failed him.

Perhaps even more surprising about this unfailing love is the fact that God promises it to these people although they are expecting punishment. Jeremiah rightly weeps for the discipline that will come in the form of the enemies who will chop Israel down. Yet despite the coming devastation he sees, he prophesies God's continuing love and the promise of future restoration with the repentance they both stimulate.

THE PUNISHED

Jeremiah's words contain the vital scriptural truth that *the presence of divine discipline is never an indication of the absence of divine love.* Even if our failure is the result of our sin, and even if we interpret our situation to be a revelation of God's wrath, we should never assume that God's love departs from his people.

One of my great disappointments in the pastorate was to see the slow ruin of a young woman as she moved through her adolescence. I'll call her Joan. She was at one time one of the glories of our church. She was radiant, bright, fun to be around—in love with the Lord. And, then, slowly at first, something seemed to change about her. A certain slyness crept into her eyes. Her bright expressiveness colored with a dark evasiveness. Her warm, endearing smile seemed to solidify into a studied stoniness and hardness of expression.

Eventually the evasiveness became lies. The slyness became rebellion. Broken curfews turned into Saturday night drunks. Stony silence turned into angry yelling. A close family seemed to go to war with itself with an endless round of arguments, tears, and slammed doors.

After a four-year nightmare of drunkenness, drugs, and increasingly prolonged absences, this prodigal daughter returned to her parents' home one night with the announcement that she was expecting a child and needed their help. The help she had spurned she now begged for. They took her in knowing that she probably planned to take advantage of them again. In many ways she did. She considered her pregnancy a punishment of God—a biologically imposed grounding—and in many ways she lashed back at God by the demands she made on her parents.

Still the change of lifestyle required by her pregnancy slowed the young woman down just enough for those who loved her to remind her of the God she had once loved and who still loved her. She had trouble accepting those words. She considered the sins she committed too great and the infant she carried too clear an indication of God's displeasure to spell anything but rejection.

Her parents believed that for them to deny the possibility that God was disciplining their daughter was not in her best interests. They affirmed that God does allow us to experience the consequences of our sin and that he turns us from paths of disobedience that will cause us or others harm. At the same time the parents affirmed as clearly what the Bible says unmistakably: "The Lord disciplines those he loves" (Heb. 12:6). God is forever seeking to protect from greater danger. He is always drawing his own back to himself. The presence of discipline does not indicate the absence of divine love. Even when God judges rebellion, his love pervades his every action, and his blessed intent covers us in the darkness of our sin (Ps. 94:12; 119:75; Rev. 3:19).

Eventually, by God's grace, the young woman understood God's care and acknowledged it. Later when she brought her child for baptism, I am sure some saw the young mother's child as a symbol of shame, perhaps even a symbol of punishment. But not I, and not her family, and not she. As the waters of the sacrament trickled down that infant's little head, we saw in the streams of water the tinsel of divine love covering shame and sin. The message to all: "God covers even the unfaithful with unfailing love." He makes beautiful what the world has made ugly, because he loves to decorate.

Each of us needs to hear anew these "old-fashioned" truths about the love of God that covers our shame because the mature as well as the young can fall into awful sin. The addictions and adulteries that tempt us and trip us can make us believe we have fallen away from God forever. Because of the seriousness or repetition of our sin, some of us may consider ourselves separated even from the potential of God's love. We may have been taught to assume that difficulties signify the withdrawal of God's affection. The message of Jeremiah contradicts each of these assumptions. Through this prophet our Lord says that even those who are deserving and experiencing discipline for their own sin are loved by their God.

III. Making the Shameful Shine

How can God act this way? How can he be loving to those who possess nothing that could make them respectable before him? The actions of some friends of mine who recently got a new puppy may help explain. They gave their dog the name Josephine Chateaubolier Sofrier St. Vincent. By the name you know that this is a special puppy. Its breed is officially listed as Heinz 57—it's a mix—a mutt. Our friends gave their dog this wonderful name to make a statement of how special it is to them regardless of what others may think of its heritage.

HIS NAME

Due to weaknesses, failures, or sin in our pasts, we may not feel very significant to God, but he wants us to recognize how special we are to him. So he gives us a special name. Speaking through Jeremiah, God says that when the Branch comes, the nation (represented by Judah and its capital, Jerusalem) will be saved, and "it" will be called "The Lord our Righteousness" (v. 16). Sometimes great Scripture truths, like the best gifts, come in the smallest packages. The prophet has made a crucial point with this little pronoun "it."

A few chapters earlier the promised Messiah is called "The Lord Our Righteousness" (cf. 23:6). But now Jeremiah announces that the despised and sinful nation will be called by the same name. God not only plans to save these people, but he will give them his own name. These people are such a mix of sinful failure, but they remain special to God, and to make sure they know that, he gives them his own glorious name.

HIS NATURE

God gives his people more than his name to make them shine with his glory. He gives them what the name means. The branch that is to come, the Messiah, is called "The Lord Our Righteousness." Christ will provide the righteousness this sinful people could not provide for themselves in two ways—by his obedience and by his sacrifice.

The righteousness of obedience. Jeremiah says that the righteous Branch "will do what is just and right in the land" even though the people of God have not (v. 15). The ancient people could not have known as clearly as we now do what this promise meant. In order to pass to his people a righteousness that they had not lived, the Messiah would have to live in a way that they had not. Each obligation they did not meet, the Lord would have to meet by his own *active obedience* in order to provide the kind of righteousness that God requires.

In the New Testament the apostle Peter describes how Jesus acted in obedience to meet the standards God has given us. In describing Christ's life, Peter relates the perfection of the Savior's service in each dimension of human obligation. Jesus, King of all creation, *submitted to the rule of earthly authorities* even when obedience to the Jewish and Roman officials cost his life (1 Peter 2:21). He *endured without evil reaction* foolish accusations and profound injustice when he neither retaliated nor threatened those who "hurled their insults at him" (v. 23). Though faced with this monstrous unfairness, he *maintained a testimony of integrity* before God and man since "He committed no sin, and no deceit was found in his mouth" (v. 22).

Not only did our Savior maintain a perfectly righteous character in his dealings with men, but he also remained completely faithful to God as he performed these duties. Rather than counting on earthly reward or regard for his sacrificial service, Jesus "entrusted himself to him who judges justly" (v. 23). Jesus obeyed without the motive of personal gain and yielded his life entirely to the purposes and discretion of his Lord.

Everything our heavenly Father requires of us Jesus did. He acted justly, loved mercy, and walked humbly with his God (cf. Micah 6:8). The righteous duties he requires of us, our Savior assumed (cf. Matt. 3:15). Recognizing that the standards of his holiness would overwhelm us, the Lord allowed his own Son to meet our righteous obligations. In the person of Jesus, our God put the burden of our obedience on himself.

The righteousness of sacrifice. To make his supply complete, the Lord had to make provision for our failures as well as fulfill our obligations. Simply because Jesus met the obligations we owe does not negate the consequences of our sins. Whether by willful transgression or personal weakness, we all stand before God guilty of failure to live as he requires. A holy God cannot ignore these faults. Since he could not retain his own holiness by approval of (or union with) what is sinful, unloving, or unholy, our inability to meet our human and divine obligations results in the penalty of separation from God. From the dawn of human history God has made physical death the earthly demonstration of the consequence of this separation from the Giver and Sustainer of Life (cf. Gen. 2:17; 3:19). Our mortality reflects the deeper realities of eternal separation from God, which the Bible identifies as spiritual death for all who do not find a new source of life (cf. Rom. 6:23; Eph. 2:1; Heb. 9:14).

God himself grieves for this separation and released his people from its pain by putting the death penalty for our sin on his own Son. The very obedience by which Jesus fulfilled our righteous obligations uniquely qualified him to assume this penalty (cf. 2 Cor. 5:21). Since "he committed no sin," he was in no debt to God. His righteousness had no limit and thus was of infinite worth. As a result our God decreed that Jesus' sacrifice would perfectly balance the heavenly books and cancel the penalty for all who ask God to account Christ's righteousness in their behalf (cf. v. 24; Isa. 53:10).

Jesus paid our penalty when his own perfection released him from any obligation to suffer for sin. On the basis of this example, the apostle calls Christians to similar selfless sacrifice. "You should follow in his steps," says Peter (1 Peter 2:21). The words reveal an often overlooked aspect of Christ's suffering that echoes from Jeremiah's prophecy. We can only follow in the steps of one who walked this earth. Peter's call to follow Christ reminds us that the King of the universe came to be born in disreputable circumstances, to live in an impoverished condition, to endure humiliating bondage to human laws, and to suffer a despicable death. Thus, though it sounds noble when Jeremiah says that a Branch will sprout from the stump of Jesse, we should remember that the fulfillment of this prophecy required that our Lord live in the misery his own people had created. The seventeenth-century Reformers captured the essence of this misery, writing, "Christ's humiliation consisted in his being born, and that in a low condition, made under the law, undergoing the miseries of this life, the wrath of God, and the cursed death of the cross; in being buried, and continuing under the power of death for a time" (*Westminster Shorter Catechism*, # 27).

By his passive submission to the conditions of this life (when he could have had heaven's glory for his home) and by his passive suffering of torturous death on a cross (when he could have called heaven's armies to his rescue), Jesus fully paid the penalty for our sin.

Christ's *passive obedience* in yielding to suffering out of submission to the will of his Father and his active obedience in meeting the standards of the will of the Father combine to fulfill the righteousness we could not achieve and to satisfy the penalty that we could not pay. Thus the result of Christ's obedience and suffering in our behalf is that his righteousness is passed to his people. We can have his name because he grants us his nature. He substitutes his righteousness for our sin and cancels our guilt by his suffering (cf. 1 Cor. 15:3; Rom. 3:25). In these ways the Lord *is* our righteousness. His name portrays both what he has done and what we now are (cf. 1 Cor. 1:30).

HIS GLORY

When God gives us his name and nature, he actually shares Christ's glory with us. From God's perspective we are robed in the righteousness of Christ. We cover our Christmas trees with tinsel that is supposed to look like silver, but it's really just tinfoil or shiny plastic. The tinsel is not really what it is supposed to represent. But when God represents us to the world by calling us by the name of his Son, he actually makes us what he calls us. He gives us the nature of his own Son and, thereby, makes us his own sons and daughters. The glory he puts on us is not just a tinfoil image. It's the real thing. It is the pure gold righteousness of his own Son whereby we now shine like stars (see Phil. 2:15). Recognizing that God truly allows us to bear the name and the nature of his own Son can change the way we look at others and ourselves.

I remember some months ago sitting in a worship service and listening to a young woman sing. Hers is one of the most beautiful voices I have ever heard. People listen to her and are moved to tears by the splendor of her music. But I have heard her weep at other times as we have talked about her struggles with sin. In the past she has been unfaithful to her husband, and as a result she has felt terrible guilt. To escape her guilt she sometimes drinks too much. When she drinks too much, she loses control. And when she loses control, her own children too often pay the consequences. Then with the guilt of that sin on her conscience, the cycle repeats itself again and again.

Her weaknesses have made her family a modern horror story, and yet there she sang of the wonderful grace of Jesus. I confess that there was a piece of me that considered this an offensive hypocrisy—a bitter irony that one so flawed could sing so flawlessly. Then I realized that once again I was looking at the tinsel on a twig. That beautiful voice was the tinsel—the representation of the beauty of God draped on a twisted tendril of humanity. Her voice, like the tinsel, was the Lord's banner for all the world to see. By it he said, "I give the despicable my name and my nature. No one is holy enough for me, so I have to gift my people with my holiness. I make the ugly, beautiful. I make the inglorious, glorious. I make that which is dark with shame shine like gold."

Our cynicism and doubt at times are stimulated by seeing the terribly flawed creatures—even leaders—in the church who dare to call themselves God's own. We look at their foibles and failings and think to ourselves, *How can they call themselves Christians?* But if we follow that line of thought back to ourselves, facing our own sins and causes of shame, we know the answer. They call themselves Christians not because of any righteousness in them, but because of their faith that the Lord is their righteousness (cf. Rom. 3:22-24).

The same faith must characterize each of us who wishes to know the embrace of our Savior. Our sin, too, denies us any claim on holiness and any right to heaven. Our own hypocrisies and failings are evident to us all if we really will peer deeply into our souls. Such honest meditation will cause us to despair of being enfolded into God's family unless we remember the name and the nature we have been given, though we are undeserving. He makes us his own, not because of any goodness in us, but because of our faith in his provision. He is the righteousness of those who trust in him (cf. Phil. 3:9). He covers us with his saving blood, the tinsel of eternity that is truly gold.

Because God does not reject what is despicable but desires to make it special, useful, and glorious to himself, we who have been unfaithful, weak, and failing can turn to him again. Knowledge of his love of making the forlorn glorious is what gives us the courage to take our sins to him in open confession and humble repentance. His forgiving heart urges us to come to him again to ask for fresh cleansing, new power over sin, and new usefulness. He who used stable straw for the King's bed can again use a sinner's heart for the King's throne.

If our sin has made us flee from him, turn from him in shame, or doubt that he will again enter the life of one who botched it so badly, then Jeremiah's message holds new hope. He who decorates twigs with tinsel yet can have a design for tousled lives. Our God loves to decorate.

When my son Jordan was seven, he became enamored with Christmas poinsettias. Something about the brilliant splash of red in the dead of winter fascinated him. He wanted a poinsettia so badly that we got him his own. Driving home with it, Jordan was the picture of a child in entranced contentment. He nestled the little plant into his lap to examine every detail. He pressed his face close to smell its center and traced the edge of each leaf with a finger. He even petted the plant as though it were a puppy. And then our car came to an intersection requiring a fast brake, and the "puppy" poinsettia fell forward out of his lap and spilled into a pool of crimson petals on the floor of the car.

Jordan looked up with horror and grief and guilt on his face. To know my Jordan is to know that he said it all with the motion of his hands. Held up in exasperation and pain they said, "Oh no, what have I done? I should have held it tighter; I should have prepared; I should protected it more. I should have done better."

When his mother saw the gestures of hurt and shame, instinctively she reached out her hand to touch Jordan. In her touch she draped those hands and her son with her love. He had been wrong to be so careless. But his expression of shame and hurt was no greater than that of hers who hurt for him. To show her care, she brushed away the dirt that now covered him with her own hands, righted the crimson petals, and put the plant into his hands again.

Our God's care holds similar tenderness. He shows it not by offering us a plant but by offering us the promise of an infant, the Branch that would shoot up from the stump of Jesse. Our tendency at Christmastime is imaginatively to hold this manger babe as we would a little puppy—to coo over him and pat his head. But our errors brought him here, and our faults would spill his blood. What horror! On our hands is the guilt of what we have done.

Because of us crimson droplets would fall in a rain of grace to pool on the earth beneath a cross. They fell not from a flower's hurt but from a Savior's wounds—wounds that we deserved. When we see what we have done, our hands go up to blind us to the horror of our own actions and to hide us from the shame of our own sin. But when our heavenly Father sees the expression of our pain, his automatic gesture is to reach out to touch us with his love. The dirt on us does not distract him. He brushes it away with the handiwork of his Son. And with the body and blood of that same Son, he drapes us with his purpose, covers us with his love, and makes us shine with his glory.

As tinsel can decorate even a twig with beauty, our heavenly Father covers our shame with his splendor. Despite our past carelessness and failing, our God loves us so much that He puts his precious Son into our hearts to receive and to cherish. Our faults and failures may make it seem improbable, even impossible, that he would deal so beautifully with us. But we must remember the message that God's Spirit blows throughout his Word: Ours is the God who loves to decorate. He sent his Son for sinners, and he still puts tinsel on twigs—such as you and I.

DISCUSSION QUESTIONS

1) How has God used insignificant things in your life to accomplish his greater purposes?
2) How has God used failures in your life to accomplish his better purposes?
3) Why is it important not to measure our potential by our pasts?
4) Why is it important to know that God did not abandon the children of Israel despite their rebellion and sin?
5) Why is it important for you to know that even when God disciplines for sin, he loves us no less?
6) How and why does God give us his name?
7) How does God share with us his nature, and why is this important?
8) What did Christ's suffering accomplish?
9) Why should you express faith in Christ's sacrifice and love for you?

6

THE SWEETNESS
OF GRACE

THE WORD IN PERSPECTIVE

Have you ever used a carpenter's plane? When as a kid I learned a little bit of woodworking from my dad, nothing pleased me more than using a plane. It seemed almost like magic to take a crooked, rough piece of lumber and, by waving this tool back and forth over it, take away its defects. Curly ribbons of paper-thin wood would rise almost effortlessly from the blade, and before my eyes the board would transform, becoming straight and smooth as silk. It was great fun. So when a carpenter came to my office recently to install a door, I could not help reminiscing a bit as he took out his plane.

When he began making those curly ribbons of wood, I said, "Isn't that the funnest thing in the world?" He looked at me like I was nuts.

"Not when you do it every day for twenty years," he said gruffly. "It's been a long time since I considered this fun."

Of course, then I felt foolish for asking. I also felt sorry for the carpenter who apparently took so little joy in his work. His lack of enthusiasm showed. When he left that day and I tried out my new door, it stuck. He had not planed the door properly. The task that he took so little joy in, he did not do well. This was no surprise, of course, because whenever our hearts are not in our duties, the work suffers.

In the verses following the passage cited below, the apostle Paul details the job all Christians have. We are to participate in the construction of a kingdom—God's kingdom. This kingdom under con-

struction requires much of us. Paul knows, however, that we will not be able to perform our tasks well if we take no joy in them. So before he tells us what to do, he provides these words of encouragement to help make sure our hearts stay in our work.

ROMANS 12:1-2

[1]Therefore, I urge you, brothers, in view of God's mercy, to offer your bodies as living sacrifices, holy and pleasing to God—this is your spiritual act of worship. [2]Do not conform any longer to the pattern of this world, but be transformed by the renewing of your mind. Then you will be able to test and approve what God's will is—his good, pleasing and perfect will.

๛

BIBLE BROKEN

She took her children to the park to break the monotony of summer days, and instead she broke her own heart. She watched her children run to the playground equipment as another car drove into the parking lot. The new car ground to a quick stop. A young, attractive woman with a beaming smile leaped out of the driver's seat and virtually skipped to a secluded picnic table near an adjoining lake.

The imagination of the mother began to race. Who could this attractive young woman be meeting in such a secluded spot with so much enthusiasm? Was this a long-awaited and carefully planned rendezvous with an over-busy husband, a lunch date with a best friend, or a tryst between secret lovers? The young mother determined to stay on the lookout for whoever got out of the next car.

No one else came immediately. The mother soon grew preoccupied with her children and forgot to watch the young woman. When she did finally glance again at the secluded woman, what the mother saw made her own heart hurt. The woman was reading a Bible. The person she had leapt from the car to meet with such enthusiasm was the Lord.

The mother recognized with pain that penetrated her spirit that she no longer had that same enthusiasm. Once the excitement of her relationship with the Lord had overwhelmed her. Once the joy of her salvation had burned warm and bright. But the fervor was gone. Faith had become dreary duty; God had become a detached, frowning bystander. Something had happened over the years of her walk with the Lord. She did not know what it was, but she did know that she would not now be one to skip to meet him. She had lost something wonderful, and she wept there in the park for her loss.

Do you know the loss of which I speak? Do you know what it means for your worship to seem terribly important but painfully dull? Can you sympathize with those learning more and more about God but caring less and less? You may still be trying to serve God,

but you find yourself doing so increasingly with bowed neck, grit-
ted teeth, and weary resolve. There is so much to be done for the
kingdom, but for you, too, perhaps duty has become drudgery, God
distant, and your love cold.

Longtime lives of faith do not have to be this way. You can love
the Lord and his purposes with a burning zeal again. God's work can
excite you again. A longtime Christian servant, the apostle Paul, tells
you how to rekindle your *desire* and *ability* to serve in the building of
God's kingdom.

I. Make Mercy Your Motivation

There is much to do in this kingdom under construction. Paul says
we are not to be conformed to the pattern of this crooked world but
rather to be transformed so that we can know God's will (v. 2). We
are to know God's will so we will do it. God expects our transformation to impact our world. The apostle's following instructions
indicate how much God expects us to do in the construction of his
kingdom on earth. He tells us our corporate responsibilities as a body
of believers (12:3-7); then he gives us our individual work assignments (12:8-21). Because God does not limit his kingdom to the
church, Paul next tells us our civil responsibilities (13:1-7); and finally
he details our moral duties in society (13:8-14).

THE EXHORTATION OF MERCY

God gives us so much to do that we might lose heart. Paul must
have known the likelihood of our discouragement, so he precedes all
these work assignments with this exhilarating exhortation: "I urge
you, brothers, in view of God's mercy" to serve him (v. 1). Paul wants
to make sure our hearts are in our work, so he encourages us with
God's love rather than driving us with any other motivation.

You can sense the special nature of Paul's opening exhortation by
comparing it to other words Paul might have used to spur us on in
our tasks. Paul did *not* say, "I urge you by the guilt you will assume

if you are negligent." He did *not* berate: "I urge you by the rejection you will face if you fail." He did *not* threaten: "I urge you by the love you will lose if you fail." No, Paul knew that if we serve God out of guilt or what the seventeenth-century Reformers called "servile duty" or "slavish fear," then our labors for the Lord would not be joyful, strong, or long.

Our own work experiences confirm the wisdom of the apostle's approach. Did you ever work for a boss who just could not be satisfied? No matter what you did, it was never quite good enough because the boss motivated by intimidation. As a result you approached every new task with a sense of dread and fear, questioning and self-doubt. What happens over the long run when you work for such a boss? You stay on your toes for a while, but eventually you wear out. You either give up or grow hard or avoid the boss. Your work suffers because you have no heart for it or for the one who assigns it. God does not want you to serve him that way. "Serve me," he says, "by keeping in view not my anger nor your shame . . . but my mercy."

THE ABUNDANCE OF MERCY

Even the word *mercy* is special. The translators of the King James Version of the Bible rendered the word in the plural. As a result many Christians have grown up memorizing this text as, "I beseech you, therefore, brethren, by the mer*cies* of God." The contemporary translations that render the word as a singular noun are not spoiling for an argument. They actually add a richness to our understanding. The word for "mercy" with which the translators wrestle communicates the truth that Paul presents in the preceding chapter (11:27). In his grace God made a covenant to take away sins. Once it applied to the Jews only. Now it applies to all who claim the Gospel of Jesus Christ. God's mercy now applies to many. The mercy has multiplied (see 11:30-32). One word can hardly contain so much love. This rich, overflowing, and abundant grace is a mercy of mercies.

This abundance of mercy that challenges the translators should overwhelm us. We should delight to serve him who provides so much for us. Yet we struggle so to keep his mercy in view that God graciously gives us opportunity after opportunity in our lives to see the wonder of his love—if we will but open our eyes.

I saw that mercy afresh during one of the most difficult weeks that my wife, Kathy, and I have ever faced. We heard a word we had dreaded applied to one of our children. That word was *asthma*.

Our son coughed a little during a Saturday night. At church the next day he started running a fever, and as his temperature went up, he started having trouble breathing. We left the service early, and by nightfall he was struggling to draw each breath.

No doctor had officially labeled the problem yet, but I knew what was happening. I grew up with asthma. I know all about the days missed from school, the constant medication, the innumerable trips to the doctor. I have known the bitter disappointment of preparing months for a sports event only to experience a sudden attack that wiped strength, breath, and opportunity from me.

I thought of all of this as I tried to help my son get to sleep that night. I rubbed between his shoulders that were hunched in the way that asthmatics naturally roll their shoulders to take pressure off their lungs. I listened to him inhale in wheezing misery and exhale through lips pursed as his body instinctively tried to create back pressure to expand bronchial tubes another micro-millimeter. Still the difficulty he was having was no greater than the pain I felt. I had already experienced each of these asthma reactions a thousand times, and my heart lamented, "Oh, my child, how I wish I could spare you what I went through."

Then I thought of the mercy. I remembered another who went through such misery that it took his breath away. I thought of other shoulders rolled in suffering against the wood of a cross. I recalled the one whose weight hung on nails so cruel that each breath was torture. He willingly took the agony my sins deserved, all so his lips pursed with pain could express, "Oh, my child, now I will spare you what I go through."

"How great is the love the Father has lavished on us, that we should be called children of God!" (1 John 3:1). Such mercy eclipses all other motivations for our service. His mercy should so fill our vision that gratitude floods our hearts with the longing to do his will. If thankfulness does not move us, then we do not truly understand who our God is and what he has done in our behalf. Without gratitude for Christ's sacrificial love, our duty will become nothing more than drudgery and our God nothing more than a dissatisfied boss. This is why Paul tells us at the outset to serve "in view of God's mercy."

THE CHALLENGE OF MERCY

Despite God's overwhelming love, mercy can quickly fade from our view. Other motivations that make our service to God distasteful and destructive all too easily preoccupy us. We can begin to focus on reasons to serve God that spoil our view of the cross almost without our ever really intending it.

Our spiritual health requires us to confess the difficulty we have in keeping the mercy fully in view. I have struggled more than once over two decades of pastoring to keep using mercy to motivate others. I had been a pastor for about five years before I began really to struggle with the recognition that so many Christians, including those in the church I served, seemed so far from the Lord because of mercy deprivation.

Recognition of the spiritual emptiness so many were experiencing was all the more surprising because both churches I have pastored are well over 100 years old. Many of the families in those churches have been members for generations. There was nothing in their outward actions that signaled any problems. After being in church so long, almost everyone knew very well how Christians should act. They faithfully observed a code of community conduct dictating that most were faithful to their spouses and did not smoke or drink to excess nor cuss in polite company. Outwardly so much seemed okay.

The matters I struggled with were their attitudes. Almost all of them took their Bibles to church, and many could put me to shame with their Bible knowledge. But that was the problem. I could not understand how people who were so knowledgeable about God could be so bitter, so guilt-ridden, so often depressed, so cold to each other, and so intolerant of the faults of newer Christians. These longtime church people said they were followers of Jesus (and many of their outward actions would give their professions some credence), yet love, joy, peace, patience, and long-suffering seemed so far from so many. I used to get so angry at those people for their lack of heart response to the Word they said they loved. Then I began to realize the problem was not so much them as it was me—and others like me.

If you are responsible for the spiritual welfare of others—a preacher, a teacher, a parent, a spouse, a committed Christian in any walk of life—you know that God gives us a difficult task. The Word of God tells us to exhort sinful people to change even though they may not want to change. We are supposed to instruct them to stop doing what is dishonoring to God. We often wonder how, and probably all of us at some point in our attempts to change others discover a very effective tool called guilt. All parents know this tool. Preachers and teachers know it, too.

There is nothing more *effective* than guilt to get people to obey the standards of God and nothing less *efficacious* in sanctifying them to God. Make people feel bad enough, fearful enough, guilty enough, and you can get them to change (or else they will leave your church, and then you will not have to worry about them). Yet nothing is less biblical than motivating believers by the guilt that makes God's love conditional upon human performance.

Early in my ministry I did not recognize how damaging such

guilt is as a primary means for motivating Christian obedience. I used lots of guilt as a pastor. And I saw people's behaviors change—for a while. Still so often I found that these people did not mature. They did not grow in faith nor seem more spiritually whole even though their outward actions may have changed. For instance, I might deal with a married couple whose relationship was coming apart because they were not being faithful to each other. I would tell them that if they changed their behaviors, God would bless them, but that as long as they pursued sinful relationships, they could not expect his love. The couple might very well cease their immoral activities with this advice, but I would later see that their lives were not necessarily better. A year or two down the road these same people were often locked into depression, pursuing other addictive behaviors, or were simply spiritually disinterested.

It took me a few years (we preachers can be notoriously dense), but finally I figured out what was happening. I was telling people that the way to get rid of their guilt before God and assure his blessing was by changing their behaviors. But what did this imply? If people expect behavior change to get rid of their guilt, whom are they trusting to take their guilt away? Themselves!

I was forcing people to question, "What action of mine will make me right with God?" No wonder their faith did not mature. Their faith was in what they could do to fix their own situations. I had let the mercy get out of view. I was encouraging people to look to themselves rather than to the cross as the place to erase guilt. Christ alone can remove the guilt of our sin. By letting people think that what they did made them right with God, I was driving the wedge of human works between them and God. The people who listened to me, though they may have changed some aspect of their lives to get my approval and secure God's affection, were actually further away from God spiritually than when I began to "minister" to them.

When mercy got out of view, grace went away, and works rightoouoncss jumped into its place before I even knew it. My people were trying to become acceptable to God by being good enough. But they could not be good enough for a holy God. Something in them knew that. That is why they were so hard and bitter and cold. I was teaching them that if they just did things right, they could make things right with God. How foolish was my instruction. The Bible says that when we have done all we can do, we are still unworthy servants (Luke 17:10). Our best works are only filthy rags to God (Isa. 64:6). I was teaching people that if they just offered God more filthy rags, he would love them more: "Here, God, here are some more filthy rags; now will you love me?"

What a cruel God I painted for them. What grace I denied those in our church by teaching them that God's love was dependent on their goodness. I was the one who made them intolerant of less mature believers. By listening to me, my people had to gauge their spiritual status by their works. And what better way is there to confirm your own righteousness than by finding fault in others? If the people in our church had bad attitudes and lost interest in matters of faith, I had no one to blame but myself. I was the one who had veiled the mercy.

THE GOD OF MERCY

We should know from our own family experiences how unproductive obedience is when primarily obtained through guilt. What happens to a child who obeys only out fear of parental rejection—a child who stays good to stay loved? He may obey when he is young, but he is scarred for life. Because the love is never more certain than the child's actions, acceptance is always in doubt. As a result, the child grows up hard or weak, hating his parents, and doubting himself. Many of us know these truths very well because we were manipulated by guilt as children, and we may still bear the scars. We hate what makes us feel guilt to gain favor.

Family relations expert Karen Sanheim tells of a teenage daughter who was given a new hair drier by her mother. But even as the mother presented the gift, she said, "Your father and I give up so much so that you will have things like this to enjoy." The girl later said that at that moment she wanted to take the new hair drier and throw it through the window. She knew that every time she used it, she would have to face the guilt of depriving her parents of something. Of course, she did not throw out the hair drier. That would only hurt her mother and lead to another round of guilt. Instead, the daughter cut off her hair. She did what she had to do to keep from feeling guilty. She punished herself.

Many Christians respond this same way. They punish themselves to get rid of their guilt. They will substitute the penance of depression and self-hate for confession. They think that making themselves feel bad enough and carrying a burden of guilt long enough will surely make them right with God. But who really wants us pressed down and paralyzed by a burden of sin? Satan. He is our accuser (see Rev. 12:10). Nothing pleases him more than for Christians to beat themselves down into idle depression or unproductive despair. The Bible does not say that our guilty feelings or compensating recriminations will make us right with God. God makes us right with God. He does not want us bowed down in despair. He is the lifter of our heads (Ps. 3:3).

No one can serve a God who only loves us when we are good. If God's love is conditional, if he is only waiting to get us when we step out of line, if avoidance of his rejection or relief of our guilt is our reason for serving him; then we may obey him for a time, but we will not like him very much. Unfortunately, a failure to love God only makes us feel more guilty and forces us into a downward spiral of greater despair and more futile resolve to make things right with him. When we sin, we decide to let the guilt consume us more. We wallow in our guilt to punish ourselves with it. We intensify our disciplines of Bible reading, prayer, and church attendance so that God will forgive us.

Despite this well-intended penance, we find we love this never-satisfied God less and less, even as we try to please him more and more. Eventually it all becomes meaningless. We become hard, cynical, judgmental, bitter, or despairing because we have made God what he could never be, i.e., a heavenly ogre intent on extracting his pound of flesh from whoever crosses him.

Paul exhorts us to keep the mercy in view because grace alone will keep our service in effect. If we try to compensate for the guilt that only Christ can remove, then we will lose the capacity to love him and to serve him rightly. God does not want us to punish ourselves to erase our guilt. He punished his Son to cancel our guilt. God will not build his kingdom on our pain because he is building it on his mercy.

THE GRATITUDE OF MERCY

Does guilt have any role among God's kingdom-builders? Yes. But we should be very sure about what function it serves. Guilt should drive us to the cross, but grace must lead us from it. Guilt makes us seek Christ, but gratitude should make us serve him. Guilt should lead to confession, but until we live in thankful obedience, true repentance never comes. The kindness of God motivates the repentance that truly promotes changed lives (Rom. 2:4). The love of Christ constrains and compels us to do his will (2 Cor. 5:14).

Mercy stimulates the gratitude that is the only enduring motivation for effective Christian service. Gratitude recognizes the love that never fades and restores confidence in our relationship with God. Here is the only true source of Christian power. How can you build if you are paralyzed with dread, beaten down with remorse, burdened by guilt, made miserable and sad? Such a condition cannot be what God intends. God intends for you to take all your sin and guilt, bring it to the foot of the cross, and lay it down. Now stand up. Lift your head. Believe that you are free of your guilt and trust that you can now do what he asks of you with joy because God's grace has released you from your burden. Lasting service comes when we serve God *from* acceptance, not *for* acceptance.

Does this unconditional love of God for his children mean that we can sin with impunity? May we determine to indulge our worst inclinations because God promises to love us anyway? No, of course not. Sin will hurt you. Satan will damage you as much as he can through the allure of temptations that lead to heartache. If you tell lies, then you will destroy your reputation and self-estimation. If you yield your body to immorality, then your family will suffer. You must fear the consequences of your sin. Still you must be more overwhelmed by the love of your God, or you cannot be holy. Only when our heart's loving response to God's mercy becomes our primary motivator do we delight to serve God. Without this delight neither true worship nor sacrificial service are possible. In the depth of God's love we find an appreciation of grace (the unmerited favor of God) that makes our service rich, sweet, and honoring of him.

Paul calls us all to the building of God's kingdom. But before we lift the first gospel hammer or drive the first spiritual nail, he makes us pause to ask ourselves this question: "Why do you do what you do?" Our fallen minds and twisted consciences might supply a variety of answers to that question—guilt, fear, pride, or personal gain. So lest we damage the kingdom or ourselves with ill-conceived notions, Paul supplies our motivation. He says to build "in view of God's mercy." If we chiefly serve him so that we will not feel bad, guilt motivates us. If we serve him principally so that we will gain his affection or avoid his punishment, self-interest motivates us. Mercy should motivate all we do, for then the grace of God motivates us.

II. Make Mercy Your Power

Mercy does not merely affect our *attitudes*. Mercy energizes our *abilities*. The grace of God provides motivation *and* enablement for the tasks God sets before us. When we recognize all that God requires of us in the building of his kingdom, we may quickly get overwhelmed. We readily fall into a mental conversation that sounds something like this: "I would like to help, but I'm not sure I can. I'm not sure that I'm able. I don't think I'm strong enough to do kingdom work."

Such thinking is not necessarily ill-considered. We are wise not to attempt tasks that we do not have the ability to complete. We need more than desire to do a good job. We need the energy to see the task through, and we need resources to accomplish it. Paul tells us where we can get both. Mercy holds the power we need. In mercy resides the encouragement needed for our drive, and the enablement needed for our service.

A generation ago young people recited the first verse of this passage from the King James Version this way: "I beseech you therefore, brethren, *by the mercies of God* to present your bodies as living sacrifices . . ." The phrasing "*by* the mercies" captures a rich dimension of the biblical writer's original intent. In the following verses the apostle Paul indicates that God will require much of us in his kingdom work. But before he describes the tasks before us, Paul gives us the tool we need to do the job. Mercy is the instrument, the leverage, that gets the job done. It is *by* God's mercy that we can accomplish what God requires. We are not only to keep mercy in view, but we are to keep it in use.

ENCOURAGEMENT POWER

Mercy becomes our power when first we recognize the freedom it provides. We cannot expect to serve God very effectively when we are carrying a load of guilt on our backs—even if we think that by carrying the load, we are somehow pleasing God. Our service becomes powerful as we recognize that Christ has released us from the burden of sin. Grace makes us truly able. We stand tall, ready, and free to do God's will when we understand that he loves us enough to take the burden from us—the burden that we could not remove even by our best efforts. God's work in our behalf provides the encouragement that makes us strong.

Mercy is the good news that God is for us (Rom. 8:31). He is on our side. He is in our corner. The mercy of God's continuous support is a powerful source of the believer's strength in the face of his own faults and frailties. Think of the strength another's support can provide in the context of the amazing feats of our nation's Olympians. Because St. Louis has become a mecca for young boxers, our town follows the Olympic boxing competition closely. Despite the great talents of these fighters, the youth of most of them makes them particularly prone to mistakes. Yet even when a boxer's own "showboating" sets him up for a sucker punch, I have never seen a coach walk out on his athlete. No matter what the fault, the coaches stay in their fighters' corners. God's grace reminds us that he always remains in our corner.

Even when we, like some of the young Olympians, have taken a blow to the chin due to our own mistakes and pride, God never turns his back on us. When we have boxed with sin, failed, and fallen, God is still for us. He does not wait for us to lift ourselves off the mat before he encourages us. God shouts from our corner, "Get up, child. Yes, you forgot what I told you, but I'm still here for you." Were God to walk away when we go down, leaving us alone and ashamed, there would be no reason to get up again. But our God promises never to leave or forsake us (Heb. 13:5). His encouragement lifts us from the paralysis that our own guilt would impose and makes us the vital warriors he desires for the kingdom's battles.

In Old Testament worship innocent animals were killed in sacrifice to atone for the sins of God's people. But dead animals could not please God nor ultimately atone for sin. So God sent his own Son as an atoning sacrifice to completely take the guilt of sin from his people once and for all (1 John 4:10; Rom. 6:10; Heb. 10:10). No longer desiring dead sacrifices, our God now calls us to offer our bodies as living sacrifices to carry out his will (v. 1). He wants people who are strong, able, and willing to fight for his causes. Therefore, God tells us to keep the mercy in view that will keep us vital and valiant in his fight. Our God's support grants us power. As we rejoice in his mercy, we find the resolve to get up and fight again. Paul merely reminds us of what we should know from ancient days: "The joy of the LORD is our strength" (Neh. 8:10). There is power in love that guilt cannot imitate. There is capability in mercy that intimidation cannot begin to tap.

Knowledge of another's unconditional support unleashes human power in amazing ways. Missionary leader Paul Kooistra tells of a study a state Department of Education once conducted. Educators wanted to know why remedial studies programs throughout the state were failing. The programs were supposed to supply extra help for students who were struggling academically in order to bring them up to the performance levels of their peers. Unfortunately, whenever children entered the program, they were stigmatized in their schools and in their own minds as problem students. Because they were put in a program for slow students, the children labeled themselves as failures. Children simply gave up once the school assigned them to the special classes. The program that was intended to promote their learning instead became an academic whirlpool. No student who entered the remedial studies ever got out of the program—with one exception. Her name was Edy.

Edy was a track star, and everyone called her "Speedy Edy." Everything about her was fast except her academic progress. She was put in the program for slow learners, but somehow she broke free of its whirlpool effects. When Edy's scores indicated she was back on peer level academically, the state officials concentrated their research on her. Everyone wanted to know what was different about the instruction that made her succeed in the remedial program when so many others failed. What made Edy tick?

The researchers talked to Edy's teacher to get details.

"What did you do with Edy that was different from what you did with the other children?"

"Nothing," the teacher replied.

The researchers pressed, "Did you use different books or vary the assigned curriculum?"

"No," said the teacher. "We all used the same materials."

"You must have done something different with Edy," said the researchers. "Think what was different about the way you interacted with her."

The teacher thought, and then almost as a question offered an answer. "Do you know that Edy runs track?"

"Yes," said the researchers. "We've heard all about Speedy Edy"

"Well," said the teacher, "when Edy runs, I go to her meets and cheer for her."

That was the difference. When her world gave her a failure label, Edy found a teacher who supported her anyway. The encouragement empowered her. The undeniable care of her teacher gave her an ability to break free of her mental bonds. As the compassion of a teacher granted Edy strength, the mercy of our God supplies ours. Our God does not merely cheer for us. He died for us. He came where we race against our own weaknesses in order to free us from our spiritual bondage, and now he sits at the right hand of the Father interceding for us even when we fail (Rom. 8:34). Intercession is not quite like cheering, but it just as clearly means that we have an unfaltering Advocate.

Christians gain spiritual power from the certainty of God's support. Self-preserving human efforts may result from fear of a God who will get you if you get out of line. But "spiritual worship"—the selfless inner desire to honor God—cannot come from threats (v. 2). Spiritually vital and enduringly vibrant service flow from a heart that sings, "I am his and he is mine forever and forever. I cannot be taken from the palm of his hand. He is for me. Mercy claimed me, and though I may lose my grasp on him, my God will not let me go."

ENABLEMENT POWER

In view of this divine mercy, we sometimes must confess that we feel pain rather than hope. If we have been guilty of serious, long-term, or repetitive sin, we feel worse because we have not done better. Our consciences may cry out, "Lord, I would love to serve you better in view of your mercy, but you know me. You know how weak I am. You know how I keep on failing. You know my temper and my tongue and how temptation seems to get the best of me. Lord, I wish I could honor you with my life. I wish I could serve you, but I can't. I just can't."

Yes, you can. By God's grace the power is already yours, and you need only understand how to plug into it. The resources for accomplishing God's purposes come in two forms—provision and assurance.

Provision. Most of my life I believe I read a key phrase of this passage the wrong way. I think that I read the verse as if it said, "In view of God's mercy, present your bodies as living sacrifices, *and then you will be* holy and pleasing to God." I believe that many others read this verse the same way. We think that by presenting our bodies as sacrifices to God, we will please him. But the verse does not talk merely about our pleasing God; it also talks about being holy. That word *holy* should give us a clue that my former reading was wrong. No matter how much we sacrifice, we cannot make ourselves holy to God. God's standard of holiness is as high as the heavens. Our best efforts will not make us "holy." If we are to be holy, it is only by God's provision. That's the point! The words *holy* and *pleasing* are not conditions of God's acceptance; they are declarations of his mercy.

By Jesus' cleansing work on the cross, God declares us to be holy and pleasing to him. The offering of our bodies as living sacrifices does not make us holy and pleasing to God. He has made us holy and pleasing to himself by his merciful provision of Christ. This is the fundamental truth that enables us not to be conformed to this world nor to succumb to its temptations (v. 2). So powerful is the nature of

God's provision for us that Paul says if our minds truly grasp it, our lives will be transformed (v. 2).

Paul began developing this thought much earlier. Two full chapters before writing these words, Paul says that the ancient Jews did not understand God's provision. Their minds were gripped with a view of God that made them read their Scriptures the way I formerly read this passage. They thought that their actions would make them acceptable to God. Paul writes, "Brothers, my heart's desire and prayer to God for the Israelites is that they may be saved. For I can testify about them that they are zealous for God, but their zeal is not based on knowledge. Since they did not know the righteousness that comes from God and sought to establish their own, they did not submit to God's righteousness" (Rom. 10:1-3).

By trying to make themselves acceptable to God, the Israelites minimized the holiness God requires and thus dishonored him. Their zeal was not based on proper knowledge. Paul says that we should not get trapped in their way of thinking. We should be transformed by the renewing of our minds with the understanding that holiness comes from God and not from us.

Renewing our minds by focus on God's provision of mercy rather than on our acquisition of acceptance provides various means of transforming power. First, we do not minimize God's holiness by assuming it is such a slight thing that we mere humans could gain it. We are forced to put our faith in him. Second, because we trust his provision for our righteousness, we need not fall into the despair that our actions will never be sufficient to earn his satisfaction. We are free to serve him without paralyzing fear.

The early church robed adult believers in white after their baptisms. The garments did not indicate that believers would never again sin. The white robes signified the holiness God provides despite our impurities. The robe covered an imperfect person. Think of the implications today. We do not have to despair of attaining the perfection that would warrant God's acceptance. By recognizing the richness of his provision, we have the resources necessary to move forward in his service. We need never say, "I can't do anything right. I always mess up. I have tried time and time again to live right, and I always fail. If I try anything, I will only look bad and get God mad, so why try?"

Some Christians are so afraid of stepping out of line that they never get in step with God. Fear of the loss of what little holiness they think they have managed to scratch out in life has led to paralysis. They are not serving God with vigor and energy because they do not want to risk losing what little mercy they have. They will not serve God well until they realize how rich are the resources of his mercy.

My father has worked with third world farmers as an agricultural adviser. He says that often it is nearly impossible to get these farmers to use advanced farm technologies because they live so close to the edge of their existence. If some new farming technique fails, they will starve. For them it is better to keep struggling along with what little they have than risk everything on something untried. Abundance beyond their dreams is within their reach, but they are paralyzed because they are so conscious of their poverty.

God does not want us to be caught in the paralysis of spiritual poverty. Through the doxology the apostle Paul uses to prepare us for the requirements of this passage, God tells us of the richness of his provision so that we will serve him with courage and vigor:

> Oh, the depth of the riches of the wisdom and knowledge of God!
> How unsearchable his judgments,
>   and his paths beyond tracing out!
> "Who has known the mind of the Lord?
> Or who has been his counselor?"
> "Who has ever given to God,
>   that God should repay him?"
> For from him and through him and to him are all things.
> To him be the glory forever! Amen.
>   Romans 11:33-36

God says in essence, "I have already declared to you that by the work of Jesus Christ, you are rich in mercy. Now build my kingdom with the energy and effort that befits those with unlimited resources. Be done with the self-doubt and fear of loss that cripples those poor in faith. I have declared you holy. Be about the business of building my kingdom. Stop saying that because you are not a Moses or were not raised in the right environment or wandered to other priorities or made some mistakes that you cannot serve God. Yes, you can."

We who are rich in mercy have God's business to do, and no one can say that we are under-financed. God's gracious provision empowers us for his service.

Assurance. Do you find yourself saying, "Lord, thanks for the wealth of mercy. You surely know I need it, and I would like to serve you better. I wish I could, but you know me. You know I can't please you. I am trapped in this sin or in this job or in this relationship. Lord, you might as well give up on me. I have. You know I can't change. You know I'll never be able to please you."

"I have already made you pleasing to me," declares the Lord.

"Me? With all my sin and shame?"

"Yes, you are able to please me," says the Lord.

It sounds amazing, but God says that sinful people please him. He has made us living sacrifices, holy and "pleasing" to him (v. 1). Because we are holy through the work of his Son, God declares that we already please him despite our imperfections. This is a wonderful assurance, and again the result is power.

In the 1980 Olympic games, Soviet coaches tricked one of their weightlifters. They *told* him the weight that he was lifting on his final lift was 499 pounds, a weight he had lifted before in practice and knew he could handle. However, in fact, the coaches had instructed Olympic officials to put 500 1/2 pounds on the bar. This was a world-record weight that the athlete had never been able to hoist before. He stepped to the bar—and lifted it. Believing that he could do the task, he did it.

There is power in believing that we are able, and we know that we are able to please God because his Word says so. We do not gain this ability to please God by some trick, but by the work of his Spirit in us. Satan would love for us to believe that we can do nothing. He wants to paralyze us with self-doubt and past shame. In contrast, God has filled us with his Spirit of power and cleansed us with the blood of his Son. He tells us in his Word that we *are* able to please him. We are able to serve him. Our lives can be a joy to him. Our service can build his kingdom. He says so. We can go about the business of God with confidence because his mercy makes our work pleasing to him.

By his mercy God claims us. By his mercy he encourages us. By his mercy he empowers us. By the mercy . . . by the mercy . . . by the mercy. So echoes the grace that makes our service sweet and our hearts strong.

MERCY RESTORED

The day after her experience in the park, the young mother mentioned at the outset of this chapter again sought some relief from the summer monotony. She took her children to vacation Bible school. She soon was to discover how much her heart was still aching from the revelations of the previous day.

When she went to pick up her children at noon, the program was running a little late, so she sat in her car listening to the voices of the children waft out the church windows. Their singing and laughter did *not* lift her spirits. Instead, the children's cheer made her remember the joylessness of her own walk of faith, and again melancholy gripped her.

She remembered when Jesus was another word for joy, when folding your hands to pray meant you were talking to God, and when you said, "Lord, I'm sorry," you really felt forgiven. Recognition of the things that once filled her heart now only made her feel more empty. Her head fell to the steering wheel, and the tears came again with a silent sigh of spiritual longing. So quiet was her grief that she could still hear the children's songs. The closing exercises of the Bible school were ending, so the children were singing their marching song—the song that was supposed to take them into the world with zeal for the Lord. When the words penetrated her consciousness, the mother drew in her breath with a startled gasp.

From a familiar song the children sang, "I will sing of the mercies of the Lord forever, I will sing, I will sing; I will sing of the mercies of the Lord forever . . ." Sudden realization flooded over the mother like a shock wave from heaven. The words of mercy lifted her head from the wheel. *That's it*, she thought. *That's what I have forgotten.*

Once she had sung that song with the joy the children now echoed. But somewhere, somehow life with its busyness, along with the guilt of a thousand failures, the negligence of ten thousand duties, and the pursuit of a million priorities other than God's had taken the words from her lips and the truths from her heart. More and more she had performed the duties she could manage for divine favors and out of human dread. Now in the song of the children, she saw a way back to the warmth she had known. Affirmation of his mercy was the way back into his arms and all the joy that was there.

She sang with the children as new joy flooded into her heart: "I will sing of the mercies of the Lord forever. . . ." Now there was cause for loving zeal again—here was new strength. She knew that in view of this mercy, she could seek him again, serve him afresh, and love him anew. By mercy God clasped her heart, captured her commitment, and reclaimed her joy.

By mercy God again made this woman's service sweet and her heart strong. Such grace God will grant us, too, as each of us questions, "Why do I do what I do?" and as we each answer, "Because of God's mercy."

DISCUSSION QUESTIONS

1) What makes our faith grow cold?
2) Why does Paul insist that mercy motivate us in our kingdom tasks? What other motivations might he have used?
3) What are the effects of guilt motivation? Why can it be very effective?
4) Does guilt have any role to play in the Christian life? How does this role change before and after conversion?
5) What does it mean to serve God from acceptance rather than for acceptance? How does this distinction affect our motivations to serve God? How does this distinction affect our counsel to those who are struggling with sin?
6) Why doesn't presenting our bodies as living sacrifices make us acceptable to God? What makes us acceptable to God? What makes us pleasing to God?
7) How does assurance of God's mercy grant Christians strength?
8) How can you plug into God's grace as a resource to serve him?
9) Why do you do what you do?

7

THE GREATNESS
OF FAITH

THE WORD IN PERSPECTIVE

What is faith? How do we apply it to the problems we face? King Nebuchadnezzar of Babylon learned from three faithful witnesses named Shadrach, Meshach, and Abednego. As every Sunday school student knows, the pagan king erected a ninety-foot-tall statue of gold on the plain of Dura. Then the king ordered all his subjects to worship the idol whenever the bands of the kingdom played a salute. Those who did not worship were promised death in a fiery furnace. At least three subjects did not heed the threat nor bow to the idol. Shadrach, Meshach, and Abednego stood up for their God and, by doing so, got a blast of the king's wrath. In their response to Nebuchadnezzar, we learn not only what human faithfulness can be, but what biblical faith truly is. We pick up the account as the king learns of the refusal of the three Hebrew captives to honor his idol.

DANIEL 3:13-30

[13]Furious with rage, Nebuchadnezzar summoned Shadrach, Meshach and Abednego. . . . [14]Nebuchadnezzar said to them, "Is it true, Shadrach, Meshach and Abednego, that you do not serve my gods or worship the image of gold I have set up? [15]Now when you hear the sound . . . of music, if you are ready to fall down and worship the image I made, very good. But if you do not worship it, you will be thrown imme-

diately into a blazing furnace. Then what god will be able to rescue you from my hand?"

[16]*Shadrach, Meshach and Abednego replied to the king, "O Nebuchadnezzar, we do not need to defend ourselves before you in this matter.* [17]*If we are thrown into the blazing furnace, the God we serve is able to save us from it, and he will rescue us from your hand, O king.* [18]*But even if he does not, we want you to know, O king, that we will not serve your gods or worship the image of gold you have set up."*

[19]*Then Nebuchadnezzar was furious with Shadrach, Meshach and Abednego. . . . He ordered the furnace heated seven times hotter than usual* [20]*and commanded some of the strongest soldiers in his army to tie up Shadrach, Meshach and Abednego and throw them into the blazing furnace. . . .* [22]*The king's command was so urgent and the furnace so hot that the flames of the fire killed the soldiers who took up Shadrach, Meshach and Abednego,* [23]*and these three men, firmly tied, fell into the blazing furnace.*

[24]*Then King Nebuchadnezzar leaped to his feet in amazement and asked his advisers, "Weren't there three men that we tied up and threw into the fire?"*

They replied, "Certainly, O king."

[25]*He said, "Look! I see four men walking around in the fire, unbound and unharmed, and the fourth looks like a son of the gods."*

[26]*Nebuchadnezzar then approached the opening of the blazing furnace and shouted, "Shadrach, Meshach and Abednego, servants of the Most High God, come out! Come here!"*

So Shadrach, Meshach and Abednego came out of the fire, [27]*and the satraps, prefects, governors and royal advisers crowded around them. They saw that the fire had not harmed their bodies, nor was a hair of their heads singed; their robes were not scorched, and there was no smell of fire on them.*

[28]*Then Nebuchadnezzar said, "Praise be to the God of Shadrach, Meshach and Abednego, who has sent his angel and rescued his servants! They trusted in him and defied the king's command and were willing to give up their lives rather than serve or worship any god except their own God.*

A New Definition of Faith

How do you win the World Series? As I type these words, my favorite baseball team is near winning the National League pennant. If I could figure out how this team could be world champions, I would be the hometown hero—and rich as well. Unfortunately for me, more credible characters already have publicized their secret for success. Some years ago when the New York Mets were the underdog darlings of the National League, two young pitchers told us how they were going to win the World Series. Tom Seaver and Tug McGraw borrowed a line from a Walt Disney character and said that the secret to winning lay in these words: "Ya' gotta believe."

A clever advertising agency picked up that phrase, too. According to its commercials, you make the best peanut butter "with a whole lot of peanuts and a little bit of magic" and then one more thing: "Ya' gotta believe."

There appears to be a consensus in our culture that good things happen because someone believes enough. Having sufficient faith that something wonderful will happen supposedly makes it happen. Unfortunately, that notion about why good things happen is often transferred without serious thought to spiritual matters, which also are framed in terms of faith and belief. Christians sometimes assume that good things happen because of an exceptional confidence in an outcome they desire. We may even have been taught at some time in our Christian lives that if we want something to happen, the way we make it happen is to build up enough faith. "Believe hard enough, and God is at your disposal," people seem to say. Others imply that if you put enough "faith nickels" in the celestial vending machine on high, then you get what you want. At times the message sounds inviting, but is it true—is it biblical—that if you believe without doubting in what you want to happen that you will get exactly what you desire?

Many Christians do believe that the Bible teaches that faith is the equivalent of confidence in outcomes. When talking about the miracles of the Bible, they will point to those holy men and women of ancient times and say, "What great faith they had. Why just look at the wonderful things that happened because of their unwavering confidence in what would occur." If this is your view of what faith is, and you are absolutely wedded to it, skip the third chapter of Daniel.

This chapter of Daniel's history tells us of three faith giants— Shadrach, Meshach, and Abednego. These three young men are heroes of courage, obedience, and faith. They stood up to the cruel and wicked Nebuchadnezzar refusing to bow to his image of gold even when their lives were at stake. Yet when Shadrach, Meshach, and Abednego stood on the brink of the fiery furnace, they did not pretend to know what was going to happen to them. The three had no desire to burn, but they did *not* claim that they would not die. Instead of offering some confident assertion about what would occur because of their great faith, these giants of faith said simply, "We don't know what will happen; we only know we will obey God and trust him" (vv. 17-18).

Shadrach, Meshach, and Abednego did claim that God was *able* to save them and would, in fact, save them from the king's hand (because even if they died, they were still in God's hands). But the three faithful men also said that even *if* God did *not* save them from the furnace of fire, they would worship only him (v. 18). These words can trouble us. We may want to say, "Oh no, Shadrach, Meshach, and Abednego. No 'ifs, ands, or buts.' Believe without doubting." Thankfully Shadrach, Meshach, and Abednego did not operate on some popular notion of what faith should be. Theirs was a biblical faith.

By their words and actions Shadrach, Meshach, and Abednego tell us what biblical faith is. Biblical faith is not a belief that *we* know what is best; it is the belief that *God* knows. True faith is not confidence in what we think is right, but confidence that God will do what is right. Such faith determines to serve God because it trusts him—whatever happens. We do not glean this new definition of faith from a popular consensus but from biblical evidence. The Bible says that faith is not confidence in a desired outcome to a particular circumstance; faith is confidence in God.

What good is such a definition of faith? Can it help us as we face today's trials? To answer let me recreate a rainstorm experience from my school days. The storm may seem light years from Nebuchadnezzar's incinerator, but both taught me much about the difference between popular belief and biblical faith.

I had found a summer job working as an assistant to a commercial photographer. A local pool manufacturer hired us to create an advertisement with lots of photographs. We needed two full days of good weather to get all the needed photos. My boss, a Christian, encouraged me to pray with him for the good weather we needed. So we prayed, and the first day of picture shooting was sunny, dry, and beautiful. We only needed one more day of good weather to finish on schedule.

It was not meant to be. The next day was dark, wet, and ugly. Sitting in my boss's station wagon, I saw his face change slowly from sadness, to dejection, and then to anger.

"Yesterday," he snarled, "God gave us a good day because we prayed in faith. Today it's raining even though we need it to be sunny. That means somebody isn't doing his job."

Now I don't know which "somebody" he had in mind (I wasn't about to ask), but there were only two alternatives. If our faith accounted for the first good day, then the reason the second day was rainy was either because our faith had shrunk or because God had failed. Either we were not doing our job, or God was not doing his job.

Great spiritual harm results from such explanations of undesired outcomes. If our God is inadequate, then we have no one to trust. However, if bad things happen because our faith is inadequate, then no one really has sufficient faith because everyone faces problems. By linking the evidence or quality of faith to easy times and happy endings, we set ourselves up for doubt and heartache because difficulty invades every life, including that of the faithful (Matt. 6:34; John 17:15).

We can be unnecessarily hard on ourselves and on others simply because we let other people tell us what faith is rather than listening carefully to the Bible. One way to get a better picture of biblical faith, the kind of faith that helps rather than harms, is to get a clear understanding of what biblical faith is *not*. Shadrach, Meshach, and Abednego expose the false premises of an unbiblical belief.

I. Faith Is Trust in God, Not Trust in Our Belief

Christians may be tempted (or taught) to evaluate the quality of their faith by how well they can convince themselves that there will be a positive outcome to a particular situation. As a result, in their prayers they may try to force all thought of negative possibilities (interpreted as doubt) from their minds. Some adopt intricate rituals to convince themselves that they have pumped up their faith enough so that God must honor their desires. They sing songs, pray longer, read more Scripture, scold themselves for any second thoughts, and use various other practices to convince themselves that they believe enough to get God to do what they think is right.

FAITH BEYOND BELIEF

In one sense these "faith" practices make us comparable to athletes psyching up for a big event. We try to convince ourselves that we really, *really* believe. Success supposedly lies in how completely we conform our minds to our goals. In another sense we resemble witches, throwing a pinch of song, an ounce of prayer, and a ton of belief into a caldron of human desires so God must do what we determine is right for him to do. Our faith is not so much in God as it is in the amount of belief we can conjure to control him.

I recently heard a dear Christian mother express what can happen to our faith if we ever begin to trust in our degree of belief rather than in God. She was running errands one weekday morning with a tribe of preschoolers in the car. After the first few stops, she recognized she was running terribly late. She would miss a doctor's appointment.

Then came inspiration—a way to get back on schedule. The next stop on the errand list was the grocery store. Getting all of the children out of their car seats, into their jackets, into the store, and doing the reverse of all that afterward was bound to turn this into a twenty-minute stop. But only a few groceries were needed. If there was a parking space right by the front door where she could watch the children through the storefront glass, then Mom could leave the kids in the car. She could zip in, zip out, and be right back on schedule.

It was time to exercise some faith. "Lord, please give me a parking space by the door," the mother prayed. "I believe you will give me a parking space. I believe."

Recounting the experience, the mother later said, "I was praying with all kinds of faith." She expressed that faith by saying again and again in her mind, "I believe, I believe."

Her faith depended on convincing herself that she had enough belief to get God to do what she wanted. She drove to the store, turned into the parking lot, and headed for the entrance with nary a shred of doubt, only to find no parking space anywhere near that front door. You may smile at this young mother's naïveté. Yet when she told of this small event in her life, she spoke through tears. "What's wrong with me?" she asked. "Have I lost my faith? I prayed with all the faith I had, and God didn't answer. Don't I have faith?"

She had caught herself in that old trap of trusting in belief rather than trusting in God. Because her faith depended on a positive outcome and something unwanted occurred, she could only assume there was something wrong either with her faith or with her God. This Christian mother was too well schooled to believe that God could fail at anything, so she assumed that she was at fault. Shadrach, Meshach, and Abednego assure us that she had not lost her faith; she had just misplaced it.

What precipitated this spiritual crisis in this young woman's life was the idea that faith resides in feelings of belief that we conjure in our minds. Faith is not a mind game. Concocted confidence in things we would like to happen is not a mark of biblical belief. Shadrach, Meshach, and Abednego said that they did not know what would happen. Yet they were great men of faith. They understood that faith is not confidence in the appropriateness of our desires or in the degree of our feelings.

Real faith locks onto God. It trusts God to do what is appropriate and right regardless of our feelings or desires. Shadrach, Meshach, and Abednego said, "Even if God does not deliver us, we will serve only him." Their words tell us that faith is not measured by the strength of our expectations, but by the strength of the conviction that whatever God ordains is right.

FAITH BEYOND DESIRE

Biblical faith calls for each of us to acknowledge that God's provision is sufficient, loving, and good even if it falls short of or contradicts our immediate desires. Since we cannot fully anticipate God's plans nor fathom his wisdom, we should not expect our wishes to rule him. Believers whose faith can withstand the trials of this world affirm, "I may not understand God's provision. I may not expect it or in this life know enough even to like it, but I trust my God whatever comes. This does not mean that I always know what will come. But my faith is in my God, and what he knows is best—not what I think is best."

This insight into faith relieves those who worry that there is something wrong with them or with their faith because what they want to happen does not always occur. We are not lesser Christians because God is wiser than we are. Nor are we inferior Christians because we trust God's wisdom more than our own.

Too many of us have been made victims of the hoax that *real* Christians do not have problems. This deception teaches that difficulties vanish for the truly faithful because what they want to happen, happens. After all, we are told, since sufficient faith solves all problems, the sufficiently faithful never suffer. This presentation of Christianity makes it sinful (or at least a mark of second-class sainthood) to weep or hurt or be disappointed. Since such emotions automatically imply that something has happened other than what we wanted, they supposedly expose one with inferior faith.

As a result of this spiritual "logic," we are inundated with literature and programming that extol the singular benefits and exclusive value of enthusiastic Christianity. This religiosity rides the waves of emotional highs, continuous smiles, and bubbling optimism. Of course, there is nothing wrong with any of these expressions of faith—solemnity is not more holy than mirth—unless someone implies that emotional highs are a sign of faith. Faith in Jesus Christ is not a feeling. Feelings change. Emotional highs ebb. Faith should not.

Shadrach, Meshach, and Abednego did not bubble with enthusiasm. Nowhere in this passage did any of the three say, "Oh boy, here we go into the fiery furnace. Isn't this great?" They were not even filled with confidence about what would happen to them. Still they were filled with faith in their God. They believed in his presence and in his care despite the likelihood that Nebuchadnezzar would burn them alive. If they lived, they knew their God was near. If they died, they knew their God was no more distant. Like Job, they would say of God, "Though he slay me, yet will I trust in him" (Job 13:15 KJV).

Our God is loving, gracious, and good. Shadrach, Meshach, and Abednego knew this because time after time God delivered his people from their enemies despite Israel's sin and rebellion. These three did not doubt God's love because he had been faithful even when his people had not. God even had promised that he would save his people from this captivity in Babylon.

Although things looked awfully grim in the present, the faith of Shadrach, Meshach, and Abednego was not shattered. Their faith was not rooted in present circumstances but in the nature of their God. The God who had repeatedly demonstrated eternal love for his people could be trusted. Shadrach, Meshach, and Abednego were not great men of faith because they were confident of easy living or good times or favorable circumstances, but because they were confident that God would accomplish his good purposes through them as they remained faithful.

Confidence in God's ultimate purposes can sustain our faith, too. We can begin to see that tragedy does not mean that God has vanished. Danger does not indicate he has failed. Difficulty does not imply he is weak. Because we know the loving nature of the one in ultimate control, our circumstances need not destroy nor dictate the quality of our faith. Difficulties may still arise, but trust in God's purposes will enable us to surmount or endure them. Grief may still come, but faith in God's eternal love gives us the strength to bear it.

God's hand is never capricious nor clumsy. True faith acknowledges that he knows and is doing what is right. Genuine trust does not pretend to know all that God must do. Faith that insists God must do things our way is not really faith in him. It is confidence in our own human frailty, and thus it is a misplaced faith that will only lead to disappointment and pain.

FAITH BEYOND TRIAL

In a rural community where my father once ministered, some members of a family grew dissatisfied with their church across town. Feeling that the church had lost its spiritual heading, they set up a church in their home. There the family taught that God would make folks rich and keep them healthy if they had enough faith. They had some proof to back their words. For several years this farming family had been under contract with a feed company to produce large quantities of hay and grain at a guaranteed price. Thus, while other farmers in the area suffered under the vagaries of a vacillating farm market, this family prospered. They were wealthy, and any who visited their home to go to church were told the reason for the wealth—great faith.

Some family members so believed in the power of faith to gain earthly desires that they began to visit the sick in the town. They would tell these ill persons—in our church and others—that the reason they were ill was that they did not have enough faith.

I do not doubt that the family starting the new church meant well. They were sincere. Still the consequences of their actions were horrible. People who were terminally ill—who needed the Lord's comfort more than ever—were told that they did not really know God at all. The evidence was their illness. If they had true faith, these hurting people were told, they would not be sick.

When our pastoral calls took us to the homes of these ill persons after they had been visited by family members from the new church, we found faithful Christians terrified and distraught. The warped interpretation of faith had enough biblical echoes to make them question their understanding of Scripture and in their desperate situations actually threatened to rob them of their confidence in God's care. Our concern was not limited to the sick individuals the family visited. Eventually the heartache came home.

A child with a birth defect was born to one of the family members. The rest of the family claimed there must be sin in the lives of the parents of this child because their prayers did not make the problem go away. These parents eventually left the church because the quality of their faith was constantly questioned due to their child's difficulty. More problems followed.

Our community, like farm communities all over the country in the 1980s, sank into a financial crisis. Suddenly the production requirements of the big feed company became impossible for this wealthy family to meet. The same contract that had provided security and prosperity for years now became a noose around the neck of its finances. In just a few months the family went bankrupt, the farm (which had been in the family for generations) was sold, and family members scattered across the country. Today they do not visit hurting families and say, "Look at the health and wealth that comes from our faith."

We should take no joy in the pain this family experienced. We should grieve for them even as we learn from them. Faith in faith alone scatters families and shatters lives. Possessing real biblical faith is just as important today as it was in the day of Shadrach, Meshach, and Abednego. We live in a fallen world where illness, difficulty, and tragedy still thrive. Christians are not immune from the consequences of being in this world. God can remove disease and difficulty from our lives today, or he may desire to use our testimonies in the midst of trial and tragedy for purposes grander than we can imagine or see. The choice rests in his wisdom and goodness. Our responsibility is to depend on him. Real faith is not confidence in our desires; it is trust in our God.

II. Faith Is Trust in God, Not Trust in What We Want to Happen

Though we may agree that faith is an expression of confidence in God, it is possible still to believe that God should conform his will to ours as long as our motives are good. Avoiding the misconception that true faith is a matter of how intensely we believe does not necessarily avert the expectation that God will honor wishes sufficiently holy. This view assumes that—although it is God we are trusting—since what we have decided he needs to do has such overriding spiritual benefits, then he must perform it. We begin counting on what we would love to happen because we think it is in God's best interests to make it happen. Because the results we desire are "for heaven's sake," we become convinced that our faith will move God's hand.

Some years ago when my brother was in the Air Force, he was hurrying back to base to avoid being AWOL. He faced a number of obstacles. He was traveling late at night on a holiday weekend in a pickup almost out of gas during the Arab oil embargo. An unbelieving friend was riding with him. When this friend saw the gas gauge needle bounce on empty, he threw up his hands in resignation and said, "That's it. We're never going to make it. We are in trouble for sure."

My brother, concerned not only for getting back to base but for the spiritual welfare of his buddy, replied, "No, we are going to make it. I have prayed to God in faith. He will get us there."

You can guess what happened. A few miles farther the engine sputtered, coughed, and died. Now the story seems funny, but at that time the humor was lost on my brother. This series of events was part of a serious spiritual crisis in his life.

"Bryan," he asked later, "why didn't God answer my prayer? I prayed in faith, believing God. Nothing better could have happened for my friend than for him to see God at work. I wasn't asking for my sake. My friend would have believed God and been saved if only God had answered. Why didn't God act?"

I do not know. What I do know is that biblical faith keeps us from being so attached to what we crave—even if we are convinced that it is for God's good—that failing to get what we want constitutes a spiritual disaster. Faith is trust in God and his plan. Faith does not require God to fulfill wishes as though our desires were his command and our human plans his divine ordinance. God knows what is necessary to bring others to himself, and when it is necessary and how. We do not. Faith does not require God to do what we would love to happen even for the right reasons.

TRUST AND TESTIMONY

Learning to trust God's wisdom above our own is not a lesson only those who are young in the faith must master. In times of trouble a willingness to rely on God's wisdom alone tries the faith of even the most spiritually astute. Rev. Jim Conway is a wonderful pastor and author whom God has greatly used in a variety of ministries. Several years ago when he was pastoring People's Bible Church in Urbana, Illinois, his daughter Becki was stricken with cancer. The doctors said they would have to amputate one leg to save her life. So the family began to pray, asking God to heal Becki's leg. They knew God is able to heal, so they prayed that he would save her leg *as a testimony* of his love. Because they desired glory for God, they believed that he would heal Becki.

So strongly did Jim believe that God would honor the family's request that on the day of the surgery he asked the doctors to test Becki's leg again before amputating. The surgeon agreed, and the family went to a waiting room eagerly anticipating the results. They were sure God was about to bring great glory to himself and great joy to them. Jim later recounted for *Moody Monthly* magazine what happened:

> A crowd of friends from the church had come to wait with us. So many came, in fact, that they made us leave the waiting room. When the surgeon came out, I knew what he was going to say, and I couldn't face it. I couldn't face all those people. So I ran.
>
> I ran to the hospital basement where no one would find me. And I cried. I yelled. I pounded my fists against the wall. I felt like the God whom I had served had abandoned me at the hour of my deepest need. Was he so busy answering prayers for parking places that he couldn't see Becki?

The experience devastated Jim, but it also drove him back to the Scriptures. There he discovered that a faith that blindly insists on what we would love to happen—even if what we want would seem to honor God—is foreign to the Bible. We should know this truth already, but sometimes in the pressure of the moment and under an aching desire for something that seems so right, our wishes take control of our thoughts. We forget the faithful men and women of the Bible who did not have everything go as their desires dictated. We must remember them again lest we define faith in such a way that we and others get hurt.

TRUST AND SCRIPTURE

No one doubts the faith of the apostle Paul. He remains the greatest missionary of all time and the greatest apostolic theologian. He opened the Gospel to the Gentiles, wrote inspired Scripture, and performed miraculous healings. Yet the Bible records at least four examples of sickness or disaster in his life that God did not prevent. Paul prayed three times that God would remove a "thorn in the flesh" with which the apostle was afflicted (2 Cor. 12:7-9). We do not know precisely the ailment. What we do know is that God did not grant the Paul's request but replied, "My grace is sufficient for you, for my power is made perfect in weakness."

Paul did not respond by doubting his faith or his God. The apostle understood that his faith would not remove all hardship and suffering from his life. He believed that God knew what was best for him and the ministry of the Gospel. Thus, if God's strength was made more evident by Paul's testimony in a weakened condition, Paul readily accepted the weakened condition and even rejoiced in his weakness, believing that God knows best (2 Cor. 12:9b). Paul's attitude reminds us that God knows far better than we what will bring men and women to a saving knowledge of himself. The most powerful testimony Christians have at times is not the fact that they live on "easy street," but that they are sustained by God when their worlds collapse.

If genuine faith brings an end to all life's hardships, then Paul's comments in the chapter preceding the reference to "the thorn in the flesh" also make no sense. There Paul launches into a virtual litany of his sufferings. He reported that he had been imprisoned, flogged, stoned, shipwrecked, sea-logged; endangered by bandits, countrymen, and circumstances of all sorts; sleepless, hungry, thirsty, cold, naked, and pressured by church concerns (2 Cor. 11:23-28). How should we respond to such hardships in the life of an apostle? Do we say, "Now, Paul, if you just had a little more faith, life wouldn't be so hard." Of course not. We know the apostle's faith was sufficient for his hard times. He did not expect his faith to keep him from all trials. Why, then, today are we so ready to contend that faith is at fault when times are hard in our lives or in the lives of those we know?

Paul also encouraged Timothy to stop drinking only water and use a little wine because of the young pastor's stomach ailments (1 Tim. 5:23). I do not mention this advice to start a debate on beverage alcohol use but to ask why Paul would give such instructions if he was truly an apostle. Why did Paul not just heal Timothy? This solution seems so obvious and appropriate. Certainly Paul had been used of God to heal on other occasions. Another time in his ministry Paul even raised a young man from the dead. Why not heal now?

Should we assume Paul was lacking in faith at this stage in his life? No. Paul's faith was intact. Remember at the very moment Paul is writing this "medical" instruction, he is also writing inspired Scripture.

Should we then assume that Timothy's faith was to blame? No. Paul commended Timothy in this letter and gave him additional pastoral instruction. If Paul had felt that Timothy's faith was weak, surely the apostle would have rebuked the young man and suggested more faith as his cure. There was no such correction.

Why, then, did not Paul heal Timothy? We do not know. All we do know is that both Timothy and Paul continued to trust God's wisdom and purpose (2 Tim. 1:2, 5). To them illness was not an automatic sign of weak faith.

The fourth Pauline example of the truth that difficulty does not mean faith is lacking also lies in his second letter to Timothy (4:20). There Paul makes a passing reference to the fact that he left a disciple named Trophimus sick at Miletus. Our minds do mental flips when we read these words—particularly if we believe that real faith rescues from all ills. "Why Paul," we ask, "did you *leave* him sick? Why didn't you heal Trophimus?"

There are no simple answers to such questions. Neither Paul nor Trophimus are said to have failed the Lord. Elsewhere in the Bible both are identified without qualification as faithful followers of Jesus. We are left only with the understanding that here, as at other times in Paul's ministry, illness was a problem (Gal. 4:13-14). But it was not a problem that impugned faith. Rather, these difficulties required and produced faith so that God's work might continue despite the trials believers in all ages must confront.

The eleventh chapter of Hebrews is often called the "faith chapter" because it cites believers famous for their faith from many periods of biblical history. Added to the list of those well known for their faith are unnamed believers who have suffered great hardships. These who have been tortured, flogged, imprisoned, stoned, pierced with swords, sawed in two, made destitute, deprived, and homeless—are all commended for their faith (Heb. 11:35-40). The New Testament writers never contend that the mere presence of difficulty indicates an absence of faith.

Even the greatest of Old Testament saints did not claim a faith that removed every human trial. Remember Elisha, a faithful prophet of God. Like his predecessor, Elijah, Elisha performed amazing miracles, routed armies, healed the sick, and raised the dead. Yet unlike Elijah, he was not taken to heaven in a fiery chariot. Instead, without a word of criticism for his faith, the Scriptures simply record that Elisha got sick and died (2 Kings 13:14). So faithful was Elisha to the Lord's work that even after he died, his bones had healing powers (2 Kings 13:21). The Bible simply refuses to make illness an automatic sign of faithlessness. Our difficulties do not necessarily prove diminished spiritual integrity or distant divine power.

Lest we begin to look for reasons to blame Paul, Elisha, or other biblical believers for their difficulties, we should remember the example of Jesus himself. Did not Jesus pray before his crucifixion that God would take "this cup" from him? Still the trial came. There was no lack of faith on the Savior's part. His faith was in his God's plans, not in the absence of pain. He prayed not only that the cup would be taken away, but also, "Yet not my will, but thy will be done." Christ wanted the trial be taken away, but his deepest desire was that God would do his perfect will even if it meant humiliation and torture.

Christ's prayer teaches us what faith truly is. Our faith is not a mental or emotional snapping of our fingers to get God to do what we think he should. Our confidence is not in what we think God should do but in God. Edith Schaeffer, the noted author and wife of the late Christian philosopher Francis Schaeffer, says simply, "We must let God be God." We cannot presume to direct God's will, as if our desires bind his hands. Our wishes are not his commands, and faith should not be so ill-defined to imply as much. Real faith trusts God's plan and purpose. If we have a resolve of faith, let it be not to trust in what we decide is right, but to trust that God in his love knows and will do what is right—in his time, his way, and according to his wisdom.

TRUST AND OBEY

The message for us today is that we are not responsible to direct God's will. Rather, in any situation we are asked only to do God's will and trust him to take care of the rest. This is precisely what Shadrach, Meshach, and Abednego did. They did not pretend to know what would happen. They certainly had no desire to be burned alive and, without question, prayed for deliverance. Still they recognized that their chief duty was obedience. Had they been in charge, no doubt they would have dictated that the golden image be destroyed, that Nebuchadnezzar rescind his edict, that the furnace fail to burn, or that any number of other things would happen to keep anxiety from their lives. None of these other things did happen. Shadrach, Meshach, and Abednego stood on the brink of the furnace ready to die but faithful, because they were still doing God's will even if they did not know what would happen to them. They understood merely that God would use obedience for his good purpose. Faith is being faithful despite what comes, not telling God what should come.

III. Faith Is Trust in God, Not Trust in Our Ability to Read His Will

Shadrach, Meshach, and Abednego teach us that believers are not more holy because they have a great certainty something will happen or correctly identify what God needs to do. A related faith concept these faithful men crystallize for us is that believers are not more holy because they think they can tell what God intends to do next. Too often Christians try to prove their faith to themselves or others by predicting God's actions. These believers link their faith to their ability to read circumstances through the filter of providential insight. Faith of this sort is measured by the conviction with which one speaks about "how God will bless" and by the specificity with which the blessing is described.

CONFIDENCE VERSUS COINCIDENCE

I once attended a prayer meeting in which a woman praised God because he was going to heal her dog. She said she knew God was going to heal her dog because the day the pet got sick, she "just happened" to read in the Psalms that God "heals all your diseases." This could be nothing less than God's "providential leading," she announced, to let her know what he would do.

Obviously this well-meaning but poorly informed woman had tied her faith to her ability to read circumstances to determine how God would act. Unfortunately the circumstances were about to change. When we next met, this same woman told the group her husband had experienced a heart attack during the week since our last meeting. "Obviously," she surmised, "God was not telling me that he would heal my dog when I read that psalm. God was telling me ahead of time that he would heal my husband."

My first impulse, I am ashamed to admit, was to laugh. What if her son got sick the next day? What would God be saying then? What if she read Numbers 14:12 tomorrow? Then I remembered how often I have heard similar, if not so naive, expressions of faith from far more mature believers.

During a college break I stayed overnight at the home of a friend when a freak snowstorm forced me to forego a trip to my home. I stayed up late into the night with my friend's family as they awaited the arrival of a daughter from another college. When she was many hours overdue, the unspoken worry on every mind was that she might have had an accident in the storm. Someone finally said, "I hope she's all right." The immediate reply from the mother was, "Of course, she's all right. I have faith in God, and I know she'll get here safely." But the daughter never did arrive that night. She did have an accident.

Well-meaning church elders say to their pastors, "Because you are God's messenger for us, and because God wants his message to go out effectively, we have prayed that God will bless your ministry. Now we know that what you propose will succeed."

Zealous, committed pastors say to their churches, "Because there is the need for an expanded gospel witness in this community, and because God wants the community to hear the Gospel, we know that God will provide the money we need for this building program . . . or this broadcasting ministry . . . or this youth outreach . . . etc."

Desire plus optimism does *not* equal faith. All kinds of projects supported with such confidence fail. The reason is that confidence in what circumstances indicate is not faith. The world in which we live is too full of twists and tragedies to equate faith with holy supposition. Such faith ultimately will damage the testimony of the one speaking and the hearts of those listening.

Stating in unequivocal terms what God supposedly will do in specific circumstances will not secure faith. Such faith remains strong only as long as the "reading" of circumstances seems correct and the projects succeed as planned. Should the reading prove mistaken, or should progress falter, then such faith itself staggers. Again the problem stems from an unbiblical definition of faith. The Bible does not point us to circumstances as a means to predetermine God's will or judge his purposes.

If prior knowledge of outcomes determines the quality of one's faith, then Shadrach, Meshach, and Abednego had no faith. Not one of them claimed to know for certain that they would not be burned alive. They were not concerned to read circumstances correctly. They were only concerned to respond correctly to circumstances. Regardless of what the king did to them—and they did not claim to know what that would be—they would obey God.

DUTY VERSUS DIVINATION

Shadrach, Meshach, and Abednego define faithfulness as a righteous commitment to *do* God's will, not as a mystical ability to *read* God's results. They did not tie their faith to expectations about their circumstances. Rather, they submitted their circumstances and their actions to God in the faith that he would act appropriately. The faithful three were more concerned to obey God than to second-guess him. Their faith was not marked by special insight into confusing circumstances, but by faithful obedience amidst those circumstances.

Shadrach, Meshach, and Abednego had a faith that accurately comprehended the tasks God assigns the faithful. God expects us to act in accord with his Word and trust him to work in accord with his perfect will. We do not have faith because all is going well. We do not lose faith because something goes poorly. Our faith is not in what circumstances might indicate, but in God's greater purposes.

One group of believers who exemplifies what it means obediently to trust in God's purposes rather than be ruled by readings of circumstances is the North African Mission. This mission agency has dedicated itself to reaching Muslims with the Gospel of Jesus Christ for most of this century. Yet only in recent years has the mission experienced any real success. Now their impact is mushrooming in the developing world. But in 1934, after a generation of witnessing, the mission counted more deaths among its missionaries and their children than it could count conversions as a result of their ministry. What if someone then had evaluated faith by circumstances?

Circumstances can never be trusted to indicate with certainty what our actions should be or what God's purposes are. The wisest king who ever lived wrote about the futility of trying to determine God's will on the basis of circumstances. Solomon said:

> *There is something else meaningless that occurs on earth: righteous men who get what the wicked deserve, and wicked men who get what the righteous deserve. . . . No one can comprehend what goes on under the sun. Despite all his efforts to search it out, man cannot discover its meaning. Even if a wise man claims he knows, he cannot really comprehend it. So I reflected on all this and concluded that the righteous and the wise and what they do are in God's hands, but no man knows whether love or hate awaits him. (Eccl. 8:14-9:1)*

If faith depends on our determining what circumstances mean, then we are all involved in a futile religion. However, since faith is trusting God enough to obey him despite apparently futile circumstances, God can work mightily through us in the midst of this world's confusion.

We do not have to know what will happen or why something has happened to have a strong, vibrant faith. Scripture permits us to be like Shadrach, Meshach, and Abednego whose words and actions say, "Our faith is so great that we trust God though we don't know what will happen. As long as we do his will, we are in his care. That is sufficient for us." Great faith does not claim to know what only God can know. It claims to know the God who knows.

RELIANCE VERSUS REVELATION

We need not trust in special divinations, revelations, or expressions of sanctified self-assurance in order to be faithful, which should be a message of great comfort to many believers. We are not lesser Christians because others claim that they know more about what present circumstances mean or what the future holds. We should be content to trust and obey as did Shadrach, Meshach, and Abednego. If this simple, trusting obedience held them in God's care through a fiery furnace, then we can rely on such faith through our trials. Others may reach for a faith that is confidence in personal desires and circumstantial outcomes, but we must rest on something far more sure and solid. Biblical faith is not the stuff dreams are made of. Real faith is tougher, more resilient, more aware of the complexities of a fallen world, and more trusting of a sovereign God who loves us.

By their example Shadrach, Meshach, and Abednego lay out a simple plan of action to help us faithfully confront the trials we face: 1) We acknowledge our needs without stipulating how God must respond or will respond; 2) We acknowledge and confess the ability of God to meet our needs in the way we desire *or* in a way he knows is better; and, 3) We commit ourselves to uncompromising obedience however uncertain or unrewarding may seem the immediate circumstances. We simply obey God and trust him to take care of the circumstances. "He rewards those who earnestly seek him" (Heb. 11:6). The rewards may not be what we expect nor come as we anticipate, but faith understands the perfection of God's plan and trusts the love that prepares it so carefully. We need not read the results to rest in him.

IV. Faith Is Trust in God Alone

Faith that honors God above our desires is not mere fatalism. We do not shrug our shoulders and say, "What will be, will be." The reason we trust God, seek him, and pray to him is that he has demonstrated his love for us. When Shadrach, Meshach, and Abednego were cast into the furnace, another person appeared with them. Three men were cast in, but Nebuchadnezzar saw four in the fire—and the fourth looked divine (Dan. 3:25). Nebuchadnezzar did not understand. We do. The very presence of God was with the three Hebrews. God delivered them even though flames were all about them.

The same God who delivered them delivers us. The divine presence in the furnace reminds us of the divine Son who came to be with us, endured the trials of this world, and suffered to deliver us from the flames of hell forever. Now we trust this God, knowing he always has our best interests in mind (Rom. 8:32). He is our Father. Why should we not trust his provision since now we know his nature is loving and good? He proves his love by the cross of Jesus.

Faith depends on this love even when human reason and vision falter. When our religious optimism has dried up, we still trust him. When we are not certain what the best turn of events might be, we still turn to him. When we are unable to predict how he will handle a situation, we still rely upon him. Because the God who is all-powerful and all-wise has shown how much he cares for us through the cross of Jesus Christ, faith finds comfort in his love even when the mind cannot search out his reasons. We trust our God because he has shown how much he loves us through the gift of his Son. Faith rests in this love.

While I was pastoring a rural church in which farmers and coal miners—people accustomed to hard lives—predominated, I learned from them this story that taught me much about the nature and foundation of true faith:

There was once a miner who, though a stalwart believer, was injured in the mines at a young age. He became an invalid. Over the years he watched through a window beside his bed as life passed him by. He watched men of his own age prosper, raise families, and have grandchildren. He watched, but he did not share the rewards or the joys of others with whom he had once worked. He watched as his body withered, his house crumbled, and his life wasted away.

One day when the bedridden miner was quite old, a younger man came to visit him. "I hear that you believe in God and claim that he loves you," said the young visitor. "How can you believe such things with what has happened to you? Don't you sometimes doubt God's love?"

The old man hesitated and then smiled. He said, "Yes, it is true. Sometimes Satan comes calling on me in this fallen-down old house of mine. He sits right there by my bed where you are sitting now. He points out my window to the strong and still-active men I once worked with, and then Satan asks, 'Does Jesus love you?' Then the Devil will cast a jeering glance around my tattered room as he points to the fine homes of my friends across the street and asks again, 'Does Jesus love you?' Finally Satan points to the grandchild of a friend of mine— a man who has everything I do not—and after I have shed a tear, the Devil whispers in my ear, 'Does Jesus really love you?'"

"And what do you say when Satan speaks to you that way?" asked the young man.

Said the old miner, "In my mind I take Satan by the hand. I lead him to a hill far away called Calvary. There I point to the thorn-tortured brow, to the nail-pierced hands and feet, and to the spear-wounded side. Then I ask Satan, 'Doesn't Jesus love me?'"

The cross is the warrant for confidence in God despite a lifelong heartache. Had any of us stood at the foot of the cross and seen the horror, we would have cried out to God to stop the suffering. God knew better. He did not stop the pain until the life of the One who hung there had bled away. The agony did not mean that God failed nor that the faith of the one who died was weak. There was great suffering, but in the suffering was a purpose so loving, so powerful, and so good that our eternity changed as a result—our sins were washed away. When our focus remains on the cross, our faith finds its true focus and will not waver though troubles come and human answers fail. Such faith does not depend on emotional intensity, on knowing what should happen, or on a certainty of what God will do. True, biblical faith simply acknowledges that God is doing what is right and serves him in love under the conviction that he loves us.

DISCUSSION QUESTIONS

1) What are some common definitions of faith that our culture promotes? How do Christians sometimes fall victim to these conceptions?

2) If good things happen because someone has enough faith, then what are the two alternatives for why bad things happen?

3) Why is it important to know that the quality of our faith is not determined by the intensity, optimism, or buoyancy of our feelings?

4) How can you prove biblically that the quality of one's faith is not determined by an absence of difficulty?

5) Why doesn't God always grant what we pray for if we are praying for what we think will honor him?

6) Why do Christians sometimes want to express faith in terms of their certainty of outcomes? Why is this dangerous biblically?

7) If we are not to dictate to God what he should do, does this mean that we cannot pray for what we desire? What should be a Christian's ultimate desire in all situations?

8) When we can make no sense of our circumstances, where must we look for confirmation of God's loving plan?

9) How does the cross of Christ give us a basis for faith when our present situations offer none?

8

THE MARVEL
OF HEAVEN

*A friend told recently about an opportunity she had to share her faith on
a plane trip. She sat next to a man traveling with a five-year-old son.
Somehow the Lord led the adults into conversation about spiritual matters, but as they talked, the child kept interrupting. Finally in exasperation the father said to his son. "Please be quiet. This lady is telling me
about heaven!" At those words the child did shush, but his eyes opened
big as saucers in wonderment at the subject under discussion. Heaven!
Even children of the world know what a wonder heaven should be. Yet
Christians who regularly celebrate the basis of their heavenly hope in routine Easter observances of Christ's resurrection can lose that sense of
wonder. This is a terrible deprivation for, as this Scripture makes clear,
"heaven is a wonderful place, full of glory and grace."*

*   We can grasp some measure of that grace by recognizing that the
benefits of heaven do not merely lie beyond some eternal threshold.
Heaven holds wonderful motivating power for present ministry and
service. Our hearts beat more fervently and courageously for God when
we acquire a clear vision of heaven. For this reason, the apostle Paul
here calls Christians to greater dedication to God's purposes by detail-
ing the resurrection truths that establish heaven's blessings. These
words should rekindle our sense of wonder in the future God prepares
for his people and re-fire our fervor to serve God now.*

1 CORINTHIANS 15:48-58

[48]*As was the earthly man, so are those who are of the earth; and as is the man from heaven, so also are those who are of heaven.* [49]*And just as we have borne the likeness of the earthly man, so shall we bear the likeness of the man from heaven.*

[50]*I declare to you, brothers, that flesh and blood cannot inherit the kingdom of God, nor does the perishable inherit the imperishable.* [51]*Listen, I tell you a mystery: We will not all sleep, but we will all be changed—* [52]*in a flash, in the twinkling of an eye, at the last trumpet. For the trumpet will sound, the dead will be raised imperishable, and we will be changed.* [53]*For the perishable must clothe itself with the imperishable, and the mortal with immortality.* [54]*When the perishable has been clothed with the imperishable, and the mortal with immortality, then the saying that is written will come true: "Death has been swallowed up in victory."*

[55]*"Where, O death, is your victory? Where, O death, is your sting?"*

[56]*The sting of death is sin, and the power of sin is the law.* [57]*But thanks be to God! He gives us the victory through our Lord Jesus Christ.*

[58]*Therefore, my dear brothers, stand firm. Let nothing move you. Always give yourselves fully to the work of the Lord, because you know that your labor in the Lord is not in vain.*

HAUNTED BY HEAVEN

I have been haunted for years now by the words of an African student named Lawrence in an elementary preaching class. For his first seminary sermon he chose a text describing the joys we will share when Christ returns and ushers us to our heavenly home.

This is how Lawrence began his message: "I have been in the United States for several months now. I have seen the great wealth that is here—the fine homes and cars and clothes. I have listened to many sermons in churches here, too. But I have yet to hear one sermon about heaven. Because everyone has so much in this country, no one preaches about heaven. People here do not seem to need it. In my country most people have very little, so we preach on heaven all the time. We know how much we need it."

It can be very healthy to view yourself through another's eyes. I think Lawrence helped me that day to see some deep truths about my culture, my church, and my faith. We do not talk about heaven very much here. It almost seems as though we are ashamed of it. Whatever happened to heaven? Streets of gold and walls of jasper get relegated to the fancies of the fanatical. The details seem too problematic to attract the sensible preacher's attention. The subject is too removed for the young—too near for the old. Our messages concentrate more on the things of this world and, in doing so, impoverish our faith. For if we take our eyes off of heaven, we will focus too much on the things of earth. When heaven's riches fade into the background of our spiritual vision, then earthly concerns that should be dim to our eyes shine too brightly. Vision too nearsighted to see heaven deprives faith of the spiritual wealth needed to do God's business here.

I recognize the danger of losing sight of heaven not just by considering my culture but also the apostle Paul's. He writes this letter to a church in the midst of that day's affluence, sophistication, and sin. He must question how he can reach the people, turn them from earth's distractions and make them see what is really important. The answer on which he settles might not be our first choice. He focuses their vision on things above—the resurrection realities that await all believers. In short, he fills their vision with the spiritual realities of heaven and thus prepares them for the spiritual challenges of earth.

Paul's message is simple: Neglect of heaven robs God of faithful service. To stay rich in faith, we must stay focused on heaven. Why? What riches does heaven hold for us? What motivations can something so seemingly distant and ethereal offer?

I. Joy in Tomorrow

Joy awaits all those who know God. He will free us from the constraints and difficulties of this life. Still our heavenly existence will not be joyous just because the external environment will be pleasant. Incessant harp-playing and streets that shimmer can only fascinate us for so long. Tomorrow will be joyous not only because our world will change, but also because we ourselves will be fundamentally different.

WE SHALL BE CHANGED

It is not entirely clear what our resurrection existence will be. After all, Paul says that he is speaking about a "mystery" (v. 51). Yet important elements of that mystery are apparent. Our perishable bodies will inherit the imperishable benefits of the kingdom (v. 50). We shall not always consist of flesh and blood subject to decay (v. 50). Rather when the "trumpet will sound," believers who are alive as well as those who have died "will all be changed" (vv. 51-52). God will clothe that which is perishable with what is imperishable—the mortal will know immortality (v. 53).

It stretches the limits of our finite imaginations to consider what this means. We shall be free of the effects of mortality. This world's pain and decay will be behind us. We will have entered into that glorious freedom for which the whole creation groans, as in the pains of childbirth (Rom. 8:21). How glorious must be that state if creation yearns for our coming into that reality as much as a mother groans for the coming of a child into the reality of this world. No, we cannot fully describe what that state will be because the Bible says, "Eye has not seen nor ear heard nor has entered into the mind of man what God has prepared for those who love him" (1 Cor. 2:9). But we can catch glimpses of what our heavenly spiritual bodies will be (cf. 1 Cor. 15:40, 44). The Bible says our future state will be one of spiritual splendor. The heavenly beings who even now gather around the throne provide us with points of comparison of what this means.

Writing about the "weight of glory" that awaits us, C. S. Lewis says that while we cannot give an exact description of the believer's future, the heavenly beings we do see in Scripture indicate that "the dullest most uninteresting person you talk to here in this life may one day be a creature which, if you saw it now, you would be greatly tempted to worship." Think of that! In the tomorrow that awaits us with the heavenly realities of the resurrection, the persons nearest to you at this moment will be so transformed that, were you to see them in that state right now, you would be strongly tempted to fall on your knees before them. Do not think that is a stretch of the truth. For the apostle John says, "What we will be has not yet been made known. But we know that when he appears, we shall be like him" (1 John 3:2). When our Lord returns, he will make us into heavenly beings that reflect his own splendor.

Such glorious truths of our future condition have rich implications for ministry today. Faithful service can result from seeing not only ourselves in light of what changes await us, but also in seeing others as they shall be. I had a passing conversation with a pastor friend some time ago in which we were comparing difficulties of dealing with those who are emotionally disturbed by chemical or medical imbalances. How hard and discouraging it can be to try to manage maladjusted behavior in people who are blind to their own difficulties and therefore see our attempts to help them as arbitrary or cruel.

My friend spoke of such a man and ended by saying, "It was wonderful that he became a Christian, but until he is with the Lord, he will be a damaged human being." It struck me then how our view of heaven can enable us to minister to others. If all we see in people so damaged by our fallen state is creatures painful to endure and problematic to pastor, counsel, or even befriend, then we will soon tire of them and the effort it takes to minister to them. But what if we see them as God does—immortal beings whose glory will one day be blinding? Is it worth investing our lives in those whom the Bible says will shine like the stars of heaven? "Yes," is our certain answer in light of these glorious heavenly truths.

The joy of the changes that are sure to come keeps us from throwing over and throwing out those who trouble and blame us. The knowledge that they shall be whole gives us purpose and enables us to minister God's love to even the most emotionally and psychologically crippled. One day we shall greet them in the beauty of that eternal state where the disasters that ruined mind and body are a distant memory. What joy awaits us because we shall be changed into immortal beings.

WE SHALL BEAR HIS IMAGE

More than physical changes await us in heaven. Paul not only says that our resurrection bodies will be glorious, but also that our relationship with the Lord shall be perfected. We will bear his image in ways previously unknown and unattainable (see vv. 48-49).

We shall be like him. Paul says, "We shall bear the likeness of the man from heaven" (v. 49). This concept flows from a familiar contrast between Adam and Christ that Paul draws in this context and others (cf. vv. 45-47 and Romans 5). Paul concludes this contrast by saying that as we bear the likeness of Adam on this earth, we shall bear the likeness of Christ in our resurrected state (v. 49).

Some of what Paul means here we have already covered. The physical nature of our resurrected bodies will be different when we are like Christ in heaven. But if we are clothed with immortality like Christ, this also means that the effects of sin that brought human death into this world have been conquered for us. To be "like Jesus" has spiritual as well as physical implications. The apostle can exult that death has no sting and sin no victory because our immortality indicates that the power of sin, that came through the breaking of God's law, has itself been broken (vv. 55-57). Bearing the likeness of Jesus means not only that death cannot defeat us, but that our sin has been conquered, too.

A mother once was trying to explain to her daughter that the earthly deaths of Christians really allow them to start living in heaven. Heaven, said the mother, is such a wonderful place that Christians don't have to be afraid of death. "So," concluded the mother, "when I die, don't sing any sad songs. Sing songs that are full of joy."

Then she looked at her daughter and asked, " Can you think of a song of joy that you could sing if I were to die?" The little girl pondered a bit, pursed her lips as she thought about the latest rerun of the Wizard of Oz she has just seen, and then grinned ear to ear. "Oh, Mommy, if you would die, we could sing 'Ding, Dong, the Wicked Witch Is Dead.'"

Of course, that was not exactly what the mother had in mind. The suggestion even hurt her feelings a little bit until she thought some more about that song from an innocent child's perspective. The song said that the power of darkness had been broken; there was no more cause for fear; and now we could rejoice. As long as the witch represented sin and not Mom, this was not such a bad song for a little girl to think about in the face of death.

"Ding, dong, the power of the Wicked One is gone." The power of sin will be vanquished. The darkness in our lives will vanish. The temptations that trap me, the pasts that hound me, the guilt that depresses me will be behind me. All these will be melted into the dust of the earth by the cleansing work of Jesus. In that day we shall be like him, and our song shall ever be, "'O death, where is thy sting? O grave, where is thy victory?' The sting of sin is gone—swallowed up in Christ's victory. Ding, dong, the Wicked One is dead to me."

But bearing Christ's image means more than that the negative aspects of our being will be taken away from us. To bear Christ's image means there is something to gain as well as something to lose. Not only shall we be like him, but as part of tomorrow's joy, we shall join him.

We shall be with him. The concept of our image-bearing is rich with further biblical implications. The idea originates among the Bible's earliest verses where God said, "Let us make man in our own image" (Gen. 1:26). In that plural statement of the Godhead, our God presents his own nature as being one of relationships into which humankind was invited. Man's relationship with God was tarnished by Adam's sin. Yet in this New Testament passage, God promises that we shall again bear his image in an unspoiled way. The effects of sin will be removed, and our relationship with him will be fully restored. The final trumpet will sound, and we will join him (v. 52). This truth must have been far more critical to the apostle than informing us of the carat weight of the gold in heaven's streets. We shall inherit the kingdom where Jesus reigns, and there will be no barrier between us and him.

An old song says, "When I get to heaven, I'm going to walk with Jesus; when I get to heaven, I'm going to see his face. When I get to heaven, I'm going to talk with Jesus, saved by his wonderful grace." Just a children's song? Yes. But the implications are not childish at all. Just think of it. We will be with Jesus with no separation at all.

A child's perspective may help us see again the joy this heavenly union should bring. When Dr. Charles Schauffle taught at our seminary, he made himself dear to my children. As a consequence, we were quite concerned about how they would be affected when a quickly advancing cancer claimed his life. We struggled over the wisdom of exposing the youngest to the potential trauma of a funeral. Our concerns were largely alleviated, however, by a conversation my four-year-old daughter had with her mother. Said Corinne, "Mommy, Jesus still lives in my heart, but now 'Dr. Charles' lives in Jesus' heart."

Though these are just the words of a child, they hold a deep truth I need to claim. The day will come when all the barriers of my sin and this world's deceptions will be removed. I will be in Jesus' heart in heaven. What will that be like? Were all the love we have ever known to be collected and distilled into one moment, it would not compare with the measure of love we shall know in each moment that we are with our Lord for eternity.

We shall be like him, and we shall be with him. If we do not fully sense the wonder of this blessing, it is because we do not find our sin as utterly repugnant as we should. We do not see how much our faults spoil us and strain our relationship with the Lord. When we lose perspective of the distance that we put between ourselves and the love he so freely offers, we lose the sense of how truly beautiful and joyful it would be to have nothing between us. Full enjoyment of God's presence leaps beyond our experience in this life. Yet being with Jesus is the essential theme of heaven.

The Bible does not mention that we shall play harps eternally or visit each other in mansions, as beautiful as those images may be for some people. The most consistent image in Scripture is that heaven is wonderful because we shall be with God there. The horror of hell is the converse; they shall be without God there. What a wonder to be with God—to know fully his acceptance, his approval, and his embrace.

The opinions of others that so trouble me some days and wrongly motivate me other days will no longer count. The opinions I hold of myself, sometimes high and sometimes low—each deceptive in its own way—will not matter. The pain of the relationships of this life, including those strained by neighbors, damaged by spouses, and even lost due to our own sin, will dissolve in the embrace of the one who is the fountain and reservoir of eternal love. He will see me as I am and will love me still. The faults, failings, and mistakes of this day will grieve me no more, shame me no more, and hurt me no more because I will be like him and with him. The heavenly realities of our resurrected state truly grant us joy in tomorrow.

II. Strength for Trial

But are the treasures of our resurrection just for another day? Does heaven only offer "pie in the sky by and by"? Not for the apostle Paul. Though the full realities of our resurrection remain future, he rejoices that the benefits begin now. Heaven not only grants us joy in tomorrow; it grants us strength for today.

Though the apostle says that he is revealing aspects of a future mystery (v. 51), he makes it very clear that there are definite implications for our lives now. Knowing what will come always affects how we face present difficulties.

The way knowledge of outcomes affects present attitudes slam-dunked into my reality at a recent preaching engagement. I spoke Sunday morning at the invitation of a pastor who is a longtime friend of mine and a lifetime fan of the Chicago Bulls. It just so happened that on the Sunday I was preaching, the Bulls were also competing in the National Basketball Association play-offs for a berth in the finals. My pastor friend was beside himself with excitement and high hopes. He is also very conscientious, however, in his observance of the Sabbath. So on the Sunday that I preached in his church, he did not watch the scheduled game. Instead he videotaped it (mindful that this practice was not beyond questioning). Then that Sunday night when all the services were over, he unwound by watching his "delayed version" of the Bulls' game.

In the early stages of the game, the Bulls were playing awfully and getting killed. I do not remember all the details, but Chicago was down something like twenty points in the first half. It looked as though this game really was going to be a trial. Yet as terrible as the situation seemed to be, I was amazed at the lack of concern expressed by my usually fanatical friend. He did not get upset. He did not hang his head. He did not yell at the coach. He never lost hope.

My puzzlement grew so much at my friend's lack of anxiety that at some point I asked, "What's with you? Aren't you concerned about the outcome of this game?"

"Not a bit," he replied. "One of the fellows at church tonight watched the game this afternoon, and he told me that the Bulls pull it out in the fourth quarter. I already know there's no reason to worry."

Knowing the outcome made the game's trials less intimidating and more bearable. No mere game captures the apostle Paul's interest here, but he takes advantage of similar dynamics. He reveals eternal outcomes so that we can face this life's greatest trials without overwhelming concern. Not only does the apostle tell us what our heavenly future holds, but he also indicates how knowing our heavenly destination grants us hope and comfort in our darkest hours.

HOPE IN THE FACE OF DEATH

The apostle says that not all Christians will die before Christ's return (v. 51). He also promises that God will raise those believers who have died to imperishable life with the faithful still alive when Jesus comes (v. 52). Though the sentences are few, they are jam-packed with indications of heavenly outcomes that grant us hope in the face of life's greatest trial—death.

These words promise *the reunion of loved ones*. Paul says, "We will not all sleep, but we will *all* be changed" (v. 51). Who is included in this *all*? Those who are still living when Christ returns *and* those who will be raised from the dead (v. 52). God will reunite the living and the dead. Death may separate us from loved ones for a time, but we will meet again. Those who have entered death have not ultimately passed away. In a special sense they await the consummation with us.

Our churches in South America keep alive the reality of our ultimate union with loved ones in annual services where the names of departed Christians are read to the congregation. After a reader voices each name, the congregation responds in unison with the word *"presenté,"* which means "present!"

"Jose Gonzales."

"Present."

"Maria Rodriques."

"Present."

In this way the family of God reminds itself of the heavenly reality that grants hope in the face of our greatest trial. Those now present with the Lord in spirit will be present with us in body at the resurrection, and as a result they never ultimately depart from us.

The apostle's words also implicitly promise *the security of loved ones.* If even those who have died are still in God's care awaiting our resurrection reunion, then consider how safe they are. Paul says, "When the perishable has been clothed with the imperishable . . . then the saying that is written *will come true:* 'Death has been swallowed up in victory'" (v. 54). God assures us that our loved ones are secure with him. His provision for them *will come true.*

Perhaps we must experience the loss of one very dear to us to grasp how precious is the promise of God's safekeeping. A few years ago I ministered to a family who had lost a beautiful thirteen-year-old daughter in a tragic farming accident. Words cannot adequately express how earth-shattering such a tragedy is for a family. But I saw the importance of God's promise of safekeeping in the midst of such pain.

The parents and I talked together in the den one evening while other children watched TV in the same room. Though we adults were not watching, at one point a commercial screamed for our attention. A graphic public service announcement told kids to "just say no" to drugs. The scenes depicted the seamier side of the drug culture and rather horrifyingly portrayed the devastation drugs can bring into a child's life. When the final scene showed a young teenage girl being enticed into the drug life, this mother who had just lost her child to another tragedy rose from her chair, shook her finger at the horror on the TV screen, and said, "You can't touch my baby. I am not afraid of you because my child is with Jesus. You can't hurt my baby; she's safe."

For Christians the saying still is true: "Death is swallowed up in victory." We know this victory when even the sting of death dies before the promises of heaven's living reality. We do not lose loved ones who die in Jesus. They are safe with him, and we shall join them again.

We rightly hate death. In one sense Christians should feel death more keenly than any others because we know its roots are in the brokenness of this world. We know any death signals how sinfully corrupted is this creation. We rightly grieve, but we can face death without despair in the light of heaven's promises. This is not important just for those near death but for all who love those who can die.

The telephone rang at recent dinner party where my wife and I were playing Twenty Questions with old friends. The long-distance call brought news from another friend that his thirty-year-old spouse was dying of cancer and was not expected to live through the night. I was asked to pray, and did. But the poignancy of the moment struck me more as I realized that I had prayed similarly for the young woman to my left when her husband had died of cancer five years before and for the couple to my right whose daughter had been killed by a drunken driver two years before that. We all wept a bit to feel the pain afresh. Our grief was real, and yet it felt so sweet to pray in the midst of that sting knowing that those that we had lost and the one we were losing will join us when we meet the Lord. We will be together again.

These truths we need more than we may know. In our churches each year we rejoice with those couples who welcome the most fragile of infants into this world. We praise God for the miracles of new life he gives us. Still, others have lost children through miscarriage, illness, and tragedy in the same year. Some children have lost parents. We all either have known or shall know the ultimate consequences of this fallen world. By heaven's grace we can face these losses without despair, knowing loved ones separated from us remain safe with Jesus until the day of our reunion.

HOPE IN THE MIDST OF DECAY

The death of loved ones tries our faith, but facing our own demise can be an even greater challenge. As one who knows firsthand of life's miseries, Paul speaks of heaven to give us strength when the hour is made dark by clouds over our own health.

What does Paul mean when he says that "the perishable must clothe itself with the imperishable" (v. 53)? In this fallen world all who are living are perishing. Aging is our continual state of being. We are frighteningly vulnerable to the diseases that already rage in some of our bodies and to the many other organisms that doctors say lie dormant in all our systems. Decay, deterioration, and disease characterize us who are born to die. We are the perishable. We do not yet know heaven's eternal state. But we shall. Our spirits will be clothed in imperishable bodies. We will hurt no more, age no more, decay no more. Though this promise never makes this world's hardship pleasant, it keeps the weaknesses of our present bodies from overwhelming us.

Rev. Bob Thomas served as the registrar for Covenant Theological Seminary through its early years. He gave most of his ministry career to the institution and became dear to thousands. When Bob's aged mother was dying, we all felt we were losing a mother in the faith. Some of her last experiences in the hospital told why. When the doctor came and told Mrs. Thomas how serious her cancer was, her eyes sparkled for a bit, and she asked to be alone. After a while she told a nurse to let her son come back into the room. When he returned, she looked at him sternly and said, "Now there will be no more tears. In my prayers the Lord has already taken me to a room above and comforted me. I trust him. Now let's get on with other things."

I would not say that we all could or should express that kind of unbending spirit. But we all need its essence. We need the assurance that God so secures our eternity that when this world's decay closes in on us or our loved ones, we can face it with the knowledge and comfort of our Father's care. This is not some abstract doctrine whose implications reside in books or await in another world. When I see my friends, colleagues, and family suffering, I need to know that God will not abandon them. When the body that houses my spirit fails me, I rejoice that my God will not. An old folk song captures the heavenly comfort that calms earthly worries in these picturesque terms:

> *Ain't gonna need this house no longer, Ain't gonna need*
> *this house no more; . . .*
> *I ain't gonna need this house no longer,*
> *I'm gettin' ready to meet the Lord.*

The image of an aging house is fitting for speaking of heavenly transitions. In another passage the apostle Paul, an experienced tent-maker who had seen what desert sun and winds can do to an earthly home, writes, "Now we know that if the earthly tent we live in is destroyed, we have a building from God, an eternal house in heaven, not built by human hands. Meanwhile we groan, longing to be clothed with our heavenly dwelling" (2 Cor. 5:1-2). This dwelling groans and decays until the manifestation of a better dwelling place for our souls. It will come! For the apostle John tells us in Revelation that those who have washed their robes in the blood of the Lamb will gather before the throne "and he who sits on the throne will spread his tent over them. Never again will they hunger; never again will they thirst. The sun will not beat upon them, nor any scorching heat" (Rev. 7:15-16). Though these bodies tatter, shred, and unravel, God covers us with his own heavenly dwelling that cannot deteriorate.

How strange it is for me at this stage in my life to recognize that

I have lost a step in running to first base. It frustrates me. More frustrating days are likely to come—the days when taking a step may be hard, days when the mind will not move forward with the facility it once did, days when disease may cripple. In those days when frustration can turn to anger or endless futile striving to keep respect in others' eyes and self-respect in my own, I do not know how I shall face it all. We all justifiably fear such days. Yet we can learn to face them with the comfort heaven supplies. We can derive strength from the biblical assurance that, though this earthly tent for our souls that we call a body decays, we still have a secure building reserved eternally in heaven and need never despair.

HOPE IN TIME OF TRIAL

We have hope that grants courage in the face of life's greatest trials—death and decay. If we can face these yoked monsters of life's ultimacies without blinking, what else can intimidate us? The heaven that shields us from the consequences of earth's greatest trials possesses resources for every hour.

We do not know all that awaits us in the remaining todays of this perishing world. Yet we can be sure there are trials to come—deprivations, dangers, failures, tragedies, broken relationships, disappointments, and persecution. How can we face it all? We persevere in the strength of Scripture's assurance that heaven's victory will come. Paul says, "*When* the perishable has been clothed with the imperishable, and the mortal with immortality," heaven's realities will blossom (v. 54). Note how definite these words are. There are no ifs but a definite "*when.*" The mortal *will* have immortality in Christ. This perspective is our source of hope and renewal in the face of any disaster.

Heaven does not make earth's trials vanish, but it shrinks them from their giant proportions with the perspective of God's ultimate provision. If we know we are safe eternally, then what threat of man can intimidate us? What challenges of this world have the power to detour us from God's purposes? C. S. Lewis advised that when Satan attempts to frighten or paralyze us with this world's trials, we should answer his threats with this retort: "Pish, posh. What can you do to me? I am an immortal being!"

Death, be not proud; decay, do not exult; disaster, do not claim victory over us. For though you may seem to conquer our bodies here, our Bible says that all of this life is but a hand's breadth of time compared with the infinity of eternity that spreads before Christians in God's kingdom (cf. Ps. 39:5).

We spend too much time stressed out over what eternity will make incidental, defeated by ephemeral setbacks that heaven's magnitude will dwarf to microscopic proportions. Embarrassing grades, frustrating finances, ministry failures, relational mistakes, life's terrible injustices—all carry legitimate pain. Yet with heaven's perspective we have strength to endure all these earthly trials without buckling to despair. This trouble will pass, and the matters of eternity alone shall last.

III. A Heart for God

Of course, merely enduring trial is not all Paul wants for us or from us. It has been said that hope hears the music of heaven, but faith dances to it. If heaven's claims cause us to give up on this world, we have not heard the angelic strains clearly enough. When we understand that resurrection realities provide joy for tomorrow (so it need not worry us) and strength for today (so it need not intimidate us), these two streams of faith converge into a greater force that heaven now provides. Knowing that there will be joy in that day and claiming the strength available in this day, our hearts should begin to beat for higher purposes than the rest of the world can even consider.

Paul wants confidence in our heavenly futures to lead to us to powerful resolve not to passive resignation. He says, "Therefore, my dear brothers, stand firm. Let nothing move you" (v. 58). Heaven rightly perceived results not in retreat from this world's concerns, but in wholehearted commitment to the purposes of God. When we rest assured of future blessing and present security, there is nothing to hold us back from committing ourselves fully to the work of ministry. The famous line of Jim Elliot rings true before heaven's gates of splendor: "He is no fool who gives up what he cannot keep, to gain what he cannot lose." An uncompromising heart on fire for God's purposes is the inevitable result of heaven's realities fully grasped.

CONFRONTING PERSONAL HURT

Paul continues his charge to stand firm with this instruction: "Always give yourself fully to the *work* of the Lord, because you know that your *labor* in the Lord is not in vain" (v. 58). In the first clause of this verse Paul describes the work that leads to God's purposes as a *task*. But we should not mistake the type of job the apostle has in mind for some incidental chore. Paul makes his meaning even more clear in the second clause of the same sentence. There he encourages us in our work by saying our "labor" will not be in vain. Paul intensifies the language to let us know that he realizes heaven's tasks may require sweat and pain in earth's contexts.

Terry Waite, envoy for the Church of England who labored for the release of Middle East hostages before he himself was taken hostage for five years, told reporters of the personal pain his task caused. In an interview after his release, the envoy explained an instance when he had a chance to escape and did not take it.

At one stage of his captivity Waite's captors kept him blindfolded in a small room so he could not later identify them. One day only one guard was left to watch him. Waite asked the guard to take him to the bathroom. When he took off his blindfold there, he discovered someone had left a loaded automatic weapon on the sink.

Waite said in the later interview, "At that point I knew I could escape, but in doing so, I would have had to use the weapon. In negotiating for the release of other hostages, I had told these men that even when you are in a tight spot, it is immoral and wrong to resort to violence. Had I taken up the weapon at that point because I was in a tight spot, I would have been no different than they. Any future opportunity of negotiating releases for other hostages would have vanished."

So at great personal sacrifice Terry Waite put back on his blindfold, called for his captor to come into the room, pointed to the gun, and told the man to take the weapon away. Many months of imprisonment, danger, and deprivation would follow. Some would say Waite was a fool for not taking advantage of his opportunity. But Waite had his eyes fixed firmly on the future that required him to carry out his mission even in the face of great hardship.

Our heavenly future should also give us incentive to carry out our tasks in the face of personal pain. Because we know eternal blessings will come, we are always insulated against the fear of absolute devastation. Still, heaven is not intended merely to insulate us against debilitating pain; it is also intended to inoculate us against an even greater foe of Christian duty than the terrors Terry Waite faced. That enemy is uncertainty. It would have been far easier to turn the gun back over to the captors if Waite had known that the outcome of his actions would be positive. Yet for all Waite knew, his sacrificial gesture was mere futility. The future not only was unknown, but it appeared bleak. Such is not the case for believers. Glory does await those who live for heaven's purposes. Thus Paul says our hearts should beat for God not only in the face of painful tasks, but also when our efforts seem fruitless.

CONFRONTING APPARENT FUTILITY

"Your labor is not in vain," the apostle says (v. 58). Why does he give that assurance? Because this apostle knows as poignantly as any that our labor for God can seem very futile. After all, Paul is writing to the Corinthians! They are ones who have allowed sin in their church "of a kind that does not even occur among the pagans" (cf. 1 Cor. 5:1).

We also know from the contents of the rest of this letter that the Corinthian church is divided by jealousies, selfish in stewardship, and misguided in worship practice. There is so much wrong here, yet Paul ministers to these people even by writing this letter. He commits himself to serving their needs. Why? They are an embarrassment, a pain. Would you want to serve such a church? You would recognize the seeming hopelessness and obvious hardship of shepherding this group. Yet in the face of such futility and pain, Paul sees and seeks heaven's purposes.

Stretching before the apostle are security and joy forevermore, and not just for him but for all those whom God will touch through him. Were heaven not in view, then the suffering God's service elicits and the sacrifice God's mission requires in this world would seem senseless and worthless. Yet with the assurance of eternal rewards in focus, Paul continues to labor despite personal pain and apparent futility.

Such resolve and commitment to duty can be true of us if we do not let heaven fade from our view. Heaven is meant to put everything into proper perspective. We are to understand that "this world is not our home; we are just passing through." Position, pleasures, prestige, and possessions will pass away. The concerns that we must treasure, claim, and serve are those that will have eternal consequences. If heaven's glories ever grow dim from our vantage point— and in this culture that easily occurs—then the things of this world will glisten too brightly and cause us to cling too tightly to them.

As each academic year at our seminary comes to a close, I have a growing sense of dread for our ministry students. I fear for some simply because of where we teach them to minister. Though our school was founded in the rural outskirts of St. Louis, it has long since been surrounded by affluent neighborhoods with successful high-profile churches and well-paid pastors and counselors. As a result the things of this world glitter too brightly near us. Students can begin to believe that what they see here is the norm for ministry. It is not. And even if it were, ministering to gain this world's security, or goods, or fame may enable one to avoid much of this world's pain, but it will provide little knowledge of heaven's gain.

Will we be "content to fill a little space" if God be glorified? Are we willing to go through the pain of itineration if God gives us a heart for cross-cultural missions? Will we resolve to endure the futility of ministering in unknown places to unappreciative people because God gives us gifts to serve those people? No one can make these commitments without a heart for God that results from knowing that heaven waits with its riches for those who serve him here. If heaven does not fill our vision, concern for the loss of this world's gain will.

We are not to help ourselves to this world's rewards nor serve them. No heart is fully committed to God's purposes whose owner needs earth's rewards. We are glory bound with greater rewards and grander purposes than this world knows or offers. As a result of God's resurrection promises, this life with its light afflictions that are but for a moment is not worth comparing with the exceeding weight of glory that shall be revealed in us (Rom. 8:18; 2 Cor. 4:10). Only with these assurances in view will we be willing to serve in ways that gain us nothing—ministering to AIDS and Alzheimer's patients, caring for the retarded and destitute, sacrificing personal wealth or position to further gospel outreach, fighting for causes that cannot humanly be won and bring us only pain and disrepute in this life. These are ministries that require faithful servants. Most will say we are willing so to serve should God call, but in truth it is amazingly easy not even to consider such ministries as options and to turn our attention solely to more personally rewarding endeavors.

Our eyes must open to heaven's vision now if we are not to be distracted from God's purposes for our lives today. Some Christians do sacrifice to care for those God calls us to support or serve. Some do not. However, we will all begin to resent our sacrifice or others' apparent lack of sacrificial service unless we refuse to live for the things of this world.

No, it is not easy to be purely motivated. For most of us it will be a constant struggle in an affluent culture to keep priorities clear. It is so interesting as my own denomination grows and some aspects become very "successful" to see what ministries really prosper. Right now the national campus ministry of our church with its young, underpaid staff seems to be responsible for more pure evangelism and discipleship than anything else we support. There are ministries with greater press and greater budgets, but few are doing as much for eternal kingdom building. Could this be because somehow in the campus ministers' youth, prayerful fervor, and sacrificial commitment—naiveté, the world would call it—that God sees hearts given fully to him?

Those whose grasp on the things of this world is light are those most often mighty in God's hands. Consider the work of evangelism in South America that is sweeping a continent into a reformation greater than that of Central Europe in the 1600s. This outpouring of the Spirit is occurring in the most destitute and marginal sectors of the population. It would be of no advantage to any one of us to serve there. Yet God is doing a great work through those who are not thinking of this world but the next. Where will be the next Reformation, and shall we be a part of it? I do not know. This I do know: There is still much work to do, but we will shrink from it unless heaven so fills our vision that we are neither intimidated nor detoured by the things of this world.

LIVING HEAVEN'S REALITY

At Southern Illinois University in Carbondale a young man named Derick MacDonald and his wife, Lisal, minister to international students under the auspices of Reformed University Ministries. Derick has had trouble raising enough support for the work. His difficulty is not because there is little work to do nor because he is not capable. He has a fine mind, preaches wonderful sermons, and has a wonderful heart for ministry. The problem lies in the apparent obscurity of his work.

Southern Illinois University (SIU) sits in the middle of the cornfields and coal mines of downstate Illinois. There could hardly be a more unlikely place for ministering to international students. However, because of a popular English as a Second Language program, it has one of the largest populations of international students of any American university. The potential for mission work at SIU is astounding. Yet it is this very potential that makes Derick's pain more acute.

Southern Illinois is in the middle of a coal mining and farming depression. The churches of the region that should be supporting Derick are among the poorest in his denomination. As a result Derick has lived on a pauper's income for years despite his great talents. He and his family suffer to stay where there are. What keeps them there amid what seems to be futile striving with little support? Stories like this:

Derick organizes Bible studies for various international groups. One study reaches African students. Two years ago Derick met an African Christian at the university. That student helped start a Bible study for other Africans. Unfortunately, the chief organizer graduated last spring and went home. More futility! Still, the group managed to start again this fall and was joined by one new person—a Moslem. He comes every Saturday for friendship with other Africans and out of curiosity. His name is Ouvara.

As Derick and the others in the Bible study got to know Ouvara better, they discovered that he is a royal prince. His father is ruler of the fifth largest tribe in a West African nation. For now this young prince meets every week with seven students to study the Bible, but after Ouvara returns, he will rule a tribe of 700,000 people.

Why does Derick MacDonald serve in the midst of futility and pain for himself and his family? Because this world will pass, and only the things of heaven will last. His joy in that tomorrow grants him strength for this trial. He gives himself fully to the work of the Lord, knowing that his work is not in vain.

May God use heaven to make the same true for you and for me. Heaven clearly seen affects all our choices, priorities, endeavors, and plans. Martin Luther said, "I keep only two days on my calendar: today and *That Day* of Christ's Consummation. I pray, 'Lord, help me live this day for That Day.'" May God so help us all to live.

DISCUSSION QUESTIONS

1) Why do some Christians think so much about heaven, and why do some think so little about it?
2) What are some of the joys that heaven holds for the future?
3) How would you describe the nature of the body you will have when you get to heaven? How does this affect some of the concerns you have for yourself and others now?
4) What does the future nature of our bodies indicate about the nature of our souls in heaven?
5) What does it mean to you that in heaven you will be with Jesus?
6) How do the future promises of heaven strengthen you for today's trials?
7) How are you affected by the knowledge that you will be reunited with Christian loved ones who have died, and that until that time they are safe with Jesus?
8) How does your assurance of heaven equip you for ministry today?
9) How does heaven help you face what the world would consider futile or painful challenges to your faith?
10) How can you live today for "That Day"?

9

THE MOTIVE
OF HELL

I was asked to speak about church growth. So I spoke about hell. The preachers at the leader training conference thought I had to be kidding. Maybe it is hard not to think so. If any preacher speaks on hell these days, people instinctively hunker down behind their Bibles and give their nearest pew neighbor a knowing poke in the ribs as if to say, "Fire and brimstone? Why, I haven't heard one of these sermons since I was a kid!"

Hell embarrasses some of us, and it seems to hurt others. Perhaps we avert our eyes when the preacher sermonizes on hell to avoid the grimace on a young woman's face who, after months of cajoling, has finally gotten her husband to come to church on the basis of the pastor's "wonderfully uplifting messages." Whether she is on the verge of tears or rage is hard to tell. But there is no question she believes that, by speaking about hell, her preacher has let her down terribly.

Hell. It seems there could hardly be a less winsome topic, and yet if we want to grow with the spiritual vitality God intends, then we must not neglect the grace implicit in God's clear warning of the eternal consequences of sin. Healthy growth will not occur in Christians nor their churches if we ignore hell as Jesus presents it in this passage.

First a few disclaimers:

Despite some current debates, I will not here try to prove to you that there is a hell. Jesus says so right here. Those wanting more proof on the existence of hell should turn to other resources.

Neither will I try to describe hell. Often Christians seem to have an almost morbid fascination with the details of hell's topography. Such discussions strike me as of little profit. Depending on the translation you use, there are as many as three separate descriptions of the nature of hell in these verses. I am content for the moment simply to say hell is eternal, total, conscious separation from the blessings of God. This definition will suffice for the purposes of this chapter.

Purpose is what I am most concerned to address. Why does Jesus tell us about hell? Answering that question should lead us all to consider how hell should affect our lives and our personal ministries to others. The significance of hell Jesus specifies with these words:

MARK 9:42-50

[42]*And if anyone causes one of these little ones who believe in me to sin, it would be better for him to be thrown into the sea with a large millstone tied around his neck.* [43]*If your hand causes you to sin, cut it off. It is better for you to enter life maimed than with two hands to go into hell, where the fire never goes out.* [45]*And if your foot causes you to sin, cut it off. It is better for you to enter life crippled than to have two feet and be thrown into hell.* [47]*And if your eye causes you to sin, pluck it out. It is better for you to enter the kingdom of God with one eye than to have two eyes and be thrown into hell,* [48]*where "their worm does not die, and the fire is not quenched."*

[49]*Everyone will be salted with fire.*

[50]*Salt is good, but if it loses its saltiness, how can you make it salty again? Have salt in yourselves, and be at peace with each other.*

‿

REAL HELL

The reality had not really begun to hit me until I saw my own wife in tears. I had seen the news reports of families embracing their loved ones as young men and women boarded ships or transport planes for conflict in the Persian Gulf. I had seen the clutching hugs, the flags waving good-bye, the tears held bravely back until a fiancé or father was out of sight and then let go with such grief it seemed that the crying might not stop. Along with the rest of our nation, I had witnessed these pictures of pain on the nightly news, but I did not really get close to understanding what it was all about until I walked into our kitchen and saw my wife's pain.

Kathy told me that she had just talked to her brother on the phone. A naval reserve doctor, he called to say his orders to go had also come. Only a few weeks earlier he and his family had moved to be near us. They had a new home, a new job, new lives, but it was all about to come unglued. They were hurting. My wife wept for them. I was beginning to understand.

Then one of my former students called. He said he just wanted to talk to someone. He, too, had received his orders. He was on his way to Saudi Arabia as a chaplain for a special infantry unit destined for the front lines of any frontal assault. When the unit was briefed about their mission, Pentagon experts told the officers to expect an 85-percent mortality rate among their men if they had to carry out the mission for which they were trained. In light of those statistics my former student—my friend—asked for advice about what to say to his wife and his six-year-old son who already had trouble sleeping when his daddy was away for weekend duty. I was understanding more what this was about.

Then I heard from my parents. "Your brother has been in the Middle East for two weeks already, " they said. Because of the nature of what he does for the Air Force, he had kept it secret, but he was already there. Finally the reality hit me square.

All the hugs, the tortured kisses, the tears—they are about loved ones dying. Whenever loved ones face unknowns that could open the door of death, the whole world pours out its concern. Fears for loved ones' lives create concerns too real to escape. But there is a deeper reality for Christians. We are in a war that is not nearly so brief or decisive as the Gulf War. The battle for souls rages about us every day of our lives. If the world pours out concern for what it only fears could lead to death, then how much more should we Christians be concerned for what we do know lies beyond the door of death. We know hell awaits those who reject Jesus. With that certain knowledge, the concern the world experiences for loved ones' lives ought to be faint in comparison to the concern Christians express for the souls of those we love.

Yet such pressing concern usually seems to escape us. We go through our daily lives among unsaved friends, coworkers, and family, and their potential hell rarely burdens our hearts. We are infrequently at great effort, or even at slight effort, to introduce them to the saving grace of Jesus Christ. And if we do exert any effort, it is often to prove ourselves to others, to endear ourselves to God, or to build our church's numbers rather than to save eternal souls from hell. Whatever happened to hell anyway? Did it just go away? Did God forget or change his mind?

If our loved ones die without trusting in Jesus Christ as their Savior and Lord, they will go to hell. There is something terribly wrong with us if we think of their eternal destinies infrequently. There is something corrupt in our faith if the prospect of their souls in hell concerns us little.

If we do not want to talk about hell because we fear it will "turn off" people who are interested in the Gospel, then we need to reconsider the message of the one who made that Gospel available. He who was more concerned with building the kingdom than any other person who has walked this earth preached more about hell than any other person in the Bible. Why did Jesus do this? We need to understand lest, by relegating hell to the ridiculous preacherisms of an older age, we forget what true spiritual growth requires. As harsh as it sounds, as foreign as it is to the spirit of the age, we need to resurrect a realistic image of hell. We need hell's realities branded on our hearts and burning in our consciences, or inevitably we will become preoccupied with personal peace and prosperity while those we love are floundering on the brink of God's eternal wrath. Hell, rightly understood, builds the kingdom of God.

I. Hell Provokes Holiness

A Saturday night knock on my study door a few years ago roused me from the sermon I was supposed to be preparing. I opened the door to find one of our community's respected businessmen. The anguished look on his face told me something was very wrong. I invited him in. He sat on our sofa, and for two hours, often in tears, this pillar of our community explained his business, which often involved him in the production of pornography.

He explained how over the years of seeing young women and even children exploited, he had agonized over whether to continue in his work. He told how the anguished eyes of a child in one picture his company had produced years ago were still burning a hole in his soul. But now, despite tormenting guilt, he determined he could not leave his job of twenty-five years. He said the financial security of his family and future required him to continue in this work where he had established a position, seniority, and a pension.

What did he want from me? He wanted absolution. He asked if he were to give a certain percentage of his income to the church whether his business would be okay with God.

To answer I asked him to read these words of Jesus: "[I]f anyone causes one of these little ones who believe in me to sin, it would be better for him to be thrown into the sea with a large millstone tied around his neck. If your hand causes you to sin, cut it off. It is better for you to enter life maimed than with two hands to go into hell, where the fire never goes out" (vv. 42-43).

No, I did not jump up and down and shake my finger. In some ways I was tempted to speak to him this way. His business had caused our community and our church much hardship. Still, I did not want him to hear *me*. I wanted him to hear the God who says there is a hell. For the sake of his soul, this man had to know that if his life was oriented to spreading the infectious filth of this world, and that if he would dare to thrive on human misery, then he was in an eternal danger that dollars could not avert. To continue unrepentant in actions or lifestyles that are contrary to the will of God puts a person on the path to hell. Hell's consequences command holiness of us all.

SIN'S LICENSE DECRIED

As clear as the message of judgment appears in this passage, the words still trouble us. So little grace seems to glisten in them. Christ appears to say that what our hands, feet, and eyes do determines our eternal destiny (vv. 43-47). This does not sound like the Gospel of grace but salvation based on good works. Is Jesus saying that being good gets you into heaven, and being bad sends you to hell? No, Jesus would not teach salvation by our works. Remember who is speaking—the one who came to die. The Christ of God knew our works would not save us.

Yet although Jesus does not teach works salvation, he does tell us not to let our theology get in the way of common sense. He does not intend for this instruction to provide a plan of salvation but to expose a fact of life: If you live for the Devil, you will live with him. Jesus saves those who call him Lord and mean it. Salvation does not provide license to sin. The Bible never grants assurance that grace resides in hearts where Christ does not reign. Satan does not control a true child of God.

Understanding our release from sin's control helps us with the portions of this passage that may trouble us even more if we are honest with ourselves. I sin. You do. Does Jesus truly mean what he says in these verses about how we are to rid ourselves of sin? Are we to cut off our hands or pluck out our eyes to prevent sin? We do occasionally hear of Christians who take the "Vincent van Gogh approach" to sanctification—just cut the offending member off.

Does Jesus advocate surgical sanctification? No. Scripture interprets Scripture. We know Jesus could not advocate holiness by horror. First, such mutilation of our bodies would be *inappropriate*. Our bodies are temples of the Holy Spirit (1 Cor. 6:19). We have no right to damage what God made to serve and glorify him.

Second, such a surgical approach to holiness is *unnecessary* for those whom God has saved. Yes, it would be better to enter heaven maimed than enter hell whole, if those were the only choices. They are not. Jesus' words assure Christians that we have been set free from the power of sin. We are not controlled by our members. Christ indicates here that we even have the ability to cut things off were they to threaten our eternity. This ability (even when not exercised) confirms that our members are not in control of us. This is the power of grace—the truth of Christ that flies in the face of Satan's lie that seeks to convince us that we cannot help sinning.

Christians are never helpless in the face of temptation. Satan would love for us to believe otherwise. Sometimes we want to believe otherwise—so that we have an excuse to sin. We plaintively cry, "I can't help it. It's just the way I am. I am so weak." This is a lie, a lie Satan can use to defeat us if we listen to it. The Bible says, "The one who is in you is greater than the one who is in the world" (1 John 4:4).

Christians are not controlled by the sinful nature but by the

Spirit of God (Rom. 8:9). In the words of the theologians, once we were *not* able *not* to sin, but after our new birth, we *are* able not to sin. This does not mean that we never succumb to the temptations Satan places in our path or that we even fully perceive the ways we fall short of God's holiness. However, we are not helpless before the sin that the Holy Spirit reveals to our consciences. Once the Spirit of God enters our hearts, power over sin enters our lives. We are not so controlled by our members that we are forced to do what leads to our own hurt.

Nature itself helps confirm this truth of the believers' spiritual power. In late autumn my family likes to travel to southern Illinois around Horseshoe Lake where the geese are flying. Each time we go I am reminded of how foolish it is to believe that God would make Christians helpless to resist the destructive forces of sin.

Highway 3, the main traffic artery through that part of Illinois, slices right across the southern flyway of millions of migrating waterfowl. When you travel far enough south down the highway, you see the grain fields the conservation department has planted for the geese that gather in this area by the hundreds of thousands. From a distance as you approach the reserve, it looks as though someone has shaken pepper over hundreds of acres. Then as you get closer, you see that the pepper grains are moving, and soon you recognize each grain as a goose.

The birds literally blanket the ground until sunset. Then at dusk there is an amazing transformation. Like huge puffs of smoke, the birds rise from the ground by the thousands and fly across the highway. Why? You would think it would be far easier to navigate during the day.

Old-timers in the region offer this explanation: One side of the highway is all game reserve. The other side of the road is private farmland where hunters gather by the score. The old-timers say that the reason the birds wait till sunset to cross that road is that they have learned that the hunters' time limit is over at sundown.

Now, listen, if a dumb goose with a pea brain and controlled by blind instinct has the ability to change behaviors that would lead to its own destruction, then how can those of us who have the mind of Christ and are controlled by the Spirit of God claim that we cannot change destructive behaviors?

Our weakness is a lie we tell ourselves, or learn to tell at Satan's knee. Believers are capable of change. We must not buy the lie that says things cannot be different. God has already made us different. Christians are no longer under the control of sin if they remember that the Spirit of God has made them stronger than any temptation.

The apostle makes our power apparent saying, " I can do everything through him who gives me strength" (Phil. 4:13). Therefore, we must not believe the lie that says we cannot walk away, change the channel, resist the sin, or keep control. We must not submit to the despair that says we are powerless against our own members and passions.

Above all, we must remember that no matter how weak we feel, God assures us in his Word that the Spirit within us is stronger than the sin that confronts us. We can change. Because God's Spirit is in us, God's strength is in us.

We can resist Satan. God gives us the means. We must as an act of faith believe that we are not helpless before our enemy. We must claim the assurances of our eternal adoption that keep us from the weakening despair of possible rejection if we fail. Then we must seek the Christian counsel (provided by prayer, scriptural instruction, and godly advisers) that God provides to shield us from temptation. God assures us he will never resign us to temptations greater than the aid he provides (1 Cor. 10:13). We are not helpless. We are not hopeless. Christians are never dead in sin.

This Gospel we have provokes holiness. This good news teaches that there is a path that leads to hell, but we do not have to take it. God grants a path of rescue. We have a Gospel that leads to righteousness and hope in controlling the evil in our lives that even we hate.

The message of hope that hell throws into vivid relief can help churches grow. The reason for this is that our world is hungry for the righteousness hell provokes. In our town someone sexually assaulted and murdered two boys, ages seven and eight. The police discovered that the murderer was the thirteen-year-old brother of one of the boys who was acting out an erotic ritual in a pornographic magazine a school friend gave him. We are sickened by the sin. We should recognize our whole society is sick of it. The free love philosophies of the late twentieth century have turned today's universities into the date rape centers of our culture. At these institutions of "higher learning," we have sophisticated our children into thinking of each other as mere objects from which to extract personal pleasure. Our beastliness does not limit itself to decadent campuses or devasted inner cities. The FBI reports that violent crime will touch one in every four American families this year. That's worse than living on the old frontier before "civilization." None of us can escape the immoralizing of our society and its effects.

We are sick to death of the evil. The stench of it sickens our society. The anger and despair in our movies and popular literature tell us that even the ones who are addicted to the sins of sensuality want to retch at the wounds this wickedness inflicts on us all. Who says that proclaiming a message that leads to righteousness and hope in the midst of this misery will not help churches and believers grow? By warning us of hell, Jesus automatically points us to a different path. His words do not merely condemn. They offer hope. They promise that if we will turn from our hellish bents, life can be better tomorrow. We are not locked into the awfulness of today.

Hell's warnings spell hope. They tell us that by God's grace holiness is possible, help is available, hell is avoidable. Such words have the potential to propagate growth and propel the kingdom forward, because they provoke the personal righteousness that the people of this world long for at the level of their own misery and pain.

II. Hell Cements Relationships

Hell's message clearly trumpeted will do more than prompt personal holiness. While personal holiness is the subject at the center of this passage on hell, the text's core is surrounded by concern for the needs of others. Jesus begins this discourse by warning about causing others to sin (v. 42). The initial focus of the passage is outward, but outward toward a very special group—"little ones," presumably the same children he took into his arms only a few moments prior to this teaching (see v. 36). Hell becomes the reality Jesus reaffirms to recommit us to the needs of our children.

CHILDREN LOVED

Because my wife and I still have young children, the irrepressible urge to protect our children from all harm still drives us. We know it is not reasonable to expect we can protect them from every hurt, but you cannot take the desire away from us. Still, we are reminded vividly from time to time of how limited our ability is to protect our children from all that threatens them.

Some time ago our youngest awoke in the night from one of those fever-induced nightmares that horrify young children. Most parents know what happens on such nights. We are shocked out of sleep near midnight with a blood-curdling scream of absolute terror. We rush into a child's bedroom to see what is the matter, but by the time we get there, the child is already back to sleep.

Who then cannot sleep? The parent. At least I struggle to sleep again after such an episode. It troubles me. To hear that much fear in my child's voice and not be able to do anything about it actually makes me sick at my stomach. Yet perhaps we need those cries in the night from our children now and then to be reminded of how vulnerable they are. For as contrary as it is to the spirit of the age, and as much as we hate to think about it, we must remember that hell awaits even our children if they mature without the Lord. We must remember that they

are susceptible to eternal terrors so that we do not forget how impor
tant our responsibilities as Christian parents or guardians are.

You will press to ever meet a more capable Christian than Mark
Pett. Superbly gifted, Mark served as a pastor, seminary founder,
Christian college board member, mission director, and denominational leader while still a young man. He was as powerful, dynamic,
compassionate, and hard-charging a Christian leader as you could
hope to meet until cancer struck him down.

During the last two years of his life, I heard reports of a consistent message Mark proclaimed as he continued to preach. He said
that facing death changes your perspective on what is really important in life. Business concerns that once seemed so important become
insignificant compared to the needs of your family when you are
dying. Mark said, "I don't get so upset anymore when the kids' noise
disturbs my sermon writing. I don't find any matters so pressing
now that my family gets put on the back burner."

A friend who heard one of those messages later said, "When I
saw Mark, gaunt and drawn from the cancer, speaking of the importance of the little ones in our lives, it was like listening to a voice from
the other side of heaven saying, 'Care for your children. There is
nothing more important than that they hear of the Lord through you.
Care for your children. There is nothing more important in this life.
Care for your children.'"

FAMILIES PRESERVED

Caring for our children as a priority of the highest order is an
incredibly difficult task for the contemporary Christian parent. Our
own ambitions, our desires, our work, the forces of our culture that
tear parents out of homes—all these pressures are so great. Yet as
Christians we must not turn our faces from the pressures hell also
asserts. In view of that eternal reality, nothing is more important than
that we endure, sacrifice, and work to help our children avoid a
nightmare that will never end.

Living as though there is a hell to come does not necessarily make this life any easier. Our Savior says everyone who lives out the implications of these truths "will be salted with fire" (v. 49). Some take this statement as a reference to purgatory. It actually is more in keeping with the spirit of the passage to hear Jesus saying that if you live as though there is a hell, life itself gets hot. From the perspective of those in biblical times, the salt analogy makes Christ's point beautifully. The ancients understood that salt could irritate and burn, but they also knew that salt could act as a preservative. Thus Christ's reference to our being salted with fire indicates that we cannot expect to preserve our dear ones from hell without experiencing some of its burning now.

My wife, Kathy, and I have good friends who have grown up in the church. They have what appears from the outside to be an ideal marriage and home. They have a house many of us would envy, along with sweet kids, loving relatives, and good jobs. But the external appearances of a picture-perfect life are very deceiving. The wife has an emotional/mental problem no one has been able to solve. She periodically steals from her own family and gambles the money away. The reasons she does so neither she nor anyone else can explain.

She has been to counselors, doctors, and pastors. Nothing helps permanently. Her actions have put her family on the edge of bankruptcy more than once. The money spent, the objects of value pawned, and the fiscal damage done will take half a lifetime to restore. Still, the worst damage she has inflicted on her family is not financial. It is relational.

Imagine your own spouse stealing from you, destroying your family's security, withdrawing money from bank accounts intentionally (but not infallibly) denied her, and lying about it for months. This young woman has done all of this not once but over and over again.

Imagine the husband's torment. What should he do? What does the world tell him to do? It screams, "Get out of that marriage. You don't have to take this. You don't have to put up with her. Leave!"

He has not left. Instead, every time she has stolen from him and ruined his financial future, he has forgiven her and taken her back. Even when she gave up on her own life and tried to kill herself, he refused to give up on her. She has made his life a living hell. Yet enduring like an Old Testament Hosea loving a faithless Gomer, this faithful husband accepts his wife back into his heart and house time after time despite her sin against him. Why? He endures this burning pain because of hell.

I asked this husband one time why he did not end this marriage despite pressure from many friends and family to do so. His words were as courageous as they were simple. He said, "She is a good mother most of the time. My children need her. But more than that, they need to know the love of their God. How can they know of a Father in heaven who forgives them if their own father will not forgive their own mother." For Christ's sake and against the gates of hell he holds on. There is nothing more important to this father than that he preserve his children from a hell greater than his own.

By refusing to hide our eyes from the realities of hell, we become even more dedicated to what is dearest to us. We too easily lose that vision. I recognize even as I write these words that due to work commitments, I have not been home for the past three nights. Preaching also took me out of town for two days before that. Because there is a hell to face, I must look at my calendar, my career, and my commitments with my family in mind. All parents must.

I will not contend that it will be easy for us to make choices that preserve our families. I will declare that there is nothing more worth preserving. Hell should make our priorities plain, and in a world full of hurting families, ultimately this message will promote healing. This component of the Gospel from which we shy can help preserve families in the face of awful trial. If we remain true to all the particulars of Jesus' message of hell, our churches can grow with the people whose families need and long to hear it.

The trials we endure because there is a hell may burn us now, but they do preserve. They are the salt that Christ himself taught us to endure for the sake of others. Yet salt not only preserves, it flavors. This passage on hell that began with concern for the welfare of others ends with an image of how that concern spreads its influence in our Lord's ministry and how it should affect ours. The analogy of salt now trips forward on itself, gaining momentum to tell us the final great effect hell should have in our ministries.

III. Hell Compels Witness

Jesus concludes his teaching on hell by urging us to be salt and to be at peace (v. 50). This seems to be a curious combination of commands until you consider the words in the contexts of hell's threat and our human situation. My friend forgives his wife and takes her back not only for his children's sake but for hers. He does not want to abandon her to her own sin. Despite what she has done, he seeks peace with her because he does not want hell for her. Hell must so motivate us. We too easily grow indifferent, too easily neglect our testimony, too easily hate. Hell should keep Christians loving despite the hurt done to us.

My historical calendar each year reminds me of the event that ended World War II. A cryptic caption on August 6 reminds me of a fuller account told by Evangelist Jimmy Lyons of what happened on that day a half century ago when my nation dropped an atomic bomb on Hiroshima. The action caused few regrets in our country at that time. We remembered too clearly the enemy's atrocities in that war. We knew of Bataan and the death march where the sick and the infirm who faltered were slaughtered. We knew of lack of mercy at Midway. We knew of the deceit at Pearl Harbor. We remembered what an enemy had done to us and did not question the bombing.

Yet on that August 6 so long ago, a young Japanese girl named Matchiko walked the streets of Hiroshima with her schoolmates. They looked up when the sirens warned of bombers, but Hiroshima had not been a central target, and they were not alarmed. The school chums did not seek shelter.

Had you had opportunity to speak with Matchiko about what you now know would happen in the next few seconds—even with Bataan and Pearl Harbor and Midway in your memory—what would you have done? You would have cried out, "Run, little girl, run! Get to safety! Run!"

But she did not run. She turned a corner with her schoolmates trailing behind, and in a millisecond they were dust. Seconds later the heat wave came that literally melted the skin off Matchiko's face and body.

This was the Matchiko we Americans came to know. We saw her burned and scarred on the newsreels. Then despite what her nation had done to us, we brought her and many more children like her to our hospitals to help them. Those people had hurt us so badly, but when we saw what the fire could do, all we wanted was to warn all the world of its horrors and to seek the peace that would enable us to help even our enemies heal.

The fire of Matchiko's hell was only seconds long. How much greater should be our efforts to proclaim warning and seek peace with those who know not the Gospel because we know of a hell that will last eternally if they do not turn from it.

It shocks me—truly it does—how angry Christians can get with bosses, with workers, and with their own families. We get so embittered that we "write them off." We will send thousands of dollars across the ocean for missions but will sit in angry silence for years across the desk from a colleague that we have condemned as unworthy of our witness. We excuse ourselves from witnessing in the name of Jesus Christ because of what someone has done to us. We do not even feel that we have to act lovingly toward such people. We may believe in love for the lost, but somehow we think it is acceptable to abandon our testimony if another has hurt, wronged, or embarrassed us.

How can we be this way? Because we have stopped seeing hell. Only when we blind ourselves to the pain that awaits others there can we allow ourselves the luxury of ignoring our responsibilities here. A vivid vision of hell keeps our testimony vibrant. Regardless of what others have done, our hearts will never allow us to claim that we have a right to abandon their souls to hell if we keep its horrors in view. When we remind ourselves of what that fire can do, we will discover that every fiber of love and compassion in us cries out, "Run, run—get to safety! Hell awaits you if you do not seek the shelter of the cross."

Faithful disciples always petition, "Please, please, God, let us see hell so clearly that we will seek peace with the persons you put in our lives who must face fire should we not warn them."

IN THE GAP

I have never seen hell more clearly than when my family traveled to my parents' home over the Christmas holidays some years ago. Late one evening a long-distance call came for me. A teenager in the church had been in an auto accident. He was not likely to survive to see the next day.

"You don't need to come," the caller said. "He's unconscious, but please pray."

I prayed, and as I did, the biblical reality of the situation began to take hold of me. This young man who was within hours of death was one of the "black sheep" of our church. I had pastored there two years, and though his parents attended, their son had never once darkened the doorway. His lifestyle showed when his father sent him over to my house to help with a construction project. At lunch he and a coworker would go out behind our woodpile to smoke pot. The boy was virtually into everything a wild nineteen-year-old could experience these days.

I remembered this history as I prayed, and that is when I saw the reality of what I was really praying about. If that young man died that night, he would go to hell (I do not pretend to have divine insight into his heart, but the evidence of his life could lead to no other human conclusion.). In my mind's eye I saw this young man on the brink of the eternal lake of fire. My wife and I prayed and decided I needed to go.

As I drove through the early dawn hours, I continued to pray, "Lord, I do not ask for his life, but please give us another chance with his soul. If it is your will, please shut the gates of hell just a little longer. Let him wake long enough to hear the Gospel one more time."

Then I arrived at the hospital, and he did not wake. But he did not die. For the next six months he lay in the hospital bed in a coma. During that time his family and church prayed not only for him but with him. We read him Scripture when there was no reaction. We prayed when there was no response. We talked without results.

Then, almost imperceptibly at first, things began to change. His eyes would twitch when he heard familiar voices. One of the first hints we had of his growing awareness occurred during prayer. When we began, he shut his eyes, and when we said, "Amen," his eyes opened.

He began to understand more. Sometimes he would point in apparent recognition toward snapshots of his family and friends on the wall by his bed. Still, his mind was not functioning fully. He could not read. So we gave him a picture Bible. When he finally talked, one of his first statements was a request for more prayer. Then after we prayed, he began to say, "Amen." When he later could write, he wrote for more prayer.

If you were to go to that young man's church today, you would see a pew with a gap in it. Designed by the young man's father, the gap is wide enough for a wheelchair. For the rest of my pastorate at that church, the gap was filled each Sunday. The young man who filled the gap still has much to learn in the Lord's house, but he lives to learn. God shut the gates of hell, allowing a soul in a damaged body time to be won.

This young man will go through life maimed, but heaven's wholeness awaits him. One more can be added to the number of heaven's hosts because a young man's family and church so clearly faced the known beyond his door of death and responded with the Gospel. So must we.

What makes churches grow? Practical programs, friendly people, interesting preaching—all this we know. Still, it is all useless without people made earnest by the consequences of hell. Such fervor comes from the fire in the belly of the people who see the fire beyond and respond with appropriate urgency. Our lips and our lives must proclaim his warning: "See it; there is hell—it is real." The warning makes Christ's beckon all the more powerful: "Come to the cross— it is life."

May a vision of hell make us bold enough to say, "Run, run to the cross. You must. You must." May God make us say what he sees. May he make us see what he says. May he make us care, make us bold, make us burn with his message so that our churches grow in the truth that saves souls from hell. May God give us a holy hate of hell that spurs us on to the holy cause of heaven.

DISCUSSION QUESTIONS

1) Why are Christians today embarrassed or horrified by messages on hell?
2) Who spoke about hell more than any other person in the Bible? Why?
3) How does the fear of hell provoke holiness?
4) How do you know that Jesus does not want us to mutilate ourselves in order to avoid hell? Can the mutilation that some attempt in order to ensure their entry into heaven be emotional and spiritual as well as physical?
5) What hope does Christ offer by indicating that we remain in control of our members?
6) How do hell's realities cement relationships on earth?
7) How can hell's realities make our lives difficult today?
8) How does hell compel witness?
9) How can you explain Christ's combination of the commands "to have salt in yourselves" and to "be at peace with each other" in the light of hell's realities?

THE PASSION
OF DISCIPLESHIP

THE WORD IN PERSPECTIVE

৵

The details of this account in the Gospel of Mark are as unsettling as they are familiar. Jesus meets a young man whom we identify from parallel gospel accounts as a wealthy government official. This rich young ruler expresses concern about Jesus' ministry, but instead of encouraging his interest, the Savior seems to put huge hurdles in the man's path to faith. Our understanding of Christ's own concerns helps explain his actions. A few verses after the record of this event, we learn that Jesus is going to Jerusalem—for the last time (v. 32). Few days remain for the Lord to impress upon his disciples the essence of his ministry and their responsibilities. Important truths and possible misconceptions must be cleared up quickly and vividly. As a result Jesus uses the rich young ruler's apparent self-interest to underscore the proper motives for faith and to distinguish the nature of true discipleship.

MARK 10:17-22

[17]*As Jesus started on his way, a man ran up to him and fell on his knees before him. "Good teacher," he asked, "what must I do to inherit eternal life?"*

[18]*"Why do you call me good?" Jesus answered. "No one is good—except God alone. [19]You know the commandments: 'Do not murder, do*

not commit adultery, do not steal, do not give false testimony, do not defraud, honor your father and mother.'"

[20]"Teacher," he declared, "all these I have kept since I was a boy."

[21]Jesus looked at him and loved him. "One thing you lack," he said. "Go, sell everything you have and give to the poor, and you will have treasure in heaven. Then come, follow me."

[22]At this the man's face fell. He went away sad, because he had great wealth.

༈

WHAT YOU DO FOR WHAT YOU GET

Can you complete these phrases?

See the U.S.A. in your _____.

The Maytag repairman is the _____ repairman in town.

Coke. It's the real _____.

Hallmark, when you care enough to give the very _____.

At McDonalds we do it all for _____.

Most of us recognize these phrases as advertising slogans. Many of us can fill in their blanks (even though some of these commercials have not aired for years), because the constant broadcast bombardment of such slogans drives them deep into our memories. Our ability to remember these ads demonstrates that whether we know it or not—or like it or not—advertising so saturates our lives that we cannot help but be affected by it. Yet despite the massive influence on our culture, few of us have been informed of advertising's basic principles or working assumptions.

Understanding how this pervasive cultural force operates may reveal much about our culture's values and their potential effects on our spiritual priorities. Especially if we have not been made wary of their influences, we need to know how commercials work. Two ingredients permeate every advertisement you will ever see, read, or hear. In explicit statements or by necessary implications, every ad presents a "What You Get" and an explanation of a "What You Do" to *get* it. If you want to *get* a dependable washer, buy a Maytag. If you want to *get* the best greeting card, purchase Hallmark.

THE CHRISTIANITY OF CULTURE

So much around us carries the message of "you must do something" to "get yourself something" that this formula for personal gain becomes a philosophy many people live. Even Christians can uncritically adopt such a mind-set. We too may approach the most fundamental commitments of our faith from a perspective of self-gain and, as a result, inadvertently adopt perspectives foreign to biblical Christianity.

Evidence of the ways Christians have been influenced by culture exists in the mixed messages we give to society. Our churches are generally quite specific about the "What You Do" aspects of Christianity. We readily talk about *repentance, obedience,* and *maintaining a right relationship* with God. However, when we begin to discuss "What You Get" as a result of doing these things, we send very inconsistent messages.

Outside of the common offering of eternal life, Christians sometimes offer an end to sorrow, termination of all material want (or, conversely, the supply of all material want), cessation of sinful desires or actions, a cure for all family ills, an escape from loneliness, freedom from guilt, certainty of purpose, absence of pain, answers to trials, and perfect health. At times it is difficult to discern if our churches are offering a daily cross or Aladdin's lamp.

Too often we sound like those awful stereotypes of used car salesmen as we try to "sell" our Christianity. Most of us at one time or another have been approached by people saying, "Do you know Jesus? He can solve all your problems. You'll never have another care." Yet just as when a dealer promises a car that "never needs oil," has "all new tires," and was only driven by "a little old lady from Pasadena," we know the offer rings false, and so does everyone else.

The problem with such promotions of Christianity is that they attempt to "sell" Jesus on the false premise of self-gratification. By offering others satisfaction of their own desires as the primary reward for their commitments, we invite people to make themselves the objects of their faith. Because no force on earth drives more and rewards less than "self," we should not be surprised that faith sought for such a cause satisfies little.

For a more rewarding concept of faith's real benefits, we must assess anew the motivations for Christian discipleship the Bible offers. What is the real goal of our Christianity? What is the real purpose of our repentance, our obedience, and a right relationship with God? Is Jesus just another McDonalds promising to "do it all for you"? Following the Lord Jesus as a disciple loses all biblical definition if our primary goal is satiation of self rather than loving service to the Lord. Our Lord calls us to selfless commitment not because he needs our service, but because he knows that life's greatest joy lies in discovering the delight of giving ourselves to him. Only when we live to honor our Lord rather than seeking to serve our desires is there any hope of real satisfaction. The Lord allows us to rest in the knowledge that loving obedience delights the one we most desire to please. Self consumes the greatest achievements and demands more.

THE CHRISTIANITY OF CHRIST

We gain a more rewarding conception of the true goals of our repentance, obedience, and relationship with God by examining the type of discipleship Christ himself promoted. The difference in some current approaches to spiritual persuasion and Christ's own becomes evident when we imagine the way many Christians might respond to this rich young man who came to Jesus asking, "What must I do to obtain eternal life?" Some might consider this "ideal evangelism." No one had to knock on any doors or hire any big-name evangelists to conduct a crusade. Without any prodding, prompting, or promotion, the rich young ruler simply requested the key to eternal life.

I suspect most of us would respond to such an evangelistic opportunity with a quick rehearsal of some gospel formula and then ask the young man to acknowledge Jesus as his Savior. We would say, "Offer this prayer of commitment, and you will receive the eternal life you desire." The approach seems innocent, even noble, because it reflects so much that we have been taught to say in reaching others with the good news of the salvation Christ offers.

However, closer examination of these words may reveal a per-

THE WONDER OF IT ALL

spective far more secular than the well-intended salvation presentation suggests. Echoing under the religious recitation may be a "What You Do" for a "What You Get" that appeals more to self-satisfaction than to the yielding of one's life in sacrificial service. Offering salvation without evaluating a recipient's heart concerns can make the Gospel a commodity Scripture will not recognize.

Jesus paid attention to such vital details when he responded to the young ruler's request for a key to eternal life. Instead of quickly directing the ruler to repeat a prayer of commitment, Jesus first registered whether the man's attitudes were consistent with a desire for true discipleship.

Picture the situation. Standing before Jesus is a young man who seems to have the best this life can offer. In today's terms, he drives up in his BMW and swaggers forward sporting a Broad Brothers' suit, Yves Saint Laurent power tie, and Gucci briefcase. He has all the authority and luxury a young man of his day could acquire, and still he wants one more *thing*—eternal life. Spiritual warning flares must be shooting up before our Lord's eyes signaling potential problems.

In the face of these mixed signals Jesus devises a test to reveal the young man to himself. Christ answers the man's greeting of, "Good teacher," by saying, "Only God is good." This last statement will stand in stark relief against what the young man will say about himself shortly.

Next Jesus seems to present a "What You Do." He tells the young ruler to keep the commandments (v. 19). On its face this instruction sounds like a condition that the young man must himself meet in order to gain eternal life. As of this moment in Jesus' ministry, shamefully few recognize that only when Christ fulfills the requirements of the law for them may they claim the benefits of holiness. This rich ruler is about to indicate that he is among the ranks of those who think that their salvation lies in their own goodness.

In the man's response to Jesus' instruction is the clue to why he would not "get" the one more "thing" he desired at this time. No, he did not confess some great sin nor refuse to obey the command-ments. Instead he seems to consider what Jesus requires as hardly a problem at all and quickly asserts that he has kept all the command-ments from his youth (v. 20).

We should not assume the ruler was consciously lying about his obedience. Jesus does not expose some despicable hidden sin in the young man's life as with "the woman at the well" (see John 4). Neither should we automatically disqualify the young man from heaven's rewards because of his wealth. Job, Abraham, Joseph, David, and Solomon demonstrate that God has the right to bless believers with wealth if his kingdom will benefit as a result. Jesus does not condemn this young man for any obvious transgression nor for his possessions. Rather, the Savior leads his disciples to under-stand that the ruler's problem was not a failure to keep the letter of the law but an unwillingness to recognize its significance.

I. The Object of Our Worship

By refusing to be humbled by the law's requirements, the rich young ruler broke the foundational commandment to have no other gods. His own arrogance blinds him to his self-idolatry. Jesus has already put the issue plainly in front of the ruler by responding to his greet-ing with the reminder, "Only God is good." Yet when the young man hears that obedience to the law is required for heaven's entry, what does he immediately reply? "I am good, too." By presenting himself as a blameless keeper of God's ordinances, not only does the young ruler fail to look deeply into his own heart, but he sets him-self up as God's equal. The implications of Jesus' recent reminder that "*only* God is good" simply escapes the notice of the self-absorbed young man.

EXPOSING PURPOSE

The obvious motives as well as the actual statements of the ruler reveal the actual object of his concerns. Why, after all, did he present himself as a conscientious observer of God's rules? The young man wanted to use his obedience as a ticket granting him entry to heaven's blessings. Though he falls to his knees before Jesus, the rich young ruler's own desires are the object of his worship. He thinks that his previous service *deserves* reward. He displays no sense of shame and no longing for repentance. In his heart the ruler still stands tall before his God and declares, "I am ready to receive the divine blessings that I have earned."

Apparently in the rich young ruler's mind the one under obligation is God. The Lord now should supply what the man wants. He has paid his bill, and now this dignitary expects some service. Oh, yes, he is willing to bow and call Jesus "teacher," but whom does the young ruler really place in servitude? His willingness to shackle God to the service of human interests signals the deepest concerns of the man's heart—and these concerns have little to do with honoring someone else.

Whose primary interests were to be satisfied by rich young ruler's expressions of faith? His were. The goal of the man's faith was his own self-gratification. We need no plainer evidence of this fact than the ruler's quick exit when Jesus asked him to sacrifice his own interests to become a disciple (vv. 21-22).

At this point we need to exercise special care in our interpretation of this Scripture. We should not take Jesus' requirement that the young man abandon his wealth as a universal norm for all disciples. On other occasions Jesus did not require his followers to abandon all ownership of personal property. He simply made it plain on numerous occasions that nothing of this world could take precedence over a true disciple's devotion to him (cf. Luke 9:23-26; 14:26; 18:24-30). Had not the young man's conceited words and actions revealed that self-serving resources stood between him and his Sovereign, then Jesus would not have needed so pointedly to reveal the man's heart priorities (cf. Luke 12:34).

DEFINING DISCIPLESHIP

The care that Jesus exercised in analyzing the real concerns of the rich young ruler warn us against making mere expressions of devotion or outward actions the defining marks of true discipleship. While Jesus requires his disciples to honor him in word and deed, he never indicates that these alone qualify anyone for eternal life. The rich young ruler is proof of this. His terminology is right. His actions are right. But his motives are dead wrong. When his heart does not bow to Jesus, the young ruler disqualifies himself from discipleship regardless of the homage his tongue and posture (or posturing) pay the Savior.

Motives that place human interests above God's are often sadly evident not only in this ancient ruler's false humility, but also in the lives of modern Christians. One young writer recently looked back on his early excursions into Christian discipleship with this assessment: "Becoming a Christian was great. I got everything—God got nothing." A local columnist in my city's newspaper recently chronicled the life of a man who identified himself as a "born-again Christian," but who was using his wife's earnings as a topless dancer to pay for a graduate degree. Less bizarre but equally distasteful hypocrisies surface in reports of a lay church leader arrested for tax evasion, a well-known Christian entertainer who confesses a history of marital infidelity, and a sports figure whose inspirational talks at local churches seem to have little influence upon his own weekly on-field tirades against opponents and officials. What unites each of these accounts is the willingness to devote words and actions to the honor of Christ only until there is some personal cost.

These cases may be extreme enough to convince us that distinguishing heart commitments from public testimonies is easy. Nothing could be further from the truth. The point of this account of the rich young ruler—and the very reason Scripture makes us struggle through some of its puzzling features to discover the real point—

is that discernment of true motives is one of the most challenging of Christian responsibilities. Jesus requires his followers to look deep into every human heart (including their own) to see if self or our Savior inspires words and actions. Failure to acknowledge the challenge involved in this responsibility keeps our faith in infant stages and robs God of genuine discipleship. Without careful examination of our impulses, the selfishness that motivated the rich young ruler can easily characterize us.

REVEALING REPENTANCE

Our own prayers of repentance provide an opportune place to test the attitudes of our hearts. In these confessions, our penitent words and prayer posture signal our attitudes before the Savior. In thought if not in actual practice we, like the young ruler, also bow before the Lord and lay our desire for forgiveness before him. Each contrite expression professes sorrow for our sin. However, to the surprise of many Christians, these words and actions do not in themselves offer proof of appropriate humility. The nature of the sorrow that accompanies our contrition ultimately reveals the priorities in our hearts and determines the validity of our repentance.

Until we can discern from what corner of our hearts sorrow for sin arises, we cannot know the quality of our repentance. What is the source of our sorrow? For whom are we sorry? These are the critical questions a disciple's heart must answer. The Bible urges obedience with the imperative that we must not "grieve the Holy Spirit" (Eph. 4:30). Our sin hurts God. Such a perspective reflects the sentiment of David who confessed that his sin was against God alone (Psalm 51:4). This means that the "godly sorrow" that characterizes true repentance is the remorse of soul that aches for the wrong we have done God (2 Cor. 7:10-11). The party for whom we are primarily concerned in biblical confession is God.

Such "concerned-for-God repentance" differs fundamentally from the ritualistic penitence of those whose confessions are self-oriented. The primary concern of those whose repentance wells from this cavern of personal regard is themselves. Such persons seek forgiveness because they think a pardon is in their best interests. Concern to avoid divine reprisal or buy heavenly approval drives these individuals to their knees. They bow before God primarily because of what they think their humility will gain or guard. If they did not think they might suffer as a result of their omission, such "penitents" might not perceive any compelling reason to confess.

These disciples of personal promotion enter God's throne room with a "looking-out-for-#1" motivation that virtually ignores the pain they have caused God and the damage they have done his purposes. While grief may accompany the prayers of such persons, the focus of their pain is their own loss or potential deprivation. The holy horror that accompanies the realization that the blood of the Son of God stains our hands, because of the divine sacrifice our sin required, never really touches the emotions of those who do not grieve for sin as Scripture requires.

B. B. Warfield characterizes self-centered repentance in his book *The Plan of Salvation*, as he recounts words of Heinrich Heine, a German poet and faith skeptic. As he lay on his deathbed, Heine was asked by a minister, "Do you trust God to forgive your sins?"

With a wry smile the poet replied, "Why, of course, that is what God is for." Though the satire drips from these words, they are not distant from our own lips when we attempt to use God's mercy to avoid facing the seriousness of our sin. One writer confronts Christians with this accusation that at times rings much too true: "You keep cows to give you milk, and chickens to give you eggs, and you keep God to give you forgiveness."

The affirmations that make the honor of God secondary to one's personal good are not Christianity but mere humanism—and greedy humanism at that. There is a type of longing after heaven and fearing of hell that is straight from the Devil because its only goal (and god) is the fulfillment of self. When personal gain and religious advantage replaces sorrow for sin and a renewed desire for God's glory as the motivation of our repentance, then self-glorification has become our aim regardless of the penitence we mouth.

GLORIFYING CONTRITION

Our needs and desires are not irrelevant to God nor inappropriate in our prayers, but the satisfaction of them cannot be the *primary* purpose of our sorrow for sin or any other aspect of our worship. God must remain the object of our faith. If we present or pursue the Gospel purely on the basis of its human benefits, then we offer in Christ's name the same relentless regard for self-indulgence that the world advocates and that its most successful disciples have already found empty. Heaped at the end of the dead-end street of narcissism are the broken families, shattered psyches, driven persons, and empty lives of the famous, wealthy, and powerful whose endeavors were self-oriented. Jesus' disciples should never lead others down this same course.

Keeping legitimate personal interests subject to concern for God's purposes is possible. Even human relationships can help teach us this dimension of God's plan for our lives. Those who find enrichment in loving and being loved must learn to care for others' interests above their own. Sacrifice accelerates this process not only by teaching what true love is, but also by stimulating selfless concern in return. My own understanding of these dynamics grew dramatically due to a series of events during high school.

In my junior year I got what every teenager from a large family wants most—a room of my own. I was out of town during the weekend on which my birthday fell. While I was away, my parents worked feverishly to complete a new bedroom in the basement. My dad put up drywall and painted. My mom refinished furniture and hung pictures. After seventeen years of sharing a room, I got the best present of my life.

Three months later my Dad learned his company was transferring him. We moved to a smaller house. My personal room vanished and never returned.

I confess that transfer did not do me a bit of good. I grieved for the loss of my room. Yet in my growing maturity, I sorrowed even more for my parents. They had worked so hard, prepared a gift so special, and loved so dearly only to have the decisions of another nullify their efforts. I read the hurt in my parents' eyes, and I hurt for them. How much greater would have been my sorrow if I had done something that somehow nullified or took advantage of their love. Had my actions caused my parents' pain after they had sacrificed so much for me, grief would have poured from my heart in their behalf.

The Bible requires no less of the children of God when we confess our sin. With our knowledge of our heavenly Father's sacrifice of his own Son to save us, and with our awareness of the pain we cause our God when we sin, godly sorrow should readily flow from our hearts. Sad to say, such selfless sorrow often eludes us even when we repent. We too easily find ourselves praying in the first person singular. "Please forgive *me*," deteriorates into a childish whine of self-indulgence because what it really means is, "Please, don't get mad at *me*, God. Remember your love for *me*. I petition you not to let *me* suffer consequences or punish *me* for what I did. I beg you to take care of *me*. Please don't spank *me*." Though we petition God, he is not in the foreground of these prayers. Self holds the seat of honor even when particular phrases seem to echo biblical truths.

Everything Christ's disciples do must be first for his glory (cf. Matt. 6:33; 1 Cor. 10:31). If his honor is not your *first* priority, and a desire to return to his will is not your *primary* compulsion, then you cannot properly repent. Biblical repentance aches for the one wronged before it pleads for forgiveness of the wrong. Genuine contrition acknowledges the damage done to God's purposes before raising its own concerns. True discipleship bows before the mercy of God rather than trying to take advantage of grace.

II. The Object of Our Obedience

If you cannot see the true object of the rich young ruler's faith in his attitude toward confession, perhaps his aim will show more clearly in the motives behind his obedience. Just as his kneeling before Jesus exposed a false humility when the man claimed, "I am good enough to merit eternal life," though Christ had just said, "Only God is good," so also the ruler's professed submission to the law did little to reveal a heart desiring to honor God.

FOR WHOSE GLORY?

As we have already observed, Christians can be quite specific about God's standards of obedience. The "What You Do" aspects of our faith may fill the sermons we hear, the Sunday school discussions we hold, and the thoughts we have about the Bible. Yet despite this frequent obedience focus, the reasons we conform our lives to God's standards may receive little attention. Do we obey God to gain his affection? Do we heap up righteousness to leverage God into blessing us? Is our obedience the bribe we offer God to stay on his good side? If our hearts even reluctantly answer yes to any of these questions, then what we consider holiness is difficult to distinguish from worldliness, and what we say glorifies God actually promotes our own interests.

We can gain a more biblical rationale for our obedience by reflecting on the ministry of the Old Testament's primary lawgiver. When the people of Israel saw the thunder and lightning, heard the trumpet, and saw Mt. Sinai enveloped in smoke as God gave Moses the Ten Commandments, the prophet could have taken advantage of their fear (Ex. 20:18). His own observance of God's instruction to ascend the mountain as the people's representative offered Moses every opportunity to elevate himself. Instead, Israel's leader consistently reminded the people that his instructions and authority were not his own (Ex. 20:20; 24:7-8; 32:26-29). When Moses would later use divine instructions in such a way as to direct credit to himself, God accounted this action as the worst offense of the prophet's life (Num. 20).

Moses' positive and negative examples remind us that when we perform God's bidding for the right reasons, not only is God's work done, but also God's name is glorified. Our obedience should magnify God. What did the rich young ruler want done as a result of his obedience? He wanted to have his work recognized and his own good magnified.

Ready condemnations of this young man are inappropriate if we have not examined the motives of our own obedience. Why do we live righteously? The Bible says our primary focus should be God's glory, not our gain. Self-protection and self-promotion fall far short of the first priorities for Christian discipleship. Such motivations make the wrong person the object of our faith. Selfishness is simply far too unworthy a purpose for lives whose "chief end is to glorify God and enjoy him forever."

FOR WHOSE GOOD?

We have every right to seek God's aid for real needs in our lives, but God's rewards cannot be the *main* motive of our obedience. Those who obey God's standards because their chief aim is "to get something out of it" are not worshiping God. They are worshiping themselves and their own desires. Heaven's rewards are a welcome by-product of righteous living, but they are not its main incentive, or else the good we do is not really righteous by heaven's standards. Good works primarily intended for self-benefit or personal acclaim are mere Pharisaism. The obedience that honors God is selflessly offered for his glory and his good. The motive of such obedience is not gain but gratitude for the grace he has already bestowed on all whom he has saved from the eternal consequences of their sin.

Before we can expect to reap the rewards of God, we must clarify in our hearts whose good we are seeking to promote by our obedience. Is God the object of our faith, or are we the objects of our faith? This is the question Jesus ultimately put before the rich young ruler, and it is the question Scripture puts before us now. Failure to answer in God's favor promotes only heartache.

I witnessed this heartache in a small rural church where the congregation lovingly reached out to children of troubled families. One class of girls blossomed under the care of a teacher who assured them that if they "accepted Jesus," God would bless them with "the desires of their hearts." Such a promise was enticing enough for all of the girls to acknowledge Christ as their Savior. If God wanted to give them what they desired, that was fine with these girls. Inevitably, however, the young girls grew into young women who wanted to marry—non-Christian young men.

The results were predictable. The church refused to perform unbiblical marriages, and the young women left the church angry, hurt, and confused. In the young women's eyes the church had performed an ugly turn of face in now requiring them to serve God rather than their own desires. They said, "You said that if we just accepted Jesus, we would get what we wanted. We want to marry these young men that we love. Why now are you breaking your promise?"

Of course, there are great rewards to be found in following God's will (Ps. 19:11). In my opinion, outside of salvation itself, there is no greater blessing on this earth than spiritual oneness with a Christian spouse. Such blessings are always discovered, however, by submitting our desires to God's desires. God fulfills his most precious promises by promoting his own purposes. Because love lies beneath all divine intentions, blessings flow into our lives as we submit to his will. Still, our fulfillment resides in the resolution to have no higher goal than the glory of God.

When we allow others to make themselves the object of their faith, we communicate a message as deceptive as the world's promises of happiness that always lies just around the corner of acquiring something else. They chase a fantasy who believe ultimate fulfillment lies in a more important title, a bigger salary, a house with another bedroom, a degree from a good college, a slimmer body, a state of ecstasy, a perfect child, or greater recognition. Even if the dream becomes reality, something will always threaten its continuance or significance. The heart that seeks completeness in the empty promises this world offers will never register full. The best things of life will always elude those whose God must serve their own unappeasable appetites.

III. The Object of His Affection

These perspectives regarding the priority of our commitments may turn upside down the notions some have about their faith. For despite the "salesmanship" often used to promote Christianity, the words of Jesus in this account indicate that we become his disciples not when we primarily seek our good but God's. Oh yes, tremendous good results when we "seek first the kingdom of God" (Matt. 6:33). Heaven's blessings rain upon those who desire the glory of God above all else (Heb. 11:6). Still, our worship is of God and none else. Placing the priorities of faith in any other order "sells" a false Christianity that inevitably will fail to satisfy.

If this message seems uncaring, we must first weigh the quality of the love that promotes what God does not. Second, we should not feel obligated to embrace the harsh alternatives of a joyless Christianity burdened by a coerced duty to a perpetually vexed deity. The way to present the priorities of Christian discipleship is not to change or shortchange the Bible's message but to highlight the grace in God's own motivations.

The gospel writer presents our Lord's message with this wonderful balance: God is the object of our faith, but we are the object of his affection. Mark says that despite the rich young ruler's pretensions, "Jesus looked at him and loved him" (v. 21). Christ brought the young man to an understanding of the true nature of discipleship out of love for him. Jesus refused to sell anything false, to offer any promise that could not be realized, or to direct worship to any god other than the one who saves. Recollection of Christ's destination on this last journey to Jerusalem will allay any doubts about the love behind his words. For the sake of this young man, and for those of us who are now allowed to eavesdrop on the conversation these many centuries later, Jesus spoke honestly of the nature of discipleship that will provide any ultimate benefit. His words and actions remind us that pandering to the false Christianity of self-gratification is not loving. It is the ultimate betrayal. Such a gospel presentation offers in God's name promises of self-satisfaction that can never be truly realized.

I faced firsthand the consequences of a gospel sold primarily with promises of personal reward shortly before writing this chapter. I was visiting a young man in prison. He will be an old man before his release. Like so many other young people today, this youth I will identify here as "Bill" had drifted into the drug culture. When he got caught up in a feud with a dealer, Bill's special forces military training automatically engaged. He fired six bullets in tight configuration directly into the other man's heart.

A minister later visited Bill while he was awaiting his trial. The pastor told the frightened young man that if he just "turned his life over to Jesus," then "everything would turn out all right." At that point Bill desperately wanted everything to "turn out all right." Of course, he had his own definition of what those words meant—no conviction, no prison, no problems. Everything did *not* turn out that way. Despite Bill's quick acceptance of Jesus as his Savior and Lord, the court meted out a trial, a conviction, and a long sentence.

When I first visited Bill at the request of friends, he had been in prison for about two years. Our mutual friends had told me about the young man's commitment to Christ, so one of my early questions as we got acquainted was, "How is your spiritual life progressing

THE PASSION OF DISCIPLESHIP

under such trying circumstances?" I was not prepared for the answer. Said Bill, "I tried Christianity for a while. But that just doesn't cut it here in prison. Jesus didn't do anything for me, so I don't care about him anymore."

I recount this conversation *not* to condemn the young man, but to indict Christians whose self-oriented presentations of Jesus' blessings distract from the true nature of discipleship and ultimately deny recipients the true rewards of heaven. Because its primary object of concern is human, devotion expressed only to gain personal favor falls far short of biblical worship. This human-centered faith faces inevitable rejection because the object of such worship can neither satisfy nor be satisfied. Self has no power to fill the bottomless pit of need generated by its own insatiable desires. If we teach others or ourselves to honor God chiefly for our benefit, then we have made ourselves the lords of our faith, and we should not be surprised at the hollowness of our devotion.

True discipleship requires a God greater than self. While desires for reward and relief are not irrelevant to our faith (for God delights in the joy we take in him and his blessings), they must never become its primary aim. At times the line may be thin between primarily seeking our reward in contrast to seeking God's honor first, from which we anticipate blessing. Only in the depths of the human heart—and often in the closet of diligent prayer—do we realize the dimensions of that line. Still, though the line may occasionally seem obscure, we must understand that it exists. Without this knowledge we can never be sure faith is not simply selfishness in religious disguise.

If the line between personal gain and biblical worship remains unclear, then ask yourself this critical question: Is God the object of my faith or am I? Only when Christ is Lord of all—the chief aim of your thoughts, words, and doings—can you experience the blessings he intends. He does not call for your worship out of his need, but out of the knowledge that your heart must serve God to find fulfillment. If your God is no greater than you, then your help is no higher than this earth, and your hope is no more enduring than this life. Without a purpose superior to self, you are shackled to a life of unquenchable selfishness.

In discipleship we entrust ourselves to the only one whose grace and power can assure that the love of heaven will enter our lives and secure our eternities. As we submit our wills to the will of our Savior, we find an escape from self and rest in him. He, who looks at us and loves us, delights in our worship because it releases us from priorities that mask heaven's true benefits. The discipleship that gives life a purpose as high as heaven leads us deeper and deeper into the eternal plan earth's trials cannot deny nor its riches gain. The object of our faith will no longer lie in question when our beings resonate with the joy of these divine intentions. Our hearts will join the refrain gratefully sung by the Savior's servants across the ages: "To God be the glory; to God *alone* be the glory."

DISCUSSION QUESTIONS

1) How should the fact that the Lord Jesus "came to serve rather than be served" affect the attitudes of his disciples today?
2) In what ways are Christians tempted to "sell" the Gospel on the false premise of self-gratification? What are the dangers of this?
3) How are our prayers of repentance sometimes characterized by self-serving motives? Is it possible to repent without doing so primarily for selfish reasons? How?
4) What are ways that our obedience can become self-oriented?
5) Why are self-protection and self-promotion inadequate motives for true discipleship? Why are they so difficult to avoid? How do churches sometimes accentuate this difficulty?
6) What are ways to test our hearts or evaluate our actions to determine if we are serving God out of selfless or selfish motives?

7) Why is it so important to determine if our discipleship seeks God's glory or our own?

8) How does the concept that "we become and even are Christians not primarily for our good but for God's" square with the way Christians are called to discipleship in your church or in churches around you?

9) Is God the object of your faith, or are you? Why is the answer important?

THE COMPASSION
OF MISSION

THE WORD IN PERSPECTIVE

৵

Top-40 radio stations that only play songs listeners most want to hear inevitably stop being heard. When the repetitive music becomes the audio wallpaper of everyday existence, people expect its presence, but the words and notes barely penetrate their consciousness. Such stations must perpetually adjust their formats and "hit" lists just so that people will keep listening and advertisers will keep paying.

When churches fall into a top-40 mentality, they present the biblical texts their people expect over and over again until the nodding assent of parishioners no longer indicates that they really hear what the preacher says. Such may be the case with this text that we typically identify as Christ's "Great Commission." Evangelicals typically demand that their ministers highlight this passage, and preachers gladly comply. But the frequent repetition of these words may reduce to a mere droning on the ears what Jesus intended as a drumbeat for the march of Christian mission.

None of us can afford to be oblivious to these truths. They hold hope designed to rescue churches and individuals from the despair too easily imposed by a world antagonistic to the Gospel. We will awaken to these assurances again when we understand that they are Christ's promise of power for his Church today and when we acknowledge that with them each Christian is equipped for the personal mission God assigns no matter how great the challenge. Accentuating the significance of this pas-

sage is the fact that these are among the last words Jesus impressed upon his disciples after he defeated death and prepared to "return to the Father."

MATTHEW 28:16-20

[16]Then the eleven disciples went to Galilee, to the mountain where Jesus had told them to go. [17]When they saw him, they worshiped him; but some doubted. [18]Then Jesus came to them and said, "All authority in heaven and on earth has been given to me. [19]Therefore go and make disciples of all nations, baptizing them in the name of the Father and of the Son and of the Holy Spirit,[20]and teaching them to obey everything I have commanded you. And surely I am with you always, to the very end of the age."

THE LION'S ROAR

One of my children's favorite Walt Disney cartoons is *Lambert, the Sheepish Lion*, the unlikely story of a lion raised with lambs. As you might suspect, though this lion lies down with the lambs, the Disney Corporation is not trying to picture the end times or advocate a millennial view. As a lion among lambs, Lambert cannot figure out what he is supposed to be, and as a result he cannot determine what he is supposed to do. Should he eat grass with fangs (which is not very healthy for the lion)? Is he supposed to play sheep tag with claws (which is not real healthy for the sheep)! Lambert has an identity problem.

Because this cartoon is vintage Disney, we know the problem will be solved, but the solution comes through harsh realities. Wolves attack the flock. When the lives of his loved ones are at stake, Lambert's real nature surfaces. He fights off the wolves, and as a symbolic expression of his newfound identity, he also finds his voice. This sheepish lion roars for the first time. Finally Lambert has discovered who he is, and the battle roar tells all that he now knows of his real capabilities.

In the familiar "Great Commission" passage above, Jesus addresses a similar identity problem his disciples are experiencing. Just a few days before this event, these followers were in sheepish hiding. Thinking that their leader had been defeated and that their lives were in jeopardy, the disciples retreated behind locked doors in Jerusalem. Now they find themselves on a mountaintop where the risen Lord, the one Scripture calls the "Lion of Judah," tells them they must be his voice to the nations. Against all odds and opposition these lambish followers must secure the Lord's flock to the farthermost reaches of the earth. Jesus commissions these disciples to tell the world who he is and what he has done.

The disciples must go from sheepish hiding to being the voice for this Lion. That is a change of identity. Jesus must know that the disciples will struggle with so radical a transformation of perspective about themselves. As a result he speaks plainly about what the disciples are to be and what their lives are to express. His words establish their identity, and because we are disciples, too, his words also tell us who we are (cf. Acts 11:26). If we have ever felt sheepish about spreading the Gospel—if we have ever wondered just what it means for us to have a role in securing God's flock—these words are a special gift. When we understand what Christ's commission means, we will not only know our identity, but we will know what God intends for our lives to express. I cannot promise that we will all roar, but I will guarantee that powerful new resolve will fill our hearts.

What are we in the light of Christ's words? Some solid images will help us understand our true identity and the resultant mission Christ establishes for us in these verses.

I. We Are a Rock

There are commitments from which we should never move. Jesus' charge establishes rock-solid principles as the foundation upon which to base our identity. The Great Commission to "make disciples of all nations" concludes with the command for the disciples to spread *Christ's* teachings (v. 20). Jesus' followers may not multiply their own teachings nor disseminate new truths of their own discovery. His disciples must anchor themselves to what Christ taught.

THE COMMANDS

This constraint in the disciples' commission becomes most evident in the first aspect of Christ's instruction to them. Jesus says the disciples must teach others "to obey everything I have commanded you" (v. 20). Note the "over-the-shoulder" glance of the Savior. He looks back at the content of his own ministry to indicate the standards his disciples must pass to others. The Lord allows only himself the prerogative to determine what others must do. What he has said rules. Neither time nor circumstances nor human philosophies are allowed to infiltrate the disciples' instruction. Whether the issues are moral, ethical, or social, what Christ has commanded at the behest of the heavenly Father is what the disciples must teach. Holy standards can only be set by a holy God. When we teach what God requires, our instruction must not move from his *commands*.

THE CLEANSING

Jesus does not limit his disciples' instructional task only to teaching commands because imperatives do not encompass all he taught. These last words of the book of Matthew themselves become part of the body of Christ's thought and include other important teaching his disciples must also communicate to others. With the instruction concerning his commands, Jesus includes a reminder of his *cleansing*. Jesus commissions his disciples to baptize future followers (v. 19). How grateful we should be for this instruction. If being a disciple only required "obeying everything" Jesus commanded (v. 20), then who could be a disciple? By itself, this standard would exclude every imperfect person from future discipleship.

Jesus responds to the apparent exclusivity of his message with a wonderful compaction of the gospel message. By speaking of baptism in the context of the divine imperatives, Jesus confirms the essence of the Gospel. A holy God not only commands holiness, but he also supplies it. Baptism signifies the wonderful work from which Christ just arose, the shedding of his own blood to cleanse us from our sin. By his blood he washes us from the guilt of failing to keep his commands. Disciples who carry the message of baptism while proclaiming the holy standards of God communicate the essence of grace.

THE CLAIM

Christ's instruction regarding his commands and cleansing still does not complete the good news committed to the disciples. With the message of cleansing comes a divine pledge that promises to make the Gospel a more intimate joy for future recipients. The Savior commands the disciples to baptize in the name of the Father, Son, and Holy Spirit (v. 19). These words do not designate a formulaic chant or magical ritual that makes the water of baptism effective. They signify a wonderful *claim* God makes on those who are cleansed by Christ's blood. When God has made us as holy as himself by Christ's cleansing, our Lord adopts us into his holy family. To signify their new family status, Christians are baptized in the name of the triune God. When a family adopts a child today, he bears their name. So, too, when we are baptized into God's family, we bear his name. God pledges heaven's love when the divine names are placed upon us. Through the words he commanded to accompany our baptisms, God proclaims that he now claims us as his own sons and daughters.

Knowing the heavenly Father's commands for us, his cleansing of us, and his claim upon us is essential in order for us to discern our true identity. This is because at a most fundamental level of human understanding, knowing our Father tells us who we are.

When I was a child, my family went on a cross-country camping vacation. One day we stopped by a lake for a picnic lunch. While my parents made peanut butter and jelly sandwiches, my brothers and I decided to play by the lake. My father gave his permission with this proviso: "Do not get on the dam."

The dam had been reinforced with a mass of concrete blocks sporting sharp edges and twisted wire that could easily slice through blue jeans and skin. Dad repeated his command with the emphasis that let us all know that he was concerned for our safety and that he meant business. But—we ended up where we had been forbidden to go.

To retrieve a ball or Frisbee (I don't remember which), one of my brothers climbed on the dam's edge. Then, as every child's nightmare dictates, his parent's warning proved prophetic. My brother slipped on the wet concrete and deeply gashed his knee.

When my father first heard our cries for help, he turned from the picnic preparations and saw where we were. I can still see the look of white-hot anger that crossed his face when he recognized that we had disobeyed him. The anger quickly changed to concern, however, when he realized that my brother was hurt. Dad came running. To keep my brother from doing any more damage to his leg, my father stepped down knee-deep into the mud at the water's edge, hugged my brother to his chest, and while the blood covered them both, we rushed to the hospital.

When he came out of the emergency room an hour later to tell us that my brother would be fine, Dad was a sloppy, muddy, bloody mess. These events occurred decades ago, yet they are as vivid in my mind as if they happened yesterday. The images remain fresh not merely because they were so dramatic, but because they so forcefully declared my identity. I now understood that I was the child of a father who gave commands for his children's good and loved them so much that, even when they disobeyed, he would cover himself with filth and blood to keep them safe.

All Christians are such children. Jesus' teachings declare to every Christian that our heavenly Father loves us enough to *command* what our safety requires. Yet due to our own disobedience that puts us in grave spiritual danger, our God—in the person of his Son— stepped down into the filth of this world to save us. In his effort our Savior, too, was covered with blood, but it was not the blood of another that stained him. He shed his own blood to *cleanse* us. The blood that washes us signals an embracing love as our God now *claims* us as his own. "How great is the love the Father has lavished on us, that we should be called children of God!" (1 John 3:1).

THE GOSPEL MATRIX

Christ's commands, his cleansing, and his claim form a vital gospel matrix. One of the greatest threats to the Gospel occurs when Christians do not understand the necessity of each fundamental in this matrix. Jesus requires his disciples to teach "everything" he communicated because exclusion of any essential warps the entire message (v. 20). Concentrating only on select portions of the Christ's message while neglecting other portions will always pose a threat to a pure and powerful Gospel.

Individual churches, church leaders, and sometimes entire movements can unconsciously damage the Gospel as they pick and choose their way through the aspects of Jesus' message that they want to honor. Analyzing the way our churches communicate Christ's message in the light of the commands, cleansing, and claims entrusted to his disciples reveals how damaging such selective emphases are to the witness of the Church. For example, more persons claim to be evangelicals now than at any time in our nation's history, yet our nation seems far from more holy. The morals evident in newspaper headlines, court records, and movie marquees remind us that contemporary Christians have often erred in spreading a gospel emphasizing cleansing without commands—in preaching family claims without responsibility.

A de-emphasis on holiness is not the true Gospel's only threat. Evangelicals may also react so strongly against the predominance of evil in our society that they begin to emphasize biblical commands without an appropriate accompanying emphasis on Christ's cleansing and the assurance of God's claim upon us. Balancing the Gospel does not mean that we should ever ignore divine imperatives. God's commands touch on all the areas of our lives—social, political, ethical, economic, relational, etc. The Church rightly addresses all of these concerns with biblical teaching and has been guilty of neglecting social and ethical responsibilities. Still, it is possible in overreaction to that neglect for the Church of Jesus Christ to become the church of special-interest causes.

I recognize the danger of some misinterpreting my intent as I reiterate Christ's insistence on a whole Gospel. I am not for one moment calling for evangelicals to ignore the ethical issues of our day. I have no desire to discourage any who use biblical principles to fight for the causes of political justice and social morality. I pray that many will applaud and support such efforts. Still, I grow fearful of the churches, movements, and Christians whose legitimate concerns about societal reform cause them to say anything less about God's cleansing of, and claim upon, his children. Christians remain responsible to examine their emphases as well as their particular stands. Concentration upon even holy commands without commensurate emphases upon Christ's atonement and the assurances of the cross always has been and always will be mere legalism. Despite the best of motives, it will lead churches astray.

Finally it is possible so to emphasize God's family claim upon us that praise for our relationship to him becomes mere euphemism for arrogance. This era of evangelical victory may promote egotism under the guise of godliness in ways often more obvious to our culture than to our churches. Blindness to our conceit is a sad product of blessings secured through many tears. A previous generation of evangelical leaders fought against mainline denominational dominance for biblical orthodoxy, church resources, and members. To the continuing dismay of our land, that generation succeeded. There are now more students in Bible-believing seminaries than in all other seminaries combined. More Christians now worship in evangelical churches than the total membership of all the mainline churches—whose membership exodus continues to number in the millions each decade. Our worship and educational facilities are no longer pauper stepsisters embarrassed by the established churches' wealth of resources.

We have won! Yet in this victory lies the tendency to make success our new God. The temptation is now to build empires rather than the body of Christ, to long for high profiles and public stature, to lust after the sweet perfume of success, and to forget that in this world those God truly claims exude the aroma of death because they resolve to die to self daily.

There are so many ways to lose our balance, and some are so subtle that at times concerned evangelicals grow fearful. We worry about where the Church may go and doubt it can stay on course. We catalog the leaders who have fallen, calculate the continuing influence of departed or aging giants who have led us before—Francis Schaeffer, Carl Henry, Billy Graham—and we wonder how we can stay true to the whole Gospel. Who will keep the next generation teaching everything that Christ commanded? Our questions can lead to panic if we do not remember that these men were not the first disciples. They remained faithful because there was a holy band that preceded them, and another before them, and still another before them. Like flagstones leading all the way back to the cross are the disciples who have stood unmoved from the teachings of Christ, and nothing requires that path to end now.

We who are disciples today are the new rock on the path of the Gospel's progress. God can use us as he has used the saints before. This awareness of our divine purpose establishes my identity and yours. Knowledge of this purpose should lead to a holy resolve that roars from our hearts to proclaim, "We shall not be moved. We are a rock founded upon the teachings of Jesus Christ. Whatever evils predominate, whatever causes become popular, whatever personal gains may be ours—they shall not shake us from our commitment to all his truths. Christ alone gives our commands, his cross is our only source of cleansing, and his claim our only hope of glory. On this rock we take our stand, and we shall not be moved."

II. We Are a River

Jesus does not complete the picture of our identity with his instruction to stand still. He requires dynamism in our lives. The Savior says, "Go" (v. 19). This two-letter imperative reminds us that Christ requires more than static commitments. Jesus wants his disciples' influence to spread. His charge requires us to see ourselves as more than a rock. We are a *river*. Christ's words suggest this identity not only by stating *our responsibility*, but also by indicating *God's expectation*.

Jesus encapsulates his followers' responsibility in the imperative to "go and make disciples." Then the Savior signals the extent of that mission with the three words that follow: "of all nations." God expects his disciples' ministry to touch all peoples. This divine expectation explains why we should see ourselves as a mighty, rolling river. God plans for our influence to spread worldwide. In the light of this expectation that further defines our identity, an additional commitment becomes apparent. If we are to flood the nations, then we should resolve, "We shall not be stopped."

This new resolution may seem contrary to earlier statements of our commitments. How can you reconcile, "We shall not be moved," to, "We shall not be stopped"? The answer lies in recognizing that since our concern is the message of the Lord Jesus Christ, when we will not be moved, then we cannot be stopped.

The seeming paradox of our mission resolutions disappears in the light of real-life gospel events. The experience of Romanian pastor Laszlo Tokes just prior to the collapse of his nation's Communist government resolves these seemingly contradicting dynamics.

The Communist dictator Nicolae Ceausescu had tried to silence the Reformed Church pastor, but Tokes would not abandon his pulpit in Timisoara. As a result on December 15, 1989, Ceausescu sent his Secret Police in force to arrest the pastor.

Fearing for their pastor's life, members of the congregation surrounded the parsonage as a human fence. The police ordered the people to disperse. They did not move. More police were summoned with more weapons. The January 19, 1990, issue of the *Christian Observer* reported what happened next: "In the afternoon, the Secret Police went with the Romanian civil police to arrest Pastor Tokes. The congregation, still surrounding the parsonage, opposed the assault. The crowd placed their children in front of the human chain thinking that surely the police would not fire at the innocent, but the police opened fire. In minutes between 200 and 300 men, women, and children lay dead."

When the people of the town, including some who had gathered at a nearby Romanian Orthodox Church, heard the machine-gunning and the screams, they ran to the scene—and closed ranks with the Reformed congregation. Factory workers and others in the community soon flooded the church grounds as well. Realization of what had happened incensed the crowd and swept it toward the town square where the Communist party had its headquarters. Police demanded that the protest end, and again ordered the people to disband. Again the people refused to move. The *Christian Observer* details what then followed: "When the Secret Police realized what was happening, they surrounded the crowd and began to slaughter them. They used machine guns, tanks, and helicopters. Before December 15 had passed, between 4,000 and 7,000 lay dead in Timisoara."

This massacre did not conclude the story. As those of us in the West now know, the resolve of these people who would not move created a flood of outrage throughout Romania that could not be stopped. Seven days later the Communist government fell. On Christmas day— only ten days after he ordered the slaughter in Timisoara—Ceausescu was executed. Pastor Tokes (who was only wounded in the original assault) still ministers, but the dictator became a victim of the river he could not stop, because of the people who would not move.

The river of gospel influence may not always rise so quickly, nor may its flow always be so easily marked. Yet if any people could ever say, "When we shall not be moved, then we shall not be stopped," it should be we who live in this era. Only twenty-five years ago I sat in a college classroom while a professor seriously argued that Karl Marx was more significant than Jesus Christ. He said, "Marx's writings have only been around for a little over 100 years. Jesus' teachings have been around for 2000 years, yet communism influences far more people than Christianity." As he emphasized his conclusions by pointing to a globe more than half-covered in red indicating regions of Communist influence, the professor was difficult to dispute. I would love to challenge him today.

I would love to question why after nearly half a century of the total domination of Eastern Europe, communism there lies in ruins. I would ask my former professor about Glasnost, the Berlin Wall, Solidarity, the demise of Ceausescu, the resurrection of Dubcek, and, if he would let me, even about Tiananmen Square. From Gdansk to Belgrade, from Berlin to the Baltic, from Poland to "Peking" the sea of red recedes, and in its wake comes a crimson tide—the message of Christ's shed blood.

Oh yes, despicable influences from the West have entered the former Soviet Bloc as well in the vacuum left by communism's demise. Without the restraints of Russian rule some of the formerly dominated peoples have perpetrated their own horrors. Yet despite these evils, a massive influx of cultic organizations, and an invasion of Western decadence, the Gospel is still flowing into the hearts of millions at an unprecedented pace.

Not only are Western mission agencies flooding East European nations with Christian messengers, but the new governments themselves are inviting missionaries to work within their borders. Sensing the ethical and moral void left by Communist government, business, and education, current leaders in Romania, Hungary, Poland, Czechoslovakia, and even Russia have solicited the aid of Western mission agencies. In recent years Russian education officials working with a coalition of seventy separate churches, mission agencies, and parachurch organizations have invited 12,000 missionaries to teach Christian ethics in that nation's 120,000 public schools. As this gospel river flows into so vast a spiritual desert, some have called this the greatest single missions effort in world history. The streams of spiritual life once dammed beyond the reach of millions for generations have been unleashed with a terrific force. Faithful Christians in those lands who in the face of overwhelming evil did not move from faithful prayer, testimony, and worship now witness how unstoppable is the Gospel for which they stood.

This river now flowing is not like the philosophy that is failing. The current of the Gospel does not fight for governments and territories. It breaks through every human barrier to claim souls, and today it moves as a mighty, rolling river for those with the eyes to see. The flow is not limited to the former Soviet Union or those nations that were in its orbit. At the present pace 3,500 churches calling themselves "Christian" will start this week across the world. Not all will teach what we would desire, but what if just half did? What if just a third did? That would still mean a thousand new Christian churches will proclaim the name of Jesus this Sunday. Additionally, another thousand more new churches will do the same next week, and another thousand will follow suit the week after that.

In our time there is a mighty river flowing with the truths of the Gospel such as the world has never seen. In Africa experts estimate there are 16,000 new Christians every day. In Asia there are more evangelical seminaries than in all of North America. Some of these seminaries meet in caves; some gather in farmhouses; but wherever they meet, they become tributaries of a greater river. In South America people are converting to evangelical Christianity at a rate not seen since the Reformation in Central Europe. In fact demographic experts report that if the rate of conversion were to stay constant, by the year 2010 there would be more evangelicals in South America than there are people on that continent. In other words, the current rate is so high that it cannot be mathematically sustained. This rapid advance of the Gospel is happening right now—not 300 years in the past nor two centuries from now. Right now in our lifetime is one of the greatest mission eras in the history of the world.

Of course, this river of influence does not flow unchallenged. Though more Muslims have converted to Christianity in the last fifty years than in the last millennium, the Islamic countries remain largely without gospel penetration. Still, the gospel river may be about to break through even these formidable levees of resistance. As a result of the Persian Gulf War, not only were more Westerners in the

Moslem world than at any time in history, there were more Christians, chaplains, *and* Bibles in the Islamic domain than at any time in world history. We should pray earnestly for what God may yet choose to do with such influences. Further, some of the largest concentrations of Muslims in the world are now in France, the United States, and the Philippines where the Gospel can be much more freely proclaimed than in the Muslim nations of the Middle East.

Even where the Gospel seems to have been stopped cold, hope remains for its renewed flow for those who do not move from faithfulness. When at Tiananmen Square the Communist government in China crushed the movement toward liberty that would have released waves of Christian influence from both within and without that country, many lost hope that this generation would see the Gospel flood the great Chinese mission field. Yet a few months after the student massacre in Beijing, my seminary received a letter from a student group at Beijing University. The students requested copies of the writings of the Christian philosopher Francis Schaeffer.

Do you think we should have sent the books? Why? We know that the Communists have reasserted their power. We also know that Beijing University's official ideals are atheistic. Common sense dictates that these few pages of Christian thought will have no real impact on so vast a nation. Yes, we know all this, but we also realize something else on the basis of Christ's words. We are a river. If we shall not be moved from the proclamation of God's Word, then we shall not be stopped.

The seminary sent the books. Seven years later we received a visit from nine evangelical seminary presidents whose institutions are in mainland China. We learned that there are many more evangelical seminaries in China. Some are very small and all struggle with various restrictions, but the Gospel is flowing. When the Communists threw out Western missionaries during Mao's revolution, Christians throughout the nation only numbered in the tens of thousands. But now, despite a half century of repression, there are—estimating conservatively—forty to sixty million.

"We shall not be stopped" is not merely a refrain that captures the content of our resolve; it is the divine assurance that motivates our personal mission commitments. When we use our resources to send Christ's servants to distant mission fields, we are not casting people into a lightless void with the dim hope that perhaps sometime, some way they will reach somebody. Nor do we bear our own personal testimonies with such faint faith. We who are Christ's disciples believe ourselves to be a mighty, rolling river. We understand that if we shall not be moved from Christ's teachings, we shall not be stopped. God expects our influence to spread. Why should we expect any less?

III. We Are a Fire

The resolutions, "We shall not be moved," and, "We shall not be stopped," summarize motivations that not only should cause us to send others out, but should also ignite our own personal zeal for Christ's mission. When Jesus inspires the zeal that causes his disciples' hearts to burn for his purposes, he kindles an image that portrays a final element of our Christian identity. We are a *fire*. This image is important because fire is a mighty power that can be unleashed by the smallest spark as long as it has the right fuel. When Christians understand their fire nature, they serve the Gospel with the assurance that their roles are never so insignificant as to be without influence in God's eternal purposes—because of the fuel he supplies.

INSIGNIFICANT SPARKS

Consider the obvious insignificance of the group Jesus addresses in the light of the task he sets before them. Jesus commissions this little band of fishermen and publicans to spread his message to "all nations." How pathetic! How can Jesus expect these poorly educated, frightened, factionalized, pauper disciples to reach the world?

Already the disciples find themselves *diminished in number*. Once there were twelve of them. Now only eleven can gather on the mountain (v. 16). When they do gather, their leader (whom they only recently thought dead) indicates that he, too, will soon depart for good. Except for an occasional foray across Palestine, even when Jesus was with these disciples, their activities were limited to an area with a radius of about seventeen miles. Now they are to reach the world without him? Absurd!

Not only are their numbers dropping, but the disciples' commitments are also eroding. The trials of the last few weeks have taken their toll on the confidence of the group. So *diminished in faith* are the disciples that even when their resurrected Savior appears before them, "some doubt" (v. 17). How can Jesus expect this cadre of quivering souls to conquer the world with the Gospel? It does not make sense for Jesus to expect blazing results from such smoking embers— unless all Jesus needs is a spark to set this world on fire for him.

IGNITABLE FUEL

Consider the fuel these apostolic sparks have available. The first and last words of Jesus' commission contain the gasoline. Jesus first says, "All authority in heaven and on earth has been given to me" (v. 18). The Lord commissions the disciples with the assurance that he has the authority to charge them. They need not proceed independently nor presumptively. The disciples rightly go into the world with the message of eternity because the one who rules heaven and earth authorizes them to do so. We fathom the importance of Christ establishing his commissioning credentials by remembering that no matter what our abilities, we cannot function without proper authority.

THE AUTHORITY OF JESUS

On March 6, 1990, the quiet morning prayer in my classroom was shattered by a sonic boom. Traveling at three times the speed of sound, a Blackbird supersonic jet was setting a coast-to-coast speed record by flying from Los Angeles to Washington, DC, in one hour. The average speed of 2,190 m.p.h. was an amazing demonstration of power—that proved that no matter what your abilities, without authority you can do nothing. The amazing spy plane was actually flying its swan song. Congress had withdrawn the authority for the plane's continued funding. As it headed for mothballs, this "last hur- rah" of the super jet was its designers' bitter acknowledgment of the futility of power without authority.

Ability means nothing without authority. This is why Jesus promises his authority as the creator God to his disciples. What he calls us to do, he authorizes as the one charged with the governance of heaven and earth. We do not have to wonder if we are overstep- ping our bounds when we speak about Jesus to the people we know and meet. Jesus, who has authority over all, commissions us to speak. We need not question if we have a right to proclaim the Gospel where social propriety, government officials, or national pol- icy declare it improper, illegitimate, or even illegal.

While Scripture requires us to speak with discretion and love, no rule of humankind can deny Christians the privilege of spreading the Gospel. The universe's highest authority has already granted us the right to proclaim Christ in every setting where hearts need him. We can speak of Jesus at family gatherings, work, or school (and send others to do the same in places far and near), regardless of human objections because he who has "all authority in heaven and earth" has given us his permission and his charge.

THE POWER OF THE SPIRIT

Jesus does not send his apostolic sparks into the world with his authority alone. He knows that they will need more fuel to accom- plish all he sets before them. The Savior understands more clearly than we that as power without authority is useless, so is authority without power. Were I to assure you that I had given my favorite baseball team my authority to win the pennant this year, you would not be worried even if you rooted for an opposing team. You would know that my authority means nothing in this circumstance, since I have no power to bring about what I authorize. Jesus has no such limitations.

What Jesus authorizes, he empowers. The words that promise his continued care for his disciples signal the source of their power. Jesus concludes his charge with this assurance: "And surely I am with you always, to the very end of the age" (v. 20). These words echo an earlier comfort that Jesus promised to provide through the Holy Spirit (cf. John 14-16). The same Spirit that served as the instrument of creation, Jesus grants to accompany his disciples. The continuing presence of Jesus promised in the person of the Holy Spirit guarantees inestimable power to the disciples.

Now you know how Jesus can expect his disciples to set the world aflame. They may only be a spark, but they burn with the authority of Jesus and the power of the Spirit. With such fuel, no matter how small the fire they start, it will not be quenched (cf. Ps. 112:6-9). Like a fire in a field driven by the wind, so is the Gospel in the world empowered by the Spirit, and Jesus has given us the right to light that fire.

UNQUENCHABLE FIRE

Consider the proof Scripture offers that the disciples' fire cannot be quenched. Jesus charges his disciples to reach all nations. The mission may seem foolish, but we do not have to question its fulfillment. We already know the conclusion of the matter. In the book of Revelation, the apostle John reports that the hosts of heaven sing these words to the Lamb of God: "You are worthy to take the scroll and to open its seals, because you were slain, and with your blood you purchased men for God from every tribe and language and people and nation" (Rev. 5:9).

The setting is the consummation, the end of the ages. John's words tell us what will happen. Yet despite the future focus, the tense of these quoted words is past. The hosts declare the Lamb worthy because of what he *has* accomplished—past tense! From the perspective of the end of the ages, what Christ told his disciples to do has happened. Disciples have been made "from every tribe and language and people and nation."

Looking back from the revelations of the future, we know that the contest for the world is ours. We may not outscore the opposition every inning, but we are on the winning team. With this certain knowledge, we may determine a last resolve that our identity as the fire of Christ elicits: "We shall not be quenched." The words are not merely a declaration of our intent; they are also a reflection of God's sure promise. We may think our efforts to tell others about Jesus are small, insignificant, and even failing, but the certainly that God can use every spark to ignite the fuel of his own purposes can keep us from despairing, doubting, and giving up.

THE WHISPER ROARED

The disciples' fire did not burn out long ago. For the words of Jesus to come true, the fire must keep burning now. These first disciples lit the fire, but wherever disciples now serve the Savior, sparks still fly to ignite the fuel provided by the authority of Jesus and the power of the Spirit.

A few years ago our family began periodically to use the mission digest of the United States Center for World Mission in our evening devotions. One evening the digest urged us to pray for Malaysia, a country the periodical said had scarcely been "touched" by the Gospel. When our eight-year-old heard that analysis, he immediately thought of his music teacher who is from Malaysia.

"Is Sang-yen a Christian?" Colin asked. We said we did not know and thought that was the end of the matter. Later that evening, however, Colin asked us to show him Malaysia in our family's atlas.

The next day Colin took the atlas with him to his music lesson. He was a little more nervous than usual, and so his mother stayed close as the lesson began. She watched as the eight-year-old went to his teacher, opened the atlas, and pointed to Malaysia. "Is that your home?" Colin asked. Sang-yen smiled and answered, "Yes." She was obviously pleased that our son was showing an interest in her homeland.

Then Colin took a deep breath and, in a quivering voice that was barely audible, said what was on his heart: "The people there have not yet been touched."

Of course, that terse an expression of the Gospel made no sense to Sang-yen. She looked puzzled. Then, assuming she had just misunderstood something, she took over the conversation and told Colin a few more details about her country before commencing the usual piano lesson.

Had most of the people of this world been able to eavesdrop on that conversation, they would have reported hearing only the nervous whisper of a child. But perceptive Christians should hear something far different. When Colin determined to share the Gospel with his Malaysian teacher, he went to "make disciples of all nations," and, in doing so, he declared himself to be a disciple of Jesus Christ. That means he no longer spoke on his own. His words came with the authority of Jesus and the power of the Spirit. Cynics might claim only to have heard a sheepish whisper from a child in a failed attempt to explain his faith. Christians should hear the roar of the Lion of Judah.

Our son heard the roar and understood its significance. He believes Jesus can use even sparks from a child's heart to build a gospel fire in another's soul. Rather than being discouraged with his first testimony, our child returned to his music lesson the next week with a song he wrote for Sang-yen. These are the words:

Jesus helps me when I'm sad,
And he loves me when I'm bad.

Yes, the words are simple, and we do not yet know what Sang-yen heard deep in her heart. Still, we know that the roar of a lion echoes a long, long way.

The Lion of Judah, Jesus Christ, is still securing his flock from the nations of the earth. His roar fills the earth everywhere his disciples go, inspiring their resolve and igniting their own battle cry. The Lion roars through the voices of his disciples who resolve, "We shall not be moved, we shall not be stopped, and we shall not be quenched." This roar comes from the hearts of all disciples who recognize that the identity, authority, and power Jesus gives them makes apparently meager efforts a mighty force.

We may think that our voices will have little effect among those we love and with whom we work. We may feel that we have failed a hundred times to say everything properly. The efforts of the missionaries we support may seem insignificant compared to the millions who need to hear. Yet anytime and anywhere a disciple speaks—though the effort seems small and sheepish—the authority of Jesus and the power of the Spirit grant that utterance a mighty voice.

The Lion of Judah still roars. He is securing his flock from all nations, languages, and families. His call has not grown faint. He roars in the lives of all those who claim the promises that make these words our unified resolve:

> We are a rock, founded on the teachings of Jesus,
>   and we shall not be moved;
> We are a river, flooding the nations with the Gospel of grace,
>   and we shall not be stopped;
> We are a fire, burning with the authority of Jesus
>   in the power of the Spirit,
>   and we shall not be quenched.

The charge Christ gives his disciples defines the mission he sets before us. Commitment and courage for the task rise with the certainty of the identity our Lord bestows upon us. We are the Lion's roar.

DISCUSSION QUESTIONS

1) In what ways do Christians fail to make a rock-solid stand for Christ's commands, cleansing, and claim?

2) How have some churches emphasized commands without balancing them with the messages of God's cleansing or his claims? How have some emphasized cleansing while minimizing the focus on his commands or claims? How have some emphasized God's claims upon them without properly stressing his commands or cleansing?

3) How can you make sure your church maintains the balance of the gospel matrix in Christ's Great Commission?

4) Why is it not contradictory for Jesus to command his disciples not to be moved and not to be stopped?

5) How is the river of Christian influence affecting your world today?

6) How do you know that you can witness with the authority of God?

7) What difference does it make to know that you can witness with the power of the Spirit?

8) How can God use you as a spark to ignite a fire of gospel proclamation?

9) How can you be sure that God's expectation for the spread of the Gospel will succeed? How does this assurance affect your willingness to be the Lion's roar?

12

THE POWER OF
REFORMATION AND REVIVAL

᠊᠊

Newsweek *magazine declares that America is at war over cultural values, and weeks later* Christianity Today *follows with its own cover article reporting the battle fully engaged. The periodicals may not agree with each other's values, but all concur that we are living through a cultural war. If you want some evidence of the culture's rifts, you have only to stand in a "Hands Across America" life chain along a major traffic thoroughfare as my family and I have done. Waves and shouts of encouragement from pro-life drivers, other gestures and profanities from those of opposing views—even toward my children—make it clear how deeply we as a people are divided and how differing are our values.*

Francis Schaeffer warned the Christian churches of the impact of eroding morals and retreating churches almost two decades ago:

> [A]ll the most devastating things in every area of our culture, whether it be art or music, whether it be law or government, whether it's the schools, permissiveness and all the rest—all these things have come climatically in our adult lifehood. . . . But the mentality of accommodation did not raise the voice, it did not raise the battle, it did not call God's people to realize that this is a part of the task—to speak out into the culture and society against that which was being so undercut and lost and largely thrown away.

With this call to arms and many similar ones, the war now rages on every front. The battles touch every area of our lives involving the most basic issues of our being—family, gender, sexuality, race, ethics, personal responsibility, and the sanctity of life itself.

The scope of the issues being debated indicate that we may have arrived at a defining moment—a watershed in history that will determine the shape of our world for many years to come. Such a realization has led to a consistent call among believers for reformation and revival in our society. Clergy and laity across denominational, socioeconomic, and ethnic lines have united their voices to summon the spiritually concerned to make a difference at this crucial time. But what really will make a difference? The magnitude of our situation presses us to search for answers in this Scripture where an apostle sought revival in a church and reform in its society at a time no less troubled than our own.

1 CORINTHIANS 1:26–2:5

[26]Brothers, think of what you were when you were called. Not many of you were wise by human standards; not many were influential; not many were of noble birth. [27]But God chose the foolish things of the world to shame the wise; God chose the weak things of the world to shame the strong. [28]He chose the lowly things of this world and the despised things—and the things that are not—to nullify the things that are, [29]so that no one may boast before him. [30]It is because of him that you are in Christ Jesus, who has become for us wisdom from God—that is, our righteousness, holiness and redemption. [31]Therefore, as it is written: "Let him who boasts boast in the Lord."

[1]When I came to you, brothers, I did not come with eloquence or superior wisdom as I proclaimed to you the testimony about God. [2]For I resolved to know nothing while I was with you except Jesus Christ and him crucified. [3]I came to you in weakness and fear, and with much trembling. [4]My message and my preaching were not with wise and persuasive words, but with a demonstration of the Spirit's power, [5]so that your faith might not rest on men's wisdom, but on God's power.

THE CHASUBLE SYNDROME

Did you know that the earliest Christians wore uniforms? These were not plaid. Rather the chasuble, a hooded cloak made of woolen material, was the common garment of the first-century disciples. In the Roman world common folk, laborers, and slaves wore chasubles as a fits-any-purpose, takes-any-abuse overall that would stand up to grime, labor, and weather. No ruler or Roman professional would be caught dead in a chasuble. So when Christians of all classes adopted the chasuble as their daily wear, they were making more than a fashion statement. They were repudiating the finery of the world and revoking the distinctions of class, rank, and influence to identify with the most common and least influential.

The chasuble became so identified with the church that when customs changed, churchmen continued to wear the garment—but not always for the same purpose. In the Middle Ages, as the power and influence of the church grew, the chasuble changed. The cloak of poor monks became the robe of rich clerics. Woolsey yielded to linen and silk. Drab colors that would hide grime eroded into brilliant hues to display wealth. Jewels and gold braid replaced crude patches and raveled hems. What once identified with the common man now distinguished the most influential.

The evolution of the chasuble is a telling metaphor of the all-too-common course of human choices, even among Christians. We gravitate to power—to holding it, to displaying it, to wielding it. We may respect humility, but we want influence—which is not wrong in all respects. God calls Christ's followers to be salt and light in the world for the sake of his name. Still, we should recognize that how we achieve that influence challenges our motives, our faith, and our obedience. God charges us to promote the cause of Christ without adopting the ways of the world. This is never easy because the world so clearly indicates what makes a difference in the ordinary course of affairs. "Amass power, exert influence, gain control," the world says.

However, Christians are called to heed what the Bible says will usher forward reformation and revival.

What does the Bible say will prompt spiritual renewal in people? As we enter the twenty-first century amidst a universally acknowledged culture war, Christ's disciples must discern and act upon scriptural priorities. At the same time, *we need to make sure the implications of our actions do not wander from the affirmations of our faith*. We must ensure that the tendencies evident in the warped evolution of the chasuble do not reemerge in us.

To guard against temptations that lie in the pursuit of human power, we need to ask again in the light of Scripture, "What will really make a difference in the cause of Christ?" Biblical answers will become clear only as we again clarify the nature of *our mission*, *heaven's means*, and *Christ's mandate*. True reformation and revival cannot come until we understand these fundamentals of our faith.

I. Our Mission

Knowing precisely what God desires for his followers to accomplish should determine our course of action. The apostle Paul's words to the Corinthian church help us discern our aim by clarifying the goals he set for himself. Paul identified his mission as *promoting the glory of God in the person of his Son*.

HIS GLORY

Divisions were tearing apart the church at Corinth. This community in the midst of Greek affluence and intellectual sophistication had unconsciously begun to reflect culture more than Christ by splintering into various factions over perceived variations in the teachings of their leaders. Party lines formed behind Apollos, Peter, Paul, and even Christ. Each group was vying for the intellectual and political upper hand that would render control of the church. Paul challenged and chastened all the cliques by reminding them *who they were* and *who God is* (vv. 25-30).

A reminder of themselves. Paul first reminded those who were trying to promote themselves that they personally had nothing to brag
about. The apostle recalled for his readers that not many of them
were wise by human standards, and few were influential when God
brought them into the church (v. 26). In our language he asked,
"Where do you get off being uppity?" Paul simply would not allow
these people to form ranks over any supposed superiority. Their
common roots and humble origins made prideful divisions ridicu-
lously pretentious.

A reminder of their Sovereign. As a correction to these persons'
attempts to glorify themselves, Paul offers a refresher course on who
alone deserves glory. He reminds the Corinthians that God has
worked throughout history so as to reserve all glory for himself. He
chose foolish things to confound the wise (v. 27), weak things to
shame the strong (v. 27), the lowly despised things—the things that
are not—to nullify the things that are (v. 28). Since God commonly
uses what has no earthly influence to determine eternal destinies, the
apostle's reasoning directs all praise toward heaven. Paul concludes
that God works through these means "so that no one may boast
before him" (v. 29). Only God should receive honor. Thus the mission
of both ancient and modern followers is to glorify him alone.

This goal and these truths reflect the priorities of the faith fathers
who revitalized orthodoxy in the Church during the great
Reformation of the sixteenth century that still echoes through biblical Christianity. The distinctive trumpet calls of that Reformation—
Sola Scriptura (Scripture alone), *Sola Fide* (faith alone), and *Sola Gratia*
(grace alone)—all resound in this passage:

• The principle of *Sola Scriptura*, which teaches that the Church
should turn to the Bible alone for its spiritual authority, reflects the
apostle's contention that God's saving "wisdom," rather than any
human determinations, provides our only hope in this fallen world
(v. 30). Affirmation of our dependence on God's wisdom instructs
Christians to turn to the Bible alone to determine matters of faith and

282	THE WONDER OF IT ALL

practice. Only in God's Word do we learn what it means to be "in Christ Jesus" (v. 30).

• In this same passage the apostle reveals the means by which we may enter a saving relationship with the Savior attested in Scripture. Our works do not bring us to God. Look at the words beginning the key clauses in verses 27-28: "But God chose . . . ; God chose . . . ; He chose . . . ." In this triune affirmation of God's sovereign action in our behalf, Paul reminds all Christians that divine work rather than human effort establishes our relationship with him. We are saved solely through faith in what God has done rather than by any contribution of our own goodness—*Sola Fide*.

• Paul underscores our divine dependence by writing, "It is because of him (God) that you are in Christ Jesus, who has become for us wisdom from God—that is, our righteousness, holiness and redemption" (v. 30). Christians stand righteous and holy before God because Christ purchased our redemption from the consequences of sin at the price of his own life. Thus all that makes us right before God comes from his own gracious hand. God secures our salvation by grace alone—*Sola Gratia*.

These rallying cries of the Reformation unite to signal one compelling purpose for Christ's Church. Since all believers' standing before God relies solely on his wisdom and influence, then our efforts should exalt him alone. *Sola Scriptura, Sola Fide*, and *Sola Gratia* indicate that God alone deserves our praise. Their sum is *Soli Deo Gloria*, i.e., "to God alone be glory." Our mission is his honor alone. His name alone—not Paul's, not Apollos's, not Peter's, and no other name—must beacon from our midst.

HIS SON

The divine name that must echo from our ranks further defines our purpose. Paul's own example indicates that *our mission is to glorify God by proclaiming his Son*. The apostle clearly spells out his mission and ours with these words of focused intent: "For I resolved to know nothing while I was with you except Jesus Christ and him crucified" (2:2).

WORDS THAT SHOCK

These last words should shock us. Even a small exposure to Paul's ministry will cause us to respond, "What are you talking about, Paul? In your teaching and preaching (including this very letter), you addressed topics as diverse as the qualifications of church officers, correct worship practices, biblical family relationships, proper stewardship of resources, how we should relate to government authorities, and dozens of other issues. You cited Israel's history and quoted Greek poetry. You wrote about your own experiences. You certainly did more than talk about Christ and his atoning sacrifice for our sins."

Apparently Paul would disagree with this assessment. In his mind all the apostle did and said had a center focus of purpose. Paul's solitary mission was the ministry of Jesus—proclaiming who he was and what he did on the cross. Paul discussed other matters only because he believed they reflected upon or resulted from the ministry of Jesus.

WORDS THAT INSTRUCT

The ministry of the apostle Paul reminds us that while there are many dimensions of the Christian mission, there is only one center focus for the work of the Church. Our pulpits are reserved for the cross.

Recognizing temptation. We live in a time that requires Christian leaders to pay careful attention to the instruction implicit in the apostle's words. Political campaigns, social activists, personality promoters, and our own interests and injuries scream for the attention of the Church. This is *not* all wrong. Few of us want to return to the head-in-the-sand days when Christ's people did not bother themselves with matters controversial or social. Francis Schaeffer rightly reminded us that concern for the holiness of God requires us to be a voice for justice and morality in our culture. Martin Luther King, Jr., justifiably charged the church with too long acting as a taillight rather than a headlight with regard to these issues. At the same time, there is always the temptation to make the church a servant of an issue, individual, cause, or party. Here we deeply err. For while we must confess that there are many matters deeply deserving of the church's attention and efforts, our ultimate mission is something fundamentally different from social reconstruction or political reform. We are about nothing else but Jesus and him crucified.

Christians must keep learning from their own history. All owe an immense debt to wise leaders who stood against overt attempts to politicize the evangelical church in the 1950s and 1960s. However, as our culture continues to polarize over issues of morality and justice, the danger of the Church becoming solely identified with certain parties and personalities encroaches again. The danger lies not so much in any particular cause, but in the persistently fed perception that the Church's primary purpose is something other than Christ.

The lines of proper influence and expression grow increasingly fuzzy. Many issues in our age demand the voice of the Church. However, balancing the need to proclaim biblical truth against the mere lust for human power necessitates careful thought and constant vigilance. The "chasuble syndrome" always threatens the Church. We should never minimize the wrestling of conscience required to make sure that we are speaking to our culture for the sake of Christ and not merely for the promotion of our own interests. Wrestle we must because our mission requires no less of us than the constant examination of our words and actions to determine whether long-term consequences will diminish our capacity to carry out the primary aim of the Church. Fortunately we do not need to thrash about blindly as we weigh our priorities. The Word of God gives us guidance in our decisions.

Staying on target. We stay on target by making Paul's example our resolve. Christians today also must maintain the focus on Jesus *and* his sacrifice for sin. The Church is about "Jesus Christ and him crucified." As important as the issues of morality and government are, whenever these issues become distinct from the cross, the Church does not merely promote a partially biblical message; it promotes an anti-Christian message. As odd as it may sound amidst the din of cultural Christianity, we must recognize that at a foundational level Christ's people are *not* about family values, traditional values, the Judeo-Christian ethic, or any other standard of morality (as highly as I regard such standards). We *are* about the failure of any standard to make us right before God. Righteousness apart from the cross is the message of every *other* faith but not ours. Our message is that people have standing before God only when covered by his righteousness alone. We are the people of the cross. The standards of Christ *and* the need of his crucifixion are wed in our testimony, and when they come apart, the message is no longer of Christ.

The cross must stay center stage. To the extent that we speak less of it, think less of it, relate less to it, or act less grateful for it, we abandon the true priority of the church. To the extent that we let other voices drown out Christ's ministry or let other issues dilute his cause, we abandon our true mission. We speak about other issues when to be silent about them would be to diminish our testimony of him. But even then the issues are not our fundamental cause. He is!

If we want revival, if we want change, if we want restoration of Christian values, then we must be willing to say with the apostle, "We resolve to be about nothing but Jesus Christ and him crucified." Christ alone—*Solus Christus*—must be the cry of our reformation if we are to be true to the values of the Reformers we say we respect.

Our churches gain nothing of eternal value if they make of secondary priority or lesser emphasis the message that Jesus died for sin and that sinners are lost eternally without faith in him. Consider this: If we were to achieve social and political goals that promote morality without an awareness of the need for atonement, we could actually create a society further from the cross than we are at present. Self-righteousness is no nearer to revival than immorality—and may actually be far more resistant to the Gospel. If our society were more moral without any more dependence on the cross, then it would be no nearer to revival than were the Pharisees!

Since the success of the Church's biblical mission hinges on focused efforts to promote the glory of God through the proclamation of his Son's person and work, Christians next must ask, "How?" What means does God give us to make the eternal differences that are the focus of the Gospel? What will bring true reformation and revival to our culture? How do we change the world?

II. The Means

No mystery lies in how to orchestrate massive change in a society—set goals, develop an organizational structure, recruit influential people, develop a financial base, create a media strategy, and then seek to amass enough popular support or political and economic power to bring about desired changes. This is the way the world works, and some Christians may be tempted to believe that such measures will accomplish their spiritual goals. They are wrong. Neither the world's goals nor its means are compatible with Christ's purposes.

NOT BY OUR POWERS

Common sense should tell us that pervasive national and cultural revival lies completely beyond human means. Currently those identifying themselves as born-again Christians comprise 15 to 25 percent of the United States electorate, depending on which poll you believe. If the numbers were twice or even three times that amount, would the numbers really guarantee revival? Remember we are talking about God's kingdom, not ours. Our mission lies in the world of souls, not in the world of the polls. Never has a religious group's ascendancy to power and the imposition of conservative moral standards offered guarantees of genuine spiritual awakening in a society.

If the Church were to possess all the power and wealth that this world can offer (and could avoid all the commensurate temptations of such influence), history offers us little hope that these resources could make any real difference in our ultimate mission to promote the glory of God through the ministry of his Son in the hearts of those around us.

OUR LIMITS

Some who have sensed the limitations of their churches have begun to look elsewhere for power over the corruption throughout our culture. The obvious place to look is the political arena. Yet as important as responsible political involvement is, we need to question the impact politics ultimately will have on our culture. Consider how our society increasingly trivializes its own political system. While party conventioners gather to deliberate which of their candidates can best frame the country's future, media commentators offer jibes and jokes about the process. Campaign reporting degenerates into sound bites where we listen not for substance but for mistakes. Candidate commercials become thirty-second orchestrations of selected facts and personal ridicule designed to leave impressions rather than foster thought. Once a candidate assumes office, the assaults of approval ratings, lobby interests, late-night talk shows, a prying press, and the specter of future campaigns largely neutralize incentive to promote meaningful change.

We should not limit ourselves to scanning the current political landscape when questioning whether political success can direct a nation toward fundamental spiritual change. Though the media typically say that evangelicals had a direct line to the White House during the twelve years of the Reagan and Bush presidencies, that is hardly the whole picture of evangelical influence. The current president and vice-president also claim membership in a denomination claiming more evangelicals than any other group. The only president who actually trumpeted his born-again commitments was in office the four years prior to Reagan, and the two presidents in office six years prior to him largely had the support of conservative Christians. The United States is approaching a third of a century of intense evangelical leverage on the nation's most powerful office. Yet this prolonged period of influence at the highest level of government coincides precisely with the time Francis Schaeffer said our culture has seemed most to unravel.

What should Christians do next if politics really hold the key to national revival? Pray for half a century of political power? Seek more and more political candidates who will advocate an approved evangelical agenda? While the protection of our children, the defense of decency, the promotion of fairness, and concern for our nation's future call all Christians to act responsibly and biblically in the political arena, we ignore the painfully obvious lessons of our own times if we think these actions will spawn genuine spiritual revival. If the impact of a generation of evangelical power exerted at the presidential level has been so minimal, do we not have to question whether churches who bank on revival through political one-upmanship invest in futility?

Looking beyond the boundaries of human power for the means of spiritual renewal does not mean that Christians must surrender to their culture nor despair of its reform. Instead, realistic assessments of the limitations of the world's means of effecting change grant us greater confidence in the spiritual resources God gives us for performing his purposes. What are the resources God provides for spiritual revival? Paul answers as he writes for a society no less secular, sophisticated, and lost than our own. Our appreciation for the divine provisions grows as we scrutinize the apostle's description of God's pattern for bringing about spiritual change.

GOD'S PATTERN

God's pattern of sparking revival first glimmers in Paul's description of the Corinthian believers. Not many of them were sophisticated, influential, or noble born before God brought his church into being through them (v. 26). What was normal for this situation Paul quickly makes clear is typical of God. He works outside the ordinary channels of human capabilities. To the Greeks, whose culture taught the importance of sophistication, power, and breeding, this was an entirely counter-perspective.

So contrary was this view to the Greeks' ordinary way of thinking that Paul was forced to drive it home with one allusion piled on top of another. The apostle wrote that God uses the foolish things of the world to shame the wise (v. 27). God did not use Socrates, Aristotle, and Plato to spread his Gospel, yet it mushroomed. Paul adds that God chose the weak things to shame the wise (v. 27). Nero, Domitian, and Pilate would level the power of imperial Rome against the cause of Christ, and yet the carpenter and his fishermen followers would shame them all. To these snooty Greeks, Paul even says that God chose the lowly (literally the low-born, slaves not rulers) and the despised (publicans and prostitutes, not the privileged and elite—the *have nots* rather than the *haves*) to nullify (make of no importance) the things that are of great importance to the world (v. 28).

The apostle's past tense repetition of "God chose" three times in these different dimensions of wisdom, power, and influence indicates that God's determination to work apart from these means was not only true in the Corinthians' case, but rather was the normal and ordinary way that God worked in history. Paul did not contend such means were the only way that God worked, but rather that such was his common pattern. The Bible makes this clear repeatedly:

• God said to Israel, "The LORD did not set his affection on you and choose you because you were more numerous than other peoples, for you were the fewest of all peoples. But it was because the LORD loved you. . . . Know therefore that the LORD your God is God." (cf. Deut. 7:7-9)

• Gideon started with 32,000 soldiers. "Too many," said God. With only the 300, who did not get on their knees to drink at the water's edge, did God save his people from the Midianites and Amalekites. His salvation focuses on his power.

• To a woman named Hannah distraught over her childlessness and thought drunk by the High Priest, God promised a son, Samuel. He would guide the nation to its greatest heights and anoint the leader who would establish the lineage of the Savior.

• When that Savior comes, he arrives in a stable in Bethlehem. An itinerant carpenter and his disgraced fiancée welcome this helpless child into the world. Though angels announce him, they speak to shepherds, not kings. In his whole adult lifetime, except for an occasional excursion, this Nazarene will rarely wander beyond what would be a few minutes' drive on a highway today. Yet with a ragtag band of fishermen, tax collectors, and cowards the carpenter's son reaches across the world and reshapes countless human destinies for eternity.

• And what about Christ's followers who are supposed to carry out his great commission of spreading the Gospel that reforms and revives? The New Testament scholar Hermann Olshausen records that what happened here at Corinth was not unique: "The ancient Christians were for the most part slaves and men of low station; the whole history of the church is in reality a progressive victory of the ignorant over the learned, the lowly over the lofty until the emperor himself laid down his crown before the cross of Christ."

God chooses the weak and despised things, the things that are not to nullify the things that are.

Paul's own example indicates how consistent God's pattern is. At the beginning of the next chapter he says to the Corinthians, "I did not come to you with eloquence or superior wisdom (1 Cor 2:1). . . . I came to you in weakness and fear, and with much trembling" (v. 3). You would think God could have chosen a better representative than this frail and shy Paul to take the Gospel to this city and to the Gentile world. Paul would certainly not have made the cut if most of us were picking the evangelism team. Yet what God did in the past he continued into the present time of the apostle and these Corinthian people. He used the least likely to perform the most impressive feats of kingdom-building.

BUT BY HIS SPIRIT

Why did God chose to work through somebody like Paul? Paul answers, "My message and my preaching were not with wise and persuasive words, but with a demonstration of the Spirit's power, so that your faith might not rest on men's wisdom, but on God's power" (2:4-5). Not by our might, but by his Spirit does God build the kingdom.

Paul reiterates the same message to the Corinthians at the end of his next letter to them. After recounting his many trials and the hurdles to his own ministry that a thorn in the flesh causes, he records God's answer as to why he needed to minister with these liabilities. God says, "For my power is made perfect in weakness" (2 Cor. 12:9). God's means for reformation and revival are not found in our powers but in his Spirit.

If any church should know that the power to build Christ's kingdom is spiritual rather than earthly, it should be we who are the children of the Reformation. The movement that spawned us cannot be explained with power, wealth, and influence. These were all lined up against our faith forefathers. Luther, Calvin, Knox, and the Covenanters worked against odds we can hardly fathom in these days. But it was not merely in these big names that the Reformation found its strength. The sparks that fueled the Reformation's flames were often thrown by the least likely persons.

• Jennie Geddis—the Rosa Parks of the Reformation. Though a simple herb woman, she alone was brave enough to object openly to the imposition of the English liturgy at St. Giles Church in Edinburgh. When she threw her sitting stool at Archbishop Laud, the ensuing riot led to the renewal of the Solemn League and Covenant in 1638 and ignited the Covenanter movement for religious freedom and biblical orthodoxy of which we are present here. Now believe me, throwing a stool at an archbishop was not a real intelligent thing to do, but God uses the foolish things of the world to confound the wise.

• John Bunyan—whose *Pilgrim's Progress* not only continues to be read by generations of school children but may have done more to frame the religious conscience of this nation than any book other than the Bible. Bunyan spent his entire life within five miles of his birthplace and wrote much of his most influential work while locked in prison, where supposedly he was powerless. God chose the weak to shame the strong.

In our heritage are many examples that allow us to rejoice that God uses his Spirit to revive and reform. However, only a little reflection on these persons, who remind us how dependent we are on God's Spirit to do his will, can lead us to frustration. If only we could bottle the power of the Spirit, then we could achieve what *we* want. Reformation and revival would be in our grasp. Yet in his wisdom God has determined that the Spirit "blows wherever it [i.e., he] pleases" (John 3: 8). God pours out the work of the Holy Spirit as he wishes, not as we choose. So if we know our mission, but we know at the same time that God's means to accomplish it cannot be controlled by our will, what does God require of us?

III. God's Mandate

God's mandate becomes apparent to us in careful analysis of the apostle's own example (1 Cor. 2:2). The words he uses to describe how he sought to engender spiritual life in Corinth may surprise you. He writes, "I resolved to *know* nothing while I was with you except Jesus Christ and him crucified." I expect Paul to say, "I resolved to *preach* nothing but Jesus crucified;" or, perhaps, "I resolved to *make known* nothing but Jesus Christ and him crucified." However, the wording is clear and unambiguous. Paul was not primarily referring to what he *said* but to what he *lived*.

The apostle chose each word so carefully. For Paul to "know" Jesus as the "Christ" (i.e., the One Anointed to rule God's people) indicates that Paul humbled himself before one he recognized as the Lord of every aspect of this world. Knowing Jesus as the one "crucified" meant that Paul recognized his own need for repentance so that God might cover his sin with the blood of the Savior. To "know" Christ in this context meant that Paul had resolved to live a humble and repentant life before his God. In fact, the word used for "know" most naturally conveys the knowledge that comes from a relationship.

Paul believed that living in a humble and repentant relationship with Jesus was the most powerful message and means that he had to win Corinth. You might think that these Greeks would only listen to those who argued with the wisdom and sophistication of their philosophers. Paul knew better and, despite the disdain it would elicit from some, still resolved "to know nothing" but Christ and him crucified when ministering among the Corinthians. The power of the Gospel was not in Paul's argumentation but in his demonstration that he knew Jesus.

The message to us is as poignant as it is simple: Reformation and revival result when God's people demonstrate that they *know* Jesus in the midst of a lost and sinful society. Herbert Farmer in his classic work, *The Servant of the Word*, writes, "God's saving approach is always through persons in relationships." No spiritual force is more powerful than each believer living for Jesus in the place that God calls him or her to serve. This is not the way of the world, but it is the way of the Lord—using the personal witness and daily walk of individuals that live with an intimate knowledge of him to redirect people's eternal destinies.

Vision of the power implicit in each Christian's daily life of devotion inspired our Reformation forefathers to teach the dignity of each vocation and "the priesthood of all believers." After all, they reasoned, how could there be second-class vocations or less spiritual callings if God could use each person in whatever place or occupation to change eternity. This great insight should remind each of us that those who "know Jesus among you" are the soldiers of the cross who alone will serve as the catalysts of revival. No force, nor any other means, contributes more to the building of Christ's kingdom and the destruction of the dominion of darkness than your personal, daily commitment to honor Jesus in the place where God has called you to live, work, love, learn, struggle, and even play.

We should recognize, however, that if we say that the real power for revival lies in each Christian's hour-by-hour, minute-to-minute personal faithfulness to Christ, some will accuse us of being caricature evangelicals who are concerned only about personal salvation and lack a real "worldview." If the accusation comes our way, we first should remember that this is the same charge leveled at Jesus by disciples who expected him to dominate the world with the forces of the world. Something warped in our human nature simply will not allow us to accept the worth of efforts that do not have the trappings of human power and minimize the importance of organizational control. Second, we should recall that a commitment to live consistently for Jesus does not mean that we must put *aside* efforts for social, moral, and political reform, but rather that we must place them *under* the commitment to live for Jesus in whatever position or situation he assigns us:

• If your calling is politics, then live for Jesus recognizing that the need for power is never cause to abandon the testimony of Christ. If a position cannot be won with truth and respect for others, let it go. We win nothing for Christ with the politics of distortion, invective, and ridicule. Such does not indicate that we know Jesus. How much I love and respect the politicians associated with our church who make their personal testimony a priority over personal or party gains. I know they pay a high price for the consistency of their witness. I pray for more like them for the sake of reformation and revival.

• If your calling is business, then live for Jesus realizing that God calls you to faithfulness more than to success. Whatever you gain at the expense of his name will mean little in terms of what is truly rewarding in this world or the next.

• God may have called you to the field of education, the arts, or the church. In each place are forces you will be tempted to counter with what the world identifies as the instruments of power and influence. Employ them all *so long as* they do not diminish your testimony of him. What you long for the most—the reformation and revival of this world—requires that you know Jesus among those that he places in your life's sphere.

At the heart of this passage the apostle Paul urges us to believe in the power of one. Each of us must grasp the wonder that the Spirit of God will use those of us uncompromisingly committed to the cause of Christ in the place of our calling in a far greater way than we could ask, imagine, or orchestrate by our own means:

• Two years ago the seminary I serve hired a new professor. He is a younger man and in future years will have the opportunity to train quite literally thousands to minister the Gospel to tens of thousands—and possibly many more—over the next generation. When the school officials interviewed him, this new professor told us something that I had forgotten. He said he had come to know the Lord through the testimony of *his* brother who had come to know the Lord through the testimony of *my* brother in high school. I remember my brother in those high school years. Sometimes he was as foolish as any of us in our teenage years. He certainly had no power by the world's standards. He had a sincere faith but no doctorate in theology nor any insider connections with the church's hierarchy. Yet almost thirty years ago, God chose this foolishness to confound our wisdom and change the eternity of many.

• Ten years ago a vet in Virginia named Jim Carl called Jesus "Lord." Recently he signed on for a three-year stint to help provide health resources for refugees of sub-Saharan Africa who have suffered the double scourges of civil war and drought. He went to help them conserve water. While there he also started a daily Bible class.

Five hundred now attend, thirsting for the living water of the Spirit as much as for the water of physical life. You would not call Jim a Bible scholar. You would not say he went to a place where he has any power. But God chose a man who "knows Jesus" among those who have nothing and are close to being nothing in order to build the kingdom against the overwhelming forces of starvation and war. God uses the weak things to shame the strong.

• This week near Washington, D.C., a homemaker I cannot name because of the sensitivity of her ministry will host a Bible study on her porch. Among the two dozen women who regularly attend are wives of justices, legislators, and executives ruling at the highest levels of our government. This simple Bible study in a home was never intended to be more than a "neighbor" ministry. Yet more profound influences for our nation, world, and millions of unborn may emanate from that porch than all the political power twelve million evangelicals think they can exert in political campaigns. God chooses the things that are not to nullify the things that are.

When we see what God can do, we know his call for each of us: We must know Jesus and him crucified among those he puts in our lives. How he will use us I cannot say. That he will use us I am certain. How could God not use ones who live repentant lives conscious of the work of his Son?

Maybe this prescription for reformation and revival does not sound very sophisticated. It is not a call for a national game plan or an organizational scheme. This is simply a challenge to live for God in whatever calling he gives, knowing that in the battle for souls—in the war for reformation and revival—the Holy Spirit can and will use the commitment of those who know him more than all the forces men and women can muster by their might. This is the glory of the Lord! As neighbor lives before neighbor and friend witnesses to friend, the Spirit of God moves through those who know Jesus.

By this personal challenge I am not in the least trying to undermine the efforts or the value of national movements for social, moral, and religious causes. I have the highest respect for those whose convictions have called them to stand for justice and morality in the public arena. I stand on "life lines" for unborn children with my family because I believe in the importance of such efforts in fighting societal evil. Still, we must make sure that we know where the real power of our faith *for the faith* resides.

The power for eternal changes resides in the heart of each one who lives for Jesus. Trust in worldly influences and political measures to perform God's ultimate purposes is misplaced. The Bible specifically tells us not to put our confidence "in princes," i.e., the powers of this world (Ps. 118:9; 146:3). The foibles, frailties, and failures of leaders we have chosen politically and ecclesiastically confirm the wisdom of that command. Each of us has a job to do—to influence eternity where we are. If God chooses to use us in a political cause, a moral crusade, or to raise one child knowing him, that is God's choice—but living for the Savior changes our destiny for eternity regardless. For Christ's followers, who see with his eyes, this perspective grants deep satisfaction because these changes that affect eternity at the heart level are what real revival is all about.

What will really make a difference amidst our culture wars? You! The power of God for reformation and revival will flow through you as you resolve today to know Jesus and him crucified above all things and among all others. Live as one who acknowledges your sin and loves your Savior. The ministry of that one flows through each one who intimately knows him and what he has done. The power of pervasive revival resides in the personal revival of each one who resolves to know Jesus well in this sin-sick world.

THE RESOLVE

Twenty years ago a leader in the Communist youth movement in Peru named Gerry (Geraldo) came into contact with a group of missionaries from our church. We know them as Harry and Florence Marshall. For two generations this young man's relatives had led the Communist movement in his country. Gerry had power, political savvy, and a liberal university sophistication that made him scoff at the simple faith of the missionaries. He spoke to them as much to humiliate them as to learn their "philosophy." Then one day the Marshalls passed along to Gerry a postcard mailed by a child in the United States. A little girl had read a prayer letter from the missionaries in which they had mentioned their conversations with the militant young leader. The postcard with a teddy bear drawn on it said simply, "I'm praying for you, Gerry." Today this former Marxist will tell you that it was the concern of that child so many thousands of miles away that "broke my back." He then bowed to the Lord Jesus.

For the last several years this same Gerry—Gerry Gutierrez—has ministered to foreign diplomats and political leaders in our nation's capitol and in the capitols of several South American countries. His efforts have led to national prayer campaigns in other countries that have been attended by some of the most influential leaders in South America. Although the government officials now involved in these efforts wield tremendous worldly power, remember where the movement that has touched them started. A child wrote a teddy bear postcard, as God once again chose to use the weak and foolish things of the world to overcome the wise and the strong. Gerry remembers, and perhaps it is for this reason that he spends most of his time now ministering to orphans and to the fledgling churches of his home country. Gerry remembers that what the world considers insignificant is precious to the purposes of God.

If God chooses to use this time for revival, it will not be because *we* voted wisely or organized well—as important as those things are. If this is to be the moment of revival, it is such because individual Christians in places unlikely to receive the world's notice know Jesus deeply. National and world revival may even begin now in your heart with a renewed desire, longing, and commitment to know Jesus deeply.

THE POWER OF REFORMATION AND REVIVAL   299

Let there be no mistake; I am *not* merely suggesting that you "brighten the corner where you are." I am challenging all of us to believe something far more significant—that profound, even pervasive, changes in the eternal order of the spiritual realm ripple and reverberate from a heart that beats with the knowledge of Jesus Christ and him crucified. The force of national revival and world reformation resides in each of us. There is no national movement, no political solution, no public figure more critical to God's cause than our personal resolution to know Jesus among those he puts in our lives. Pervasive revival always and foundationally results from personal revival. Each of us can be the difference this world needs at this moment in history, because revival at its heart is the contagion of personal holiness and dedication to the Savior that no organizational structure can mimic. The infectious faith that sparks revival resides in our personal commitment to know Jesus above all else in the place God calls us to live and work. The results of this personal revival we may not be able to measure at the polls. No one is likely to record it in the history books, but in eternity these spiritual changes are all that matter.

In the spiritual realm where the powers of the earth do not hold sway, you are what will make the difference. This day, this hour, this moment make this your resolve: "I will live as one who knows Jesus." You may think that you do not have the wisdom to convince anybody of anything, but remember that God uses the foolish things of this world to confound the wise. You may think you have no power to make an impact, but remember that God uses the weak things of the world to shame the strong. You may think you have nothing to offer, but remember that God uses the things that are not to nullify the things that are. From this spiritual wisdom flows the spiritual power that sparks reformation and revival. If the knowledge of the Lord is to fill the earth as water covers the sea, it is because this commitment wells in each of us: "I will live as one who knows Jesus."

DISCUSSION QUESTIONS

1) How do the culture wars raging about us tempt us to seek earthly solutions to spiritual problems?

2) Since God brings true reformation and revival through his Spirit, in what ways do Christians grow inordinately pleased with certain political victories and inappropriately despairing with certain political setbacks?

3) If God relied upon human wisdom, power, and significance to bring about reformation and revival, what would this do to his glory? What would it do to ours?

4) How would we treat people who apparently lack wisdom, power, and influence if God indicated that they did not have a significant role to play in the building of his kingdom?

5) If we could control the operations of God's Spirit in bringing about reformation and revival, what temptations would we face? How strong would these temptations be?

6) Why should Christians address any social, moral, or political issues if our sole mission is the proclamation of Christ's cross? How should this sole mission affect our approach to the other issues?

7) What is the most important thing you can do to bring about reformation and revival? How does this affect what you do and say on a daily basis? Why are these things significant?

8) What does it mean for you to "know Jesus and him crucified?"